12. (M.S.C) 990210

A History of Abingdon

A HISTORY OF ABINGDON

BY JAMES TOWNSEND, M.A.

Formerly Abingdon Scholar of Pembroke College, Oxford

With a New Foreword by J. M. Cobban, T.D., D.L., M.A., J.P.

Republished by S.R. Publishers Ltd. 1970

Original Edition published by Henry Frowde
London
1910

© 1970 S.R. PUBLISHERS LIMITED

EAST ARDSLEY, WAKEFIELD

YORKSHIRE, ENGLAND

ISBN 0 85409 597 7

Reproduced and Printed in England by
Redwood Press Limited
Trowbridge and London

FOREWORD

by JAMES COBBAN
Headmaster of Abingdon School

Since James Townsend wrote this book, Abingdon has had to face the impact of two World Wars (from which it emerged almost unscathed) and to come to terms with the more insidious challenge of the modern age. It says much for the wisdom of the civic authorities that so much of the Abingdon that Townsend loved still remains.

Of course there have been changes. The traditional local industries of brewing, leather working and printing still flourish. But the M.G. cars, made in Abingdon, have given the town a wider fame. There is an RAF aerodrome just north-west of the town still in active operation, though not as busy as it was when part of the striking force for D-Day was being launched from it. The erection of large atomic establishments at Harwell and Culham has led to an influx of new, and highly specialised, citizens. Two housing estates to the north of the town were built to meet their needs. In the centre of one of them, a simple plaque marks the site of the manor house of Fitzharris. The Council has built its own housing estates south of the river Ock and to the north beyond Fitzharris. There has been much private building too which has helped to swell the population of the town to the 18,000 mark. The branch line to Radley is now closed to passenger traffic; the derelict canal has been filled in. But the main road from Oxford to Newbury still passes through the centre of the town, carrying an ever-increasing burden of heavy traffic. An inner relief road, nearing completion, will divert some of it from the main streets. Some day a more extensive by-pass will remove all the through traffic.

But the Corporation has recently banished all cars from the market place and replaced them by carefully-sited trees, so there the ghost of James Townsend could stand in safety and look around. To the north he would find that the ancient Bury Street has been transmogrified into a car-free shopping precinct. The Corn Exchange which disappeared in the process was mourned only by devotees of Victoriana. Turning round, he would see that the County Hall had had a complete face-lift. Beautifully restored by the Ministry of Works, it was re-opened by Her Majesty the Queen in 1956; it houses a most attractive museum. (To a long record of royal visits must be added also the visit which Princess Margaret paid to Abingdon

(v)

School in 1963.) St. Nicolas' Church shows externally no sign of the fire which damaged it so severely in 1953. It now bears on its walls a tablet in honour of St. Edmund of Abingdon. The municipal buildings have been opened up by the removal, in 1938, of a row of houses and shops which enclosed Roysse's Court. Considerable improvements have taken place within them. In 1911 the then Mayor, Alderman Preston, constructed a Mayor's Parlour out of an old lumber-room, and later refurbished the old School Room. Crystal chandeliers were installed in the Council Chamber to mark the Queen's visit in 1956, and later an illuminated cabinet was built under the gallery of the Roysse Room to display the Corporation Plate. More recently, extensive reconstruction has taken place to link the old buildings with a new Civic Hall, which extends eastwards towards the Abbey Meadows, now a public park.

Since the war the Friends of Abingdon, a flourishing civic society, has done much to beautify the remains of the outbuildings of the Abbey. At one end of them has been constructed the little Unicorn Theatre, with an Elizabethan stage, where a series of productions of the lesser known operas of Handel has in recent years attracted a more than local fame.

St. Helen's Church, attractively sited on the river, owes to Alderman Preston the restoration in 1935 of the rare painted ceiling in the Lady Chapel. To meet the needs of the growing population in the north of the town a daughter-church, Christ Church, was imaginatively created in 1961 out of an ancient tithe-barn of the Abbey. Not far from it is a new Methodist Church, built in modern style in 1959. It is more ecumenical to record that the local Congregational Church has now cast in its lot with the Trinity Methodist Church in Conduit Road.

Since Townsend wrote, Abingdon has become even more of an educational centre. Abingdon School is now a boys' direct-grant school with 630 on the roll (curiously, ten times the number ordained by its refounder, John Roysse, in 1563). Its range of buildings, seen from Park Road, is impressive. There is also a girls' direct-grant school (the School of St. Helen and St. Katharine), a coeducational county grammar school (called after Sir John Mason, one of the most famous of Abingdonians) which was one of the first schools in the country to introduce the teaching of Chinese, a College of Further Education, and two secondary modern schools, each practically within a mashie shot of the next in line—not to mention half a dozen primary schools scattered further afield.

Yet there is still much to remind the visitor of the continuity of history. The Master and Governors of Christ's Hospital continue to meet in their Jacobean hall to administer the almshouses and their estates in the north west of the town. The present High Steward of the Borough is yet another Earl of Abingdon. The Recorder has a less honorific office, for Abingdon has retained its Quarter Sessions. The members of the Corporation still celebrate royal visits and royal occasions by hurling buns from the roof of the County Hall. On Mondays the market place is gay with stalls. There is still a cattle market in Abingdon but it has been moved to a new site near the disused railway staton. On a Saturday in mid-June the Morris Dancers tread their way rhythmically down Ock Street and elect their own 'Mayor'. When the Fair comes to town in October, High Street and Ock Street are closed to all traffic, in gallant defiance of this mechanical age.

It is perhaps symbolic that I write these words in the room which is traditionally the oratory of Peter Heylyn, of whom Townsend has so much to say, within the first few minutes of what all but the pedants regard as a new decade. The town of Abingdon is conscious and proud of its traditions and its heritage. It looks forward confidently to the challenge of the future.

Lacies Court, Abingdon
January 1st, 1970.

In nomine dñi nostri ihu xpi redemptoris mundi. Anno dominice incarnationis .dccc.xxxv. Indictione .xiii. Ego re-

verber̄ter occidentalium saxonum rex monasterium illud, mercatū quinquaginta manentium ad abben dune cum licentia et consensu tocius gentis et unanimitate omnium optimatum. hec donatio fuit facta in pascha in dor kecestre et postea ipse eandem donationem libavit in altari confirmauit. anno imperii nri xxxiiii. Et siquando in nomine pris et filii et spc sci ut nullus superius mat hominum ibi superbia uticiam neterpsium pastum requiratur ut sitrex homines quos dicimus tegniun nec eos qui accipitres por tant ul falcones ul cauallos du cant siue canes. Per penam inter rete sup eos quoniam audeat nec princeps nec graphio uiolentam tem prefatam ul alicuius oneris molestiam mittere audeat atut in diebus nris ul successorum nim̄ip. Si paliquo delicto accusat̄ homo di eastre ille custos solus cum suo dominio si audeat illum castiget. Sin autem ut recipiatur alienam ut neteam heius merestrendimis con-

orcione prefatum debetum cum sim plo precio componat. Aliud plurib. Ne cui hominum prim atiquid ibi tributur neq; in pascestidis neq; in refectiones set ab his omnibus liber pmaneat. de illa autem tribulatione que witereden nominatur sit liba. m si tamen singli ptum soluerit ut talia accipiant. fures quoq; cis appellant weregeld de totas si foris ra piant precium eius dimidiu illi eccle et dimidiu regi detur. Et si mittis rapitur totum reddatur ad eccliam. Similr de hecitate pegnorum idest gallog et brittonum et totum similium eccle reddatur precium cuius sanguis pegnorum idest weregeld dimidiam pre rex teneat omni dia eccle audicere re cant. Silua quoq; omnis q̄ illi eccle subburbanis eius supperit in omni ty causis sit liba et nō secretus i ao re gis ul principis eorum eia aliqua pre matie grossi ul gracet set ab omnib; defensa et litera maneat. Siquis a pristeps statutis noluerit obedire sciat se alienum ee a consortio sce di eccle a participatione corpor et sanguinis dni nri ihu xpi paucion tatem leti perciplt u digne eme nuerit qd contra di eccliam fecist.

✠ Ego Ecgbeat rex .cces. et sublscps̄.
✠ Ego aethelwlf filii regis .cces. et subs.
✠ Ego aelfstan epc .cces. et sublscps̄.
✠ Ego rethun epc .cces. et subscps̄.
✠ Ego kinred epc .cces. et sublscps̄.
✠ Ego wlflaf abb .cces. et subscrips̄.
✠ Ego eadwald abb .cces. et subs.

XXXI

A
HISTORY OF ABINGDON

BY

JAMES TOWNSEND, M.A.
FORMERLY ABINGDON SCHOLAR OF PEMBROKE COLLEGE, OXFORD

LONDON
HENRY FROWDE
1910

OXFORD: HORACE HART
PRINTER TO THE UNIVERSITY

ABBENDONENSIBVS
ABBENDONENSIS
HOC OPVSCVLVM

PREFACE

THE object of this book is to give a continuous sketch of the history of Abingdon in a single volume, founded partly upon original research among a mass of unpublished documents, partly upon the authoritative editions of important documents, such as the Abingdon Chronicle.

The buildings of Abingdon have been so often reproduced, that it seems more useful to illustrate this book with a few specimens of the older documents. The two photographs of the Chronicle are by Mr. Macbeth, of Ludgate Hill ; the other two are by Mr. W. J. Vasey, of Abingdon.

To turn to the most pleasant of all themes, I wish to acknowledge gratefully and humbly the assistance of many friends. Documents and papers have been placed at my disposal by the Vicar and Churchwardens of the two Churches, by the Mayor and Corporation, and by the Master and Governors of Christ's Hospital in Abingdon. Mr. Bromley Challenor, the Town Clerk, encouraged me to start my work and gave me much help. The Rev. T. Layng helped me in the School history. Alderman C. A. Pryce gave me the use of his many prints and books. Mr. H. G. Bell, of Wimbledon, lent me his valuable advice and aid throughout. Mr. A. O. C. Pryce read diligently the manuscript and proofs and worked at the index. I have also to acknowledge much courteous assistance from the staff of the great libraries. At the same time I must be responsible for my own failings in dealing with a period of more than twelve centuries.

JAMES TOWNSEND.

GLENBURN, ABINGDON,
May 3, 1910.

CONTENTS

ILLUSTRATIONS

HISTORY OF ABINGDON

CHAPTER I

THE SAXON PERIOD

675–1066

At certain periods during the great days of the Abbey, and again for a moment in the Civil War, the local history of Abingdon flows along with the main stream of national history. At other times the interest is more local, centred in the growth of local institutions, in old customs, old buildings, and old forms of speech and thought. Occasionally it may be thought by the unsympathetic to be degenerating into the story of the parish pump. It is well to remember that the events of the greatest importance are not always the most picturesque, or of the most striking dramatic interest.

The so-called Dark Ages have left behind them many monuments in stone and in metal, which excite the admiration of the builder and artist, and furnish the historian with unpremeditated evidence about the past. They have left also records in a material that has often proved more durable than stone or brass—the laborious parchment of royal charters, of monastic account-books, of legal instruments. Such evidences are sometimes the more valuable, because they were not intended for such a purpose.

Besides, there are the histories proper, the chronicles and lives, written sometimes by men contemporary with the facts they record, sometimes by men of a later age, who yet had access to records that have since been destroyed.

The history of Abingdon is for more than eight centuries chiefly the story of the great Benedictine Abbey. The chief document for the earlier part of this is the Chronicle of Abingdon Abbey. This *Historia Hujus Ecclesiae Abbendonensis* or *Chronicon Monasterii de Abingdon* has been edited in two stout volumes by the Rev. Joseph Stevenson in the Rolls Series, 1858. There are two manuscripts of it

Sources of Information.

Chronicle of Abingdon Abbey.

B

extant, both in the British Museum.[1] Both are of the thirteenth century, written in double columns on vellum in folio ; the first is dated by Stevenson as half a century earlier than the second. The earlier manuscript begins from the beginning of the world :

Ab initio	homo	genuit	vixit
C.XXX.	Adam	C.XXX.	DCCCXXX &c.

The writing is clear, and the initials coloured, but there are few illuminations. Where papal bulls are quoted there are drawings of the seals of the Popes in rough pen and ink work. The later manuscript is more finely illuminated, with burnished gold in the initials. On the first page, which is unfinished, there is a bold picture of knights in battle on foot, in blue armour with green or red surcoats upon a background of gilt, brown, and blue squares. It is a page of a French manuscript, unconnected with our manuscript. The pictures in the initials of Claudius B. vi. are very interesting and elaborate : e. g. Our Lady sitting in a snake-chair, or the truculent portrait of Egbert, King of the West Saxons, seated on his throne delivering a charter to the Abbey. His face is indigo, the throne gold, the footstool green, the sword blue with gilt hilt, the background blue.

This Latin Chronicle is a dull but impartial history of the ' lands and possessions given in pure and perpetual alms to God and the blessed ever-Virgin Mary and the house of Abingdon and the monks there serving God for ever '. The earlier part, down to the Norman Conquest, is simply a cartulary or transcript of title-deeds, with a slight sketch of the circumstances leading up to the grants. After the Conquest there is less of charters, and more of original narrative : the biographical sketches of the Abbots become fuller and more frequent.

The work covers five hundred years (675–1189), from the foundation of the monastery to the accession of Cœur-de-Lion, where it abruptly stops.

It is accepted by historians such as Freeman[2] as a first-rate authority. The accuracy of its transcripts can be checked by eight of the original documents, which survive in the Cotton Collection at the British Museum ; also by nine careful transcripts in Archbishop Parker's Collection at Cambridge, made about 1558, from originals still in existence. The comparison gives a fair estimate of the author's

---

[1] Cotton, Claudius C. ix, and Claudius B. vi.   [2] *Norman Conquest, passim.*

methods and honesty. There are some obvious blunders : e. g. Edward
the Confessor is mistaken for Edward the Elder. But Stevenson and
other experts take a favourable view of the accuracy and honesty of
the chronicler. The account of the great Bishop Æthelwold is defective,
and must be supplemented by a manuscript life at the Bibliothèque
Nationale at Paris.

Stevenson also prints in the same volumes :

> Ælfric's Life of Æthelwold,
> De Abbatibus Abbendoniae,
> De Consuetudinibus Abbendoniae,
> De Obedientiariis Abbatiae Abbendonensis.

This *magnum opus* is supplemented by the Worcester Chronicle,[1]
to which a monk from Abingdon contributed ' Additamenta ' about his
old Abbey.

The Cambridge Chronicle of Abingdon covers the period from 1218–
1304.

Of the half dozen manuscript copies of the great Anglo-Saxon
Chronicle which still exist, one was, according to tradition, made at
Abingdon.[2] In it there are about half a dozen references to ' Abbandune '—chiefly records of the burials of the great at the Abbey or of
the hallowing of abbots. These brief statements indicate that the
abbacy of Abingdon was sometimes exchanged for the bishopric of
London and the primatial see of St. Augustine.

The name of Abingdon has been variously derived as Abbots' town, Name of
Abbey town, Abba's town, and Abben's town.[3] There is no accepted Abingdon.
derivation. The spelling Abbandune is found in its oldest English
form in the Anglo-Saxon Chronicle. Abbendonia is its latinized render-
ing. Many variants occur from time to time in the various writers
quoted in this book, e. g. Abendon, Abyndon, Abindon, Abyngdon,
Abington, &c. Uniformity in spelling is quite a modern practice. In
the parchments of the Middle Ages two or three spellings of the same
name sometimes occur in the same page. In the letters and memoirs
of the eighteenth century variations in spelling seem to have been
an artistic accomplishment to break the monotonous repetition of
a word. If Abingdonians signed their own names in a puzzling variety

---

[1] Printed in *Anglia Sacra*, vol. i.
[2] Brit. Mus. Tiberius, B. i, Chronicon Abbendoniae.
[3] The Chronicle suggests ' Mansio Abbenni ' or ' Mons Abbenni '.

of ways, they agreed with the practice of the greatest of all English writers.

The Abingdon Chronicle begins with the account of the conversion of the British King Lucius by the missionaries of Pope Eleutherius, and the coming of the Irish monk Abbennus to found a religious house at 'Mons Abbennus'. Of course Ireland was then the most cultured and civilized part of Western Europe. But this account is regarded as belonging to legend rather than to history.

All the historical indications suggest that Abingdon Abbey was a purely Anglo-Saxon foundation. Wessex and Sussex were the latest members of the Heptarchy to adopt Christianity. The famous Wilfred of Ripon engaged in an impetuous mission to the savages of Sussex, and under his influence Birinus worked among the 'utter pagans' of Berkshire.[1]

The same spirit that led the monks to face the nine months' winter of an Alpine pass, led them to clear the forests and drain the swamps of Berkshire. For monks were not hermits, but parts of an organized society, cultivators as well as teachers.

The first site of the Abbey is said to have been at 'Suniggewelle'.[2] When the building there did not progress satisfactorily, the site was changed to Abingdon, whose name hitherto had been Seouechesham or Seuekesham.[3]

About A.D. 675, Cissa, who was the sub-king of Wilts and Berks under Centwine, granted to Hean his nephew twenty hides (2,000 acres) of land, stretching from the Thames towards Cumnor, on condition that he should found a monastery there. About the same time Hean's sister, Cilla or Ceolswitha, founded the nunnery of Helnestoue[4] upon or near the site now graced by St. Helen's Church. This was in honour of St. Helen, the mother of Constantine, who had discovered the Holy Cross, of which the nails were found at a later date near Abingdon. Hence the connexion between St. Helen's Church and the cult of the Holy Cross, which is of such interest and importance in the civic as well as the ecclesiastical life of the town during the Middle Ages. Soon after the death of Cilla this nunnery was moved up the Thames to Wightam or Witham, and, a century later, during the wars of Wessex and Mercia, it was finally dispersed.[5]

Bede says ' Gevissorum gentem ingrediens, cum omnes ibidem paganissimos inveniret ' . . .
[2] Stevenson, i. 3.   [3] Ibid., 6.   [4] Ibid., 8.   [5] Ibid.

Hean appears to have procrastinated for many years, until Ini, the successor of Centwine and Ceadwalla, put pressure on him, and about 699 he built and walled the Abbey. These early buildings were not of a grandiose nature, but probably humble structures of wattle and thatch. The Worcester Chronicle, following Ælfric's Life of St. Æthelwold, speaks of 'a modest little monastery'.[1]

The earliest building was 120 feet in length, circular at the east and west ends.[2] This early monastery contained twelve monks.

The Abbey served as a bulwark on the Mercian frontier, and some- *Early his-* times suffered in consequence. In 752 Cuthred of Wessex defeated *tory.* Ethelbald of Mercia at Burford (Oxon.), but in 772 Offa of Mercia defeated Cynewulf at Bensington, broke up Helnestowe, and injured Abingdon Abbey.

A century later Abingdon was involved in the Danish invasions. The Berkshire Downs are famous as the scene of Alfred's struggle with his barbarous rivals. In the years 866–71 the Abbey, enriched by so many grants and charters, was sacked by the Danes. The monks escaped, as it would seem, with their charters. The chronicler relates how a certain holy image expelled the pagans from the refectory, pelting them with a miraculous shower of stones.[3] The Abbey was soon restored, but for some reason Alfred, after his victory of Essendune, 'took away violently' from the monastery the township of Abingdon and most of its other possessions.[4]

The chronicler relates that in 939 King Athelstan kept Easter at Abingdon with his full court, and received amongst others an embassy from Hugh Capet, King of France, which brought various gifts of gold and silver, and other gifts sweeter than gold and silver and precious stones, namely precious relics, which the King entrusted to the Abbey : to wit, a part of the crown of thorns, and a part of the staff of our Lord, also the standard of St. Maurice, with the precious finger of St. Denis.[5] William of Malmesbury, in describing the same embassy, mentions among the splendid gifts spices, gems, emeralds, coursers with golden bits and bosses, an onyx-vase, &c.[6]

In the reign of Athelstan's successor (c. 941–6) a pleasing miracle

---

[1] 'Modicum monasteriolum.'   [3] *De Abbatibus*, Stevenson, ii. 272.
[2] Stevenson, i. 48.   [4] Ibid., i. 50, ii. 276.
[5] Ibid., i. 88. The editor suggests in the index, Hugh, Count of Paris, father of Hugh Capet.
[6] William of Malmesbury, Rolls Series, i. 150.

Meadow at Iffley.

took place. A meadow, named Beri, on the Thames near Iffley,[1] was in dispute between the monks of Abingdon and the folk of Oxfordshire. The monks, after solemn prayer, hit upon the following plan of convincing all of their right. They placed upon the stream flowing past their church a shield bearing a light, and this shield was followed by a few brethren in a boat. It proceeded, apparently upstream, inclining now to one bank, now to the other, ' as if pointing out with its finger the adjacent lawful possessions of the house of Abingdon.' On reaching the meadow of Beri it left miraculously the main stream of the Thames, and circumnavigated the meadow by a side-stream, proving to the folk of either county the right of the monks—an agreeable and dramatic method of settling a question of legal rights.[2] In the later inroads of the Danes in the tenth century, Abingdon Abbey again suffered disaster, and about 944 it fell into entire desolation.[3]

St. Ethelwold.

About 955–9 the Abbey was again restored by St. Æthelwold, one of the greatest rulers connected with its story. The best life of Æthelwold is that by Ælfric the Abbot, himself an alumnus of Winchester, who wrote it within twenty years of Æthelwold's death. This Ælfric had been a monk at Abingdon, and rose to be Archbishop of Canterbury. The eleventh-century manuscript is preserved in the Bibliothèque Nationale at Paris, a clearly written document, very pleasant to peruse in comparison with later documents, with some errors in the local names. It is printed in Stevenson.[4] The parents of Ethelwold, or Æthelwold, were prosperous inhabitants of Winchester. To pass by the miracles of his birth and infancy, the lad attracted the favour of King Athelstan, and was ordained at the same time as Dunstan by Ælfege, Bishop of Winchester. Later on, Ethelwold became a monk of Glastonbury : in the words of the biographer, ' he gave himself up to the discipline of the magnificent man, Dunstan, abbot of that same monastery.' It is then stated that he desired to go abroad to study more perfectly the sacred books or the monastic discipline.[5]

But Eadgiva, the queen-mother, advised Eadred the King not to allow such a man to go out of his kingdom. Accordingly, in 955, the King decided to give him ' Abbandun ', where the little monastery had

---

[1] Gifteleia ; Parker mentions eighty-three spellings of Iffley.
[2] Stevenson, i. 88.   [3] Ibid., 120.   [4] Ibid., ii. 253–66.
[5] Ælfric ' disposuit ultramarinas partes adire causa se imbuendi seu sacris libris seu monasticis disciplinis perfectius,' Stevenson, ii. 257.

fallen into desolation and neglect.[1] Ethelwold then commenced at Abingdon his life-work : the establishment in England of the strict rule of St. Benedict. With the consent of Dunstan he brought clerks from Glastonbury to Abingdon Abbey, and the strict system of monachism was first introduced into England at Abingdon, spreading from that model Abbey to Glastonbury, Winchester, Thorney, Borrow and Stamford. At Abingdon he practically founded a new institution, with accommodation for fifty monks.

Ælfric gives a naïve description of a miracle performed by Ethelwold upon the occasion of a royal visit. The King was accompanied by many Northumbrian thanes, who were hospitably entertained by the Abbot. The doors being shut that no man might escape his share of the mead, the servants poured out the beverage all day long to the guests, yet the liquor did not fail a handbreadth in the vessel, to the grave discomfiture even of the northerners.[2]

Ethelwold began his work of rebuilding Abingdon Abbey, under the reign of King Edgar, in 959, raising ' an honourable temple in honour of St. Mary the mother of God and the ever-virgin '.[3] Ælfric describes him as a great builder, both while he was Abbot and when he was Bishop. A miraculous escape of Ethelwold from an accident during the building operations at Abingdon is related by Ælfric.[4]

The Chronicle of Abingdon Abbey and the *De Abbatibus* speak of Ethelwold as a skilled artificer in metals. He made two bells, which hung beside those larger bells of Dunstan, another cunning craftsman, in the church. He also made with his own hands an organ, an altar-table, crosses, &c. Also a golden wheel adorned with lamps and little bells, ' tintinnabula,' apparently for ceremonial use.[5] His church is described in *De Abbatibus* as having a round east end, a round west end, and round tower.[6]

These Saxon buildings were replaced by the Norman buildings of Faricius, in the reign of Henry I, a century and a half later. In the

---

[1] ' Abbandun, in quo monasteriolum habebatur antiquitus ; sed erat tunc destitutum ac neglectum, vilibus aedificiis consistens, et quadraginta tantum mansas possidens ; reliquam vero terram ejusdem loci (hoc est centum cassatos), praefatus rex jure regali possidebat.'
[2] ' Inebriatis Northanhymbris suatim ac vesperi recedentibus.' Stevenson, ii. 258.
[3] *Ælfric.*   [4] Stevenson, ii. 259.   [5] Ibid., i. 344, ii. 278.
[6] Ibid., ii. 277 'Cancellus rotundus erat, ecclesia et rotunda, duplicem habens longitudinem quam cancellus; turris quoque rotunda erat.'

same passage in *De Abbatibus*, Ethelwold is said to have built the mill
' under the court ', as well as to have constructed an aqueduct under
the dormitory to the water called Hokke. In digging in the Thames
the workmen found ' near the monastery of St. Helen's ' in the deep
sand, in a sort of sarcophagus, the iron cross known as the Black Cross.

In connexion with his reforms Ethelwold sent Osgar, one of the
clerks who had accompanied him from Glastonbury to Abingdon, to
Fleury, to study the strict rule of that Benedictine house.[1]

In 963 Ethelwold was appointed Bishop of Winchester by Edgar,
and ordained by Dunstan, now Archbishop.[2] At Winchester Ethelwold continued the work he had commenced at Abingdon, until his
death in 984. He expelled from the old monastery and the new
monastery there alike the clerks of evil life, and introduced monks
from Abingdon.[3] Capgrave's Chronicle describes the same work in
other words : ' Ethelwold, bischop of Wynchester, put chanones
seculer, and othir seculer, out of the monasterie, and set in munkis.'
While Dunstan appears to have worked largely by the persuasion
and attraction of his gentle genius, Ethelwold seems to have been
a stern disciplinarian, aiming at the same end by harsher methods.
The many miracles related of him must be regarded as a proof of the
deep impression that his work and character made upon his age. There
is a beautiful relic of Ethelwold in the possession of the Duke of Devonshire, namely, St. Ethelwold's Benedictional. This is a beautifully
illuminated tenth-century manuscript, one of the finest of the period,
written by Godeman for the head of the Church of Winchester, the
great Ethelwold, ' truly understanding how to preserve the fleecy lambs
of the Church from the malignant arts of the devil.' Its illuminations
include Ethelwold bestowing the blessing, and show the cock on the
top of the buildings. The Benedictional was a solemn service of
obsecration made on the fraction of the host.[4]

Later Saxon Period.   After the great days of Ethelwold the history hastens on to the
growth of Norman influence, paving the way for the Norman Conquest.
In 1043 Siward, Abbot of Abingdon, was ' blessed ' secretly by Archbishop Eadsige, who wished to retire on account of ill health and feared
that an unsuitable successor might be appointed. The fact that

---

[1] *Ælfric*, Stevenson, ii. 259, ' ad monasterium Sancti Benedicti Floriacense
ut mores regulares illic disceret.'
[2] Stevenson, ii. 260.   [3] *Ælfric*, Stevenson, ii. 260.
[4] *Archaeologia*, 1832, xxiv. 1.

King Edward and Earl Godwin were alone privy to his action suggests that this was an attempt to resist the wave of Norman influence. In 1048 Siward resigned his archbishopric on grounds of health and retired to Abingdon. Eadsige, his predecessor, resumed his sway at Canterbury.[1]

The spring of 1047 is mentioned by the Anglo-Saxon Chronicle as a period of great mortality at Abingdon.

In 1050 the Confessor gave the Abbey of Abingdon to Ralph, or Rudolf, a Norwegian bishop and kinsman of the King.[2] His predecessor Sparhavoc had been appointed Bishop of London, but was refused consecration by the Archbishop under plea of instructions from Rome. Sparhavoc is described as a skilled worker in gold and silver, and it is suggested that he appropriated gold and gems entrusted to him for the execution of a crown.[3]

A pleasing anecdote is told of Edith, the queen of Edward the Confessor. The King with his mother and wife were being entertained at Abingdon. When they were being shown over the whole monastery, they found the ' boy-monks ' in the refectory taking food before the regular refection on account of their tender years. When Edith questioned them and found they had but bread, she induced the King permanently to endow the boys with something better for their ' matutinellum ' or little breakfast.[4]

It is interesting to note that already in Saxon times the Thames was the highway of traffic between Oxford and London. In the time of Abbot Ordric (c. 1052) the navigating stream became so blocked up beneath the walls of Abingdon Abbey that ' boats could scarcely pass to Oxford '. At the request of the citizens of London and Oxford the Abbot allowed a new channel to be dug through the meadow to the south of his church. Each boat paid a toll of a hundred herrings during Lent.[5] The new navigating channel apparently turned south from the main stream at Thrupp above ' Bertun ', and rejoined the main stream at the top of the Culham Reach. This remained for centuries the channel of navigation.

In the Saxon period the Abbey was the burial-place of many of the great : Cissa, the Sub-King of Wessex ; St. Edward, king and martyr ;

---

[1] Anglo-Saxon Chronicle, *ad annum*. Probably Siward was associated with Eadsige as a colleague in the archbishopric ; cp. Stevenson, i. 451.
[2] Ibid.
[3] Ibid., and Stevenson, i. 463.
[4] Stevenson, i. 460, ii. 283.
[5] Ibid., ii. 282, and i. 481.

St. Vincent, martyr ; Bishop Sideman of Crediton,[1] and other bishops and ealdormen.

Work of the Monks. Stevenson, in the introduction to his second volume of the Abingdon Chronicle, draws a favourable picture of the monks of that age. In contrast to the rude chieftains, who were only interested in war and the chase, the monks encouraged agriculture. St. Benedict thought it good that men should be daily reminded that in the sweat of their brow they should eat bread, and day by day they toiled in the field as well as prayed in the church. After the service of Prime the monks received each his allotted task in the chapter-house, and they went out, two and two, and in silence, to their task in the fields. From Easter to October this lasted from six until ten o'clock or noon. As more lands were granted to the society, and as more fields were cleared for cultivation, the surplus farms were leased to lay occupiers. The monastery was a centre of civilization as regards both mental culture and physical comforts in that rude age. Its popularity is shown by the many large grants and bequests received before the Conquest. Within its society a career was offered to the low-born boy of ability as well as to the boy of wealth and family. It displayed locally that impartiality which the national church in its best days exhibited towards all classes, even towards the sovereign.

Bishoprics. A word of explanation may be not amiss as to the bishoprics, in which Abingdon has been included. Originally Abingdon, as a part of Berkshire, was in the diocese of Wessex (635–705), of which the see was established by Birinus at Dorchester, Oxon. In 676 the see of Wessex was transferred to Winchester, Dorchester being the see of Mercia, until it was replaced by Lincoln at the Conquest. In 705 the vast see of Wessex was divided between Winchester and Sherborne. The authorities differ, but the balance of evidence assigns Berks to Winchester (705–909). In 909 Berks was included in the little bishopric of Ramsbury, or Wilts (909–1058), of which the see was not fixed, but sometimes at Ramsbury, sometimes at Sonning. In 1058 Ramsbury was united with Sherborne (1058–75), and generally governed from Sherborne. After the Conquest in 1075 the see of this diocese was moved to Old Sarum (1075–1221). In 1221 it was moved to New Sarum, or Salisbury, which was the cathedral city of Berks until 1836. Since 1836 Berks has been in the diocese of Oxford.[2]

[1] Anglo-Saxon Chronicle, *ad annum*, 977.
[2] Freeman, i. 36, ii. 406, iv. 418, 421. Cp. *Victoria History : Berks*, ii. 1–4.

A SPECIMEN CHARTER [1]

Carta Regis Eadwardi Anglice

Eadward king gret his bisceopas and his abbotes and his heorlas, and thegnas the on tham scyran syndon the Ordric abbud heafth land inne ; and hic kythe eow thaet ic haebbe geunnon him in to sancta Mariam mynstre, (i) sake and (ii) socne, (iii) toll and (iv) team, and (v) infangnenetheof binnan burgon and buton burgon, (vi) hamsocne, and (vii) grithbryce, and (viii) foresteal, ofer his agen lande.

And ic nelle nanum men gethafian thaet him aeng thara thinga of anime the ic him geunnen haebbe.

Interpretatio in Latinum

Eadwardus rex salutat suos episcopos, et suos abbates, et suos comites et barones, qui in illis vicecomitatibus sunt ubi Ordricus abbas habet terram infra ; et ego ostendo vobis quia ego habeo permissum sibi ad sanctae Mariae monasterium, (i) litigium, (ii) exquisitionem, (iii) teloneum, et appropriationem, et (v) infra captum latronem, infra burgum et extra burgum, (vi) domus assaltum, et (vii) pacis infractionem, (viii) obviationem, super suam propriam terram.

Et ego nolo ulli homini permittere ut ei aliqua harum rerum auferat quae ego sibi concessi habere.

[1] Writ of Edward the Confessor, c. 1065, in Saxon and in Latin. Stevenson, i. 464. Powers so extensive remind us of the Benedictine Abbot quoted in Gibbon : ' My vow of poverty has given me an hundred thousand crowns a year ; my vow of obedience has raised me to the rank of a sovereign prince.'

CHAPTER II

THE NORMAN CONQUEST

1066-1189

THE effects of the Norman Conquest were felt heavily in Abingdon.
Freeman, in his great work on the Norman Conquest, has taken Berkshire as the typical instance of the social changes that took place,
partly because Berkshire was a typical Saxon district, and partly
because the Chronicle of Abingdon Abbey affords so much material.[1]

The chronicler records the appearance for a week of 'the unusual
star, which they call a comet' at Easter, 1066, which was taken as
foreboding the two invasions of that autumn.[2] We do not know if
any Abingdonians helped Harold to meet Hardrada at Stamford Bridge,
but at the Battle of Hastings many military tenants of the Abbey fell
fighting under Harold's standard. Among them figure the wealthy
Turkill of Kingston Bagpuize, and Godric of Fyfield, sheriff of Berkshire. Their lands passed into the possession of Henry de Ferrars, for
the Conqueror developed his policy of filling up the tenancies with
Norman and other suitable occupiers, who succeeded to all the rights
and duties of their predecessors, as if by legal succession.[3] Freeman
points out that Henry de Ferrars availed himself of the confusion
of the times to take also lands that should legally have reverted to the
Abbey, just as William himself did in the case of the Isle of Andersey.

The Abbey fell naturally under the Conqueror's displeasure, and its
church was plundered of its ornaments.[4] But the Abbot Ealdred
retained for a time his place, paying homage to William. About 1070
William sent Ægelwine, Bishop of Durham, to be kept prisoner at
Abingdon Abbey, where he died the following winter.[5] He had
surrendered at Ely with Earl Morcar, leaving Hereward the Wake to

---

[1] Freeman, *Norman Conquest*, vol. iv.
[2] Halley's Comet, which appears in the Bayeux Tapestry. Stevenson, i. 482.
[3] Stevenson, i. 484.   [4] Ibid., 485.
[5] Ibid., 485 ; Anglo-Saxon Chronicle, *ad annum*.

go on with his hopeless struggle. About the same time a band of the Abbey tenants started to join Hereward, but their patriotism met with an early disaster. They were surrounded on the march, taken prisoners by the King's troops, and treated with severity as rebels.[1] The King's displeasure visited Abbot Ealdred as their lord, so that he was deposed and imprisoned in Wallingford Castle, and afterwards committed for the rest of his life to the milder custody of Walkeline, Bishop of Winchester.

Ealdred was succeeded by Ethelhelm, a Norman from Jumièges—with a curiously English name. This abbot attended William's military expedition into Scotland to force Malcolm to acknowledge William as overlord.[2]

The Abbey found itself forced to hire mercenaries to serve as a bodyguard to the Abbot in the troubled district, and to supply its quota to the garrisons of Wallingford Castle and Oxford Castle. In Saxon times some twelve vassals and twelve shields were all that it had to furnish to the King's host. With the Conquest this number largely increased. Accordingly, the Abbey soon dropped into the practice of granting its lands to be held on military tenure, and we see the feudal system, not suddenly created by edict, but gradually growing up as a convenient system, which had commenced here as elsewhere before the Conquest.[3]

Under a Norman Abbot the Abbey again prospered and enjoyed William's favour. According to the chronicler, William I, and later on his son William II sojourned often at the Isle of Andersey, when he came into this district, yielding to the charm of the river with its green meadows.[4] This Isle of Andersey lies between the two channels of the Thames, and is crossed by the causeway from Abingdon Bridge to Culham Bridge. It has an interesting record. It was appropriated by King Offa of Mercia, as a pleasant site for a palace, for which he gave the monks in exchange the manor of Goosey. Later on the huntsmen and falconers of King Kenulf annoyed the Abbot and his tenants, so that Abbot Rethun acquired Andersey from the King in exchange for the manor of Sutton and one hundred and twenty pounds of silver. It was from Kenulf's maiden sisters that the Abbey received the gift of Culham.[5]

Favour of the Conqueror.

Isle of Andreseia or Andersey.

---

[1] Stevenson, i. 486 'Circumventi in itinere captique incarcerantur, et satis misere affliguntur.' [2] Ibid., ii. 9. [3] Ibid., 3–6.
[4] Ibid., 49 ; cp. Index, *passim.* [5] Ibid., 273–4.

Just before the Conquest (c. 1050) Andersey was granted by the Abbey to a wealthy secular priest, named Blacheman, or Blaecman, who built there a church of St. Andrew (whose name is connected popularly with Andersey), with monastic cells, the buildings being adorned with frescoes and carvings within and without, and sheltered by a fine lead roof.[1] After the Conquest Blaecman risked all to share the fortunes of the widow of Godwine in the western rising. When that failed he fled the country, and William, in restoring to the Abbey its former possessions, retained Andersey, which did not return to the possession of the Abbey until Henry I, at the instance of his wife Matilda, gave it to Abbot Faricius, that he might use the lead of the buildings in his new church of St. Mary.[2]

Leland,[3] who visited Abingdon in Henry VIII's reign immediately after the dissolution, mentions the castle in the middle of Andersey, where the King's ' hauks and hownds ' were kept before the Conquest. He says there was then a barn on the site, known as the ' castelle of the Rhae à flu. praeterlabente '.   This suggests the name of Rye Farm.

Antony Wood, quoting the Reg. Abend. f. 132, which we do not possess, states that William I resided at Abingdon in 1076.[4] Many writers speak of William I as keeping Easter, 1084, at Abingdon, and leaving Prince Henry to be educated at the Abbey, where he earned the soubriquet of Beauclerc. But the chronicler of the Abbey says that the King's son Henry, his brothers being in Normandy with their father, passed Eastertide at Abingdon, with Osmund, Bishop of Salisbury and Miles de Wallingford, surnamed Crispin.   Robert d'Oiley took charge not only of the royal party, but also of the household of the Abbey.[5]

Robert d'Oiley. This Robert d'Oiley, the keeper of Oxford Castle, who afterwards built a bridge at the north of Oxford, persecuted for a time the Abbey. Among other depredations he deprived the Abbey of a certain meadow of Tadmerton, over which the monks grieved bitterly, confiding their grief to Our Lady. She caused d'Oiley to see a vision, in which he was taken to the meadow and so roughly entreated, that he was glad to restore the meadow and sue for pardon.[6] Robert D'Oiley became a friend and benefactor of the Abbey, and was buried within its walls

---

[1] Freeman, iv. 143–4 *n.* ; Stevenson, i. 474.
[2] Stevenson, ii. 52.   [3] *Itinerary*, ii. 13 and vol. vii.
[4] *Hist. of Oxford*, i. 130.   [5] Stevenson, ii. 12.
[6] Ibid., 7, 13, where vivid details are given.

with his wife.   Both he and Miles de Wallingford married Saxon
heiresses, thus confirming their position.

The following episode illustrates the lawless state of the times.   In
the days of Abbot Ethelhelm some military tenants of Abingdon, going
to Normandy in the King's service, were captured at sea in their
oared-galley by pirates, and robbed of everything but life, some of
them even having their hands chopped off.   The King ordered the
Abbot of Abingdon to make provision for at least one of these.[1]

The great Domesday Survey of the Conqueror indicates that the **Domesday.**
Abbey was then the greatest landlord in Berkshire, except the King.
Of this survey an early writer pathetically remarks : ' So very narrowly
he caused it to be traced out, that there was not one single hide, nor
one yard of land, nor even—it were shame to tell, though it seemed to
him no shame to do—an ox, nor a cow, nor a swine was left, that was
not set down in his writ.'

The Abbey is set down as holding in its own hands thirty-one
manors in Berkshire alone, besides having others in fee.   Its Berkshire
estates spread over Cumnor, Witham, Barton, Shippon, Dry Sandford,
Bayworth, Sunningwell, Kennington, Chieveley, Welford, Leckhamp-
stead, Weston, Boxford, Beedon, Benham, Marcham, Frilford, Tubney,
Besilsleigh, Garford, East Hanney, Goosey, Lyford, Draycott Moor,
Milton, Appleford, Sutton Courtney, Little Wittenham, Winkfield,
Whistley, Farnborough, Chilton, Kintbury, Watchfield, Uffington,
Sparsholt, Longworth, Charney, Shellingford, Pusey, East Lockinge,
West Ginge, Buckland.[2]

William Rufus bestowed his friendship and favour upon Abbot **Rufus.**
Reginald, to whom he gave the church of Sutton.[3]   Abbot Reginald
acquired for the Abbey certain lands at Scipena or Shippon by the
payment of thirty pounds of ' denarii ' to Hugh, Earl of Chester, who
stipulated that he and his family should be enrolled in the Book of
Commemorations.[4]

Upon the death of Reginald in 1097, Rufus kept the abbacy vacant
until his own death three years later.   The prior Motbert managed
affairs in the interval, and the King and the prior brought the Abbey
to a low ebb.   The revenues fell, the buildings became ruinous, and the

---

[1] Stevenson, ii. 6.   [3] *Victoria History : Berks.*
[2] C. 1090.   Stevenson, ii. 26.
[4] Ibid.,   19–20   ' Viculus   est   burgo   Abbendonensi   contiguus   Scipena
dictus,' &c.

number of monks fell from fifty to thirty-two.[1] The chronicler states that Motbert, following the evil practice of that age, managed the internal and external affairs of the Abbey, not in the interests of the Church, but for the pocket of the King; and he seems to relate with complacency the shooting of Rufus when he was enjoying the pleasures of the chase : ' dum cibatus venatum exerceret.'[2]

Faricius.

Henry I, after his succession to the throne, gave the abbacy to Faricius, the greatest of the successors of St. Ethelwold at Abingdon. Faricius was a native of Arezzo in Tuscany, a skilled doctor, who attended King Henry and his queen Matilda, a distinguished scientist and scholar, and a wise and active man of affairs. Before he came to Abingdon, he was a monk at Malmesbury, where he held the office of cellarer. He is the author of a Life of St. Aldhelm. He was consecrated Abbot of Abingdon by Robert, Bishop of Lincoln, on All Saints Day, 1100, and his rule there until his death in 1117 was marked by important reforms, by great building operations, and by the general prosperity of the society.[3]

When Faricius arrived at Abingdon, he dismounted from his horse at the Ock Bridge, and proceeded barefoot to the great church of St. Mary. As the Archbishop Anselm was in exile, Faricius immediately after the mass laid his pastoral staff upon the altar, until the return of the Archbishop to England.[4]

The ceremony of admission of an abbot of Abingdon is prescribed in the *De Obedientiariis*. The abbot-elect put off his shoes at the door of the church, and proceeded barefoot up the nave to meet the procession of the members of the house. Escorted by them, he knelt at the topmost step of the entrance to the choir ; then he was placed in his stall by the Bishop or his deputy. The monks proceeded to bestow twice kneeling the kiss of peace upon the Abbot, who stood staff in hand. Finally, he put on his shoes in the vestry, a chapter was held, and a sermon preached by the Bishop. At the ensuing feast the Convent had every man a measure of wine, a whole loaf, and three

---

[1] *De Abbatibus*, Stevenson, ii. 285. In ii. 289, twenty-eight is the number given.

[2] Stevenson, ii. 42, 43 'Ea tempestate infanda usurpata in Anglia consuetudo ut . . . honor ecclesiasticus fisco deputaretur regio.' 'Motbertus . . . curam rerum infra extrave ministrabat non ecclesiae provectibus, sed regii marsupii mercibus.'

[3] For Faricius cp. Stevenson, ii. 44 seq., and ii. 285 seq. There is an article on him in the *Dictionary of National Biography*.

[4] *De Abbatibus*, Stevenson, ii. 286.

ANNO gͬ ab incarnatione xp̃i. m̅l.
c. predicto henrico regnante.
quarto mense principatus ip-
sius id: nouembri die celebri
...ans omnium sc̄orum. p ma-
...um ep̄i lincoliensis Robti
domnum FABRICIUS ex malmesbiriensi ce
nobio monachum abbendoniam direxit.
et ut debitam illi subiectionem deferrent mo-
nachis mandauit. ualiorem eis fore nusq̃m
ut rebatur posse se puide patronum conser-
uans. hec estimatio quantum su̅ in re appli-
ata: quandiu ecc̄e huius aliq̃d durauerit
monimentum. tamdiu eadem uera pcessis-
sise p̄dicabit. hic itaq; genere tuscus. urbis
arretie ciuis. pbatissimus officio medicus.
adeo ut eius solius amadotum confectioni-
bus rex ipse se credebo sepe medendum. esc̄ari
prudentia qd̄ hoc tempore regimini ecc̄la-
rum pnecessarium sto cauatissimus. littera-
rum ad pme scientia optime eruditus. huic
etiam sese pcellas medicis regina. sed et tot angtie
maiores natu crediderunt. Tante u̅ affabilita-
tis et urbanitatis erat. uo p parum uideo
auditorib; plixum ipsi eloquium. Agilis
ipse ad queq; exercitia. mire frigoris et calo-
ris patiens. sobrietatis integre a puero ad
uite finem studens. ac p hoc memoue p̄-
dicabile et pspicacis. Qd̄ u̅ multas honore
colligitur diuitum scilicet consangui-
tate potiri. parentum caterua in plato-
ne ambiri. qa talib; obsequiis cu̅ occurrere.
id totum iste refutans. sola prudentie
disciplina constipatus. tam ecc̄lasticis
quam scolarib; intantu̅ circa s̄ pecte uiris
occurrebat. ut multo ampli̅ ipsu̅ unicu̅
q̃s quemlibet popularem uideres om̄s
honorare. seruire. et circa eum quasi p

admiratione morum et dictorum nobiliu̅ mul-
titudinem coire. Coram rege constitutus se-
ria honestatis mox inserebat. nec erat diffi-
cile imperatu. que fieri ab eo quercbat.
Adeo cuncta quę agebat: eade̅ conuenebã-
t quidem hec di gr̃a uniuersa. ei pie conci-
lerat. quę puesstab; ecc̄e qn̄ regendam
suscepat omnino fideliter impendebat.
Hec quisq̃ placuorum a tempore sc̄i patr
adelwoldi ut studiosissimi abb̄is wlf-
gari eo peurat̃ circa hui loci ualitates
intrinsecus siue foinsecus p̄ futur. nec in
his quandiu uixto tripuit.

INFRA quidem monasterium huiusmo-
do studio contulit. uo cuncta pene frim
habitacula que aut nimiu̅ uetustate
diruta aut minus erant capacia a fun-
damentis reedificata. amplitudine et
qualitate satis honestiora contexeret.
Sanctuarium oratorii quã peuratione ualu-
it augmentauit. Stetauit id sc̄e di genitrie
imago p eum reuerenter cõpacta. et sc̄oru̅
reliquis cauato loco insignita: a dõno
u̅ Radulfo cantuariorum archiepo sa-
crata. Textus quoq; euuangticus. artifi-
cio optimo redimitus opere. et argento puro quedam. alia ex argento et de-
sup deaurata uasa officio altaris plura.
alia ex serico ptima. alia ad honandos
ipsos ecc̄e ambitus. reliqua induen-
dorum sacerdotum leuitaru̅ cantoru̅q;
usib; congrua: idem conspicientib;
testificant. Accedit ad hec et sc̄a patr
nr̄i ADELWOLDI pium patrocinium. spa-
tula scilicet et cum brachio. Que du̅ et
sacre relique a ueteri in noua capsam
p uenerabilem eidem sedis antistitem
Willm̄ cognõto Giffard du̅ sollēpniu̅

handsome dishes of fish.[1] The monks always received kneeling the
commands of the Abbot, and listened kneeling to a letter from him, if
he were absent. Everything was done to enhance the dignity of the
Abbot, who was regarded as a great spiritual prince, with almost
absolute power.[2]

Faricius proceeded to introduce many internal reforms, increasing Norman
the number of the monks to eighty.[3] He rebuilt all the buildings of buildings.
the Abbey, from the foundation—cloister, chapter-house, dormitory,
lavatory, cellar, kitchen, two parlours, one at the east, near the
chapter-house, one at the west, under the Abbot's chapel. He rebuilt
also almost the whole of the church, with the lower portion of the
tower.[4]

The Abingdon Chronicle gives the same list, except that it mentions
two towers and the Abbot's lodgings and chapel. It says that the
timber was fetched from Wales, near Shrewsbury, the double journey
taking six or seven weeks for the teams of twelve bullocks.[5]

Such description of the buildings in their glory, as we have, comes Leland.
from John Leland, who was employed as the King's antiquary between
the years 1534 and 1543, to report on ancient buildings, manuscripts,
&c. In his exhaustive tour of England, he visited Abingdon more
than once, and saw the lately dissolved Abbey. The east parts of the
Norman Church were still to be seen.[6] Again, speaking of Faricius's
church, Leland says that the old Saxon church had stood more northerly
where afterwards the orchard was.[7] These Norman buildings of
Faricius were gradually superseded by the building which went on
steadily in the thirteenth, fourteenth, and fifteenth centuries. But
we can see a delightful instance of Faricius's work upon a smaller scale
in the church of Uffington.[8]

The Chronicle and *De Abbatibus* describe at length how Faricius
enriched the Abbey with relics and ornaments, and strengthened its
endowments with numerous domains, obtained from Henry I and his
queen, 'sometimes with a prayer, sometimes with a price'—'tum

---

[1] 'i galonem vini unicuique: placentam integram: tria fercula piscium
honorabilia.'
[2] *De Obedientiariis Abbatiae Abendoniae*, Stevenson, ii. 336 seq., a *locus
classicus* for Benedictine institutions.
[3] *De Abbatibus*, Stevenson, ii. 287.   [4] Ibid., 286.
[5] Stevenson, ii. 150.   [6] *Itinerary*, ii. 13.   [7] Ibid., vol. vii.
[8] Stevenson, ii. 142 'opus ecclesiae, quod ibi lapideum a fundamento in-
choaverat'.

prece, tum pretio ' ; for the rule of Faricius was looked back to as the
golden age of the great house.

Library.

In *De Abbatibus*, Faricius is stated to have increased the library of
the monastery, and to have caused service-books and other ecclesiastical books to be copied by scribes in the scriptorium. Among the
authors quoted as copied at Abingdon are Augustine and Gregory,
Jerome and Chrysostom, Cyprian and the venerable Bede.[1]

On the death of Anselm, Henry desired to raise Faricius to the
archbishopric of Canterbury, but yielded to the remonstrances of the
bishops, who probably anticipated in Faricius a reformer of abuses,
and an upholder of strict discipline. *De Abbatibus* states that he was
actually elected, and that the objection of the Bishops of Lincoln and
Salisbury was that it was unseemly that the archbishop should be
a fashionable ladies' doctor.[2]

Writs of
Henry I.

Henry I was probably a frequent visitor at the Abbey; for instance,
there are charters dated at Abingdon in 1110, at Sutton in 1106, at
Besselsleigh (Leia) in 1108.[3]

An interesting writ of Henry I is dated ' in the year in which the
King gave his daughter to the Roman Emperor ', i. e. in 1110. It confirms to the church of St. Mary at Abingdon the mill of Henora on the
south bank of the Ock, in the manor of Sutton, near a bridge at the
entrance of the town of Abingdon, used when the Ock was in flood.
The miller had been annoying the Abbot sometimes by flooding his
meadows, sometimes by keeping back the water from the Abbot's mill
below.[4]

The case of the Mill of Langford and William the miller *v.* the
Abbey of Abingdon, is taken as important in its bearing on the right
of the King to dispossess a private owner, by a writ, with no hint of
prior judicial proceedings,[5] one of the grievances that found a voice in
the Magna Carta of the next century.

A curious little writ was addressed by Henry to all constables and
to all the faithful of the court : ' I forbid any to lodge in the town of
Abbendune save with the leave of Abbot Faricius.' [6]

Abingdon was not the Abbot's only place of residence : he had

---

[1] Stevenson, ii. 289.

[2] 'dicentes non debere archiepiscopum urinas mulierum inspicere.' Ibid.,
ii. 287.

[3] Ibid., ii. 533, 536, 538.   [4] Ibid., 64 ; cp. ii. 109.

[5] Ibid., 123.   [6] Ibid., 80. Dated at Oxford, c. 1107.

a residence outside the walls of Winchester.[1] He had also a residence in 'Westminstrestret', overlooking the river between Westminster and London, near the church of St. Innocents, which was also his.[2]

We find Henry confirming the Abbot in his jurisdiction over the Hundred of Hormer,[3] which goes back into Saxon times. This jurisdiction reached almost to the walls of Oxford, so that the Abbot used to hold court at Grandpont.

Faricius and his times occupy a lion's share in Stevenson's second volume, and with reason, when we consider the importance and variety of his activities. He is remembered for many things, but not least as a great builder, and it was not unnatural that he should dwell at the last on the text from the Vulgate, 'Lord, I have loved the honour of thy house.'[4]

Death of Faricius.

After the death of Faricius the abbacy was held vacant for four years, during which the venerable Warenger, prior since the time of Abbot Reginald, ruled the house. In 1121, Henry, on his return from Normandy, appointed Vincent a monk of Jumièges.

Abingdon Market.

Vincent and his successors had to fight hard for the right of a full market at Abingdon ; and in this struggle, which lasted during the next two reigns, it is pleasing to notice that the Abbey and the townsmen of Abingdon were fighting on the same side.[5] In the chronicler's account, certain malignant persons approached the King and persuaded him that the Abbot had no rights over the Hundred of Hormer, and that there was no market by ancient use in the town. The King's justices promptly placed the whole Abbey in forfeit.

Abbot Vincent proceeded to lay before the King the Abbey charters, and on the strength of these, supported by a gift of three hundred marks of silver, raised by stripping the gold and silver table of St. Ethelwold, he obtained from the King writs establishing his rights of market at Abingdon, his jurisdiction over the Hundred of Hormer, and his right to hold his court in Oxford. King Stephen, in 1146, confirmed this right of market among the rights of the Abbey. In Henry II's reign the men of Wallingford, supported by the men of Oxford, represented to the King that Abingdon had no right of market, except for certain trivial commodities, and obtained a prohibition of the market.

---

[1] Stevenson, ii. 111.   Ibid., 15, 75, 192.
[2] Ibid., 115.   [4] Ibid., 290.
[5] Ibid., 163, 180, 217, 227–8. Cp. Stevenson's Introd., vol. ii.

They then came to Abingdon with the constable of Wallingford on a Sunday—for markets and fairs were connected with the holy days of the Church, a practice illustrated by the market-crosses of England —and attempted to expel by force the country-folk and all who had their wares exposed for sale. The Abingdonians, taking seriously the defence of their market, and ' taking courage I know not whence '[1], drove their adversaries far from the town. The men of Wallingford appealed again to the King, who being abroad referred the matter to Robert, Earl of Leicester, and thirty-four elders of Berkshire, as a jury. The evidence was conflicting : the men of Wallingford limiting the market to bread and beer—' cervisia ',—those of Oxford admitting more than this, but casting doubt on the trade by barge and cart, with the exception of the Abbot's barges for his own use. The Earl of Leicester, in reporting to the King the indecision of his jury, added his own decisive evidence that ' he had himself witnessed the full market in the reign of Henry I, and further back in the reign of William, when he was a boy, being educated at Abingdon '.[2] The opponents would not accept their defeat, but approached the King at Reading, pressing their case with pertinacity. This was too much for Henry II, who was not the mildest of men. He drove them violently from his presence,[3] forbad all renewal of the appeal, and issued a writ in 1158, granting Abbot Walkelin, formerly a monk at Evesham, full right of market at Abingdon, only excepting the barges other than those of the Abbot.[4] Thus ended an interesting episode in the growth of the trade of Abingdon, in which the Abbey figures as the active patron of the town.

Details
Henry I.

It remains to add a few details of this period. Abbot Vincent built baths for the monks, to replace the more primitive arrangements.[5] A little meadow was set aside in the hands of the camerarius or chamberlain to provide ' hay under the feet of the monks at the baths '.[6]

In 1131 the next Abbot Ingulf, ex-prior of Winchester, is a witness

[1] ' assumpta nescio unde audacia.'

[2] ' cum adhuc puer esset, et apud Abbendonam nutriretur regis Willelmi tempore.'

[3] ' rex indignatus, eosdem a se turbulenter abegit.'

[4] ' mercatum plenissimum . . . navibus tantum exceptis, abbate tantummodo suis utente.'

[5] Stevenson, ii. 290 ' Hic, antequam monachi surgerent, implere solitus erat lavatorium aqua.'

[6] De Consuet. Abbend. Stevenson, ii. 300 ' Habet etiam pratellum de Stocgrave, unde invenit foenum sub pedibus monachorum quando balneant.'

among others at the Northampton Council of a charter of Henry I
to the church of Salisbury.[1]

The troubles of the civil war between Stephen and Matilda find
their echo in the pages of the Abingdon chronicler.[2]   On March 3, 1141,
Ingulf was among the supporters of Matilda at Winchester Cathedral.[3]
The Abbey was fined by Stephen, and its money-chest broken open
and robbed to pay his troops.   The money taken was a hoard accumu-
lated by Ingulf to restore the coffer of St. Vincent, the gift of Canute,
which had been stripped of its gold and silver to relieve the poor in
time of famine.[4]   A little later the Queen-Empress, escaping from the
siege of Oxford, across the frozen river, fled on foot through the snow
to Abingdon, and thence on horse to Wallingford Castle.

Stephen
and
Matilda.

In Henry II's firm hands the country had peace.   In April, 1165,
the Archbishop of Cologne passed through Abingdon on his way to
interview the Queen and Princess Matilda.

Henry II.

The writer of *De Abbatibus* estimates briefly the Abbots after
Walkelin.   Geoffrey was insolent, and hated by the monks, which led
the King to depose him.   This was the Bishop of St. Asaph, the famous
historian, known as Geoffrey of Monmouth.   Some writers state he
was buried at Abingdon.   Roger, the Prior of Bermondsey, was suspicious and cruel.   Alfred, the Prior of Rochester, was modest and
witty, but a miser even in a time of terrible famine.   Hugh was a monk
of Abingdon, who proved an Abbot without reproach.[5]

In the gap between Roger and Alfred the King appointed Thomas
de Esseburne custodian of the Abbey, and his unjust rule led to the
compiling of the valuable Consuetudinary.   The celebrated Chief
Justice, Ralph de Glanville, protected the monks in this crisis.[6]

With the charter of Richard I upon his accession, we come to the
end of the Abingdon Chronicle and the *De Abbatibus*, and are left to
find our way through the next period with other guides.

[1] Quoted by Gasquet, *Henry III and the Church.*
[2] Stevenson, ii. 178.
[3] William of Malmesbury, Rolls Series, ii. 573.
[4] Stevenson, ii. 210, 291–2.   [5] Ibid., 293.   [6] Ibid., 237, 297.

CHAPTER III

ST. EDMUND OF ABINGDON[1]

1170-1240

EDMUND RICH, who exercised a deeper influence on the imagination of Englishmen than any other Abingdonian has done, was born at Abingdon on November 20, the feast of St. Edmund the King, about the year 1170. He was the son of Edward or Reinald Rich. Of his three brothers, Robert wrote one of his biographies. His two sisters, Margaret and Alice, became prioresses of Catesby. Edmund's boyhood seems to have been spent at Abingdon and Oxford. His mother Mabel enticed him by little allurements to practise extreme asceticism like herself, to wear sackcloth, to fast on Friday, to refuse food on Sunday and other feast-days until he had sung the whole psalter. The family was apparently in easy circumstances, but Mabel's severe discipline did not make the home a comfortable one to the father. To quote Hook's *Lives*: ' We are not, however, surprised to find that the more self-indulgent old merchant preferred a monastery to such a home as that which Mabel latterly provided for him.' So the father withdrew to the greater comfort of the monastery of Evesham, or more probably Ensham near Oxford. Edmund and Robert were sent to be educated at Paris, then closely connected with Oxford. But the mother either could not or would not provide them with much money, so that the lads had to beg their way from place to place. Mabel's girdle was regarded many generations later as a treasure to be bequeathed as an heirloom. The next few years of his life were spent at Paris and Oxford in study and in teaching. The cathedral of Notre-Dame de Paris had recently been completed in the magnificence of the new pointed style, and serves as a link between the Paris of St. Edmund and the Paris of to-day. Of the Oxford of his day we are still reminded amid many changes by the castle, the town walls, the tower of St. Michael, the small crypt of St. Peter's in the East, and Christ Church Cathedral—

---

[1] Cp. *Dictionary of National Biography*, and Hook's *Lives of the Archbishops*, &c.

then St. Frideswide's Priory. At Paris Edmund played the part of Joseph to a fair siren, and behaved with less than his usual chivalry. He invited to the assignation the University authorities, who proceeded to lay bare the back of the frail maiden and the offending Eve was whipped out of her. Edmund practised austere self-discipline, wore garments of rope-cloth and horse-hair, and showed himself careless about teacher's fees both at Paris and Oxford. He was devoted to his pupils, nursing them in sickness and selling the treasures of his library to give to needy scholars. Edmund taught at first in the secular learning of Oxford, and was one of the pioneers in the revival of the study of Greek. Roger Bacon, the great scientist, speaks of him as ' Edmund, the first in my time who read the Elements—of Aristotle— at Oxford.' Later on Edmund joined the Austin Canons of Merton, and abandoned the vanity of secular studies for theology. He at once became famous as a preacher. Among his penitents was William Longsword, Earl of Salisbury, son of Henry II. Oxford had fallen on evil days owing to the tyranny of King John and the turbulence of the students and townsmen. Its existence as a seat of learning was threatened by the migrations of students to other places. St. Edmund with the friars took a great part in restoring its high character for learning and conduct. Three centuries later another Abingdonian, Sir John Mason, took a leading part in saving Oxford from confiscation in the days of the dissolution of the monasteries.

In 1222 Edmund left Oxford to become treasurer of Salisbury Cathedral and prebend of Calne. During the eleven years that he held this post he must have taken a share in the work of building the most graceful of all English cathedrals. At this time he was engaged in preaching the crusade all over England with marked success. In 1233 he received at Calne the news that he had been appointed Archbishop of Canterbury by the pope, to whom a disputed election had been referred. In the words of Capgrave : ' The pope cassed the eleccion. Thanne were the munkis at her liberte to have a new eleccion ; and thei chose Maister Edmund Abyngdon, a holy man, which was thanne tresorer of Salisbury.'

Prince Edward, afterwards the great Edward I, was confirmed by him, and perhaps in later life derived from him something of his crusading zeal and his popular sympathies. As archbishop he supported the barons of the national party against Henry III's favourites, and rebuked the King for the murder of the Earl Marshal. He excom-

municated the famous Simon de Montfort for his clandestine marriage
with Eleanor, the King's sister. He was the champion of the English
church against the tax-gatherers of Rome, and was further involved in
constant disputes with his own monks.

He finally broke down under the stress of all these struggles, in-
volving an unsuccessful visit to Rome to plead his causes in person. At
last, like his great predecessors Thomas à Becket and Stephen Langton,
he retired from his troubled life to an exile of despair at Pontigny, and
lived in seclusion as a simple monk. As a boy he had seen visions in
the fields of Abingdon and Oxford. The end of his life at Pontigny and
Soisy was also vision-haunted. Death came to him at Soisy on
November 16, 1240, and his body was carried back to Pontigny, where
his shrine may be seen behind the High Altar.

The miracles reported at his tomb, and still more, his holy character,
led at last to his canonization. This was hotly opposed, but finally
allowed owing to the warm support of Louis IX. It was not his political
capacity so much as the charm of his character that attracted the
affection of his own and succeeding generations. He spent the ' amerce-
ments ' of his see in portioning his poorer tenants' daughters. He
would tolerate neither bribery nor gifts, was a good steward of the estates
of his office, and was hospitable in spite of his personal austerity. To
the end he wore a cheap tunic of grey or white in preference to purple
and fine linen. The chronicler quaintly remarks that, when he was
primate of all England, he did not blush to take off his own shoes.

Among his writings must be mentioned his ' Constitutions ', which
give an interesting account of his reforms and aims, and throw light
on the manners of that age. He also wrote *Speculum Ecclesiae*, or the
Mirror of the Church. A black letter quarto of Latin sermons, undated,
c. 1521, with nice woodcuts, contains ' A Myrour of the Chyrche made
by Saynt Austyn of Abyndon '. St. Austin is a slip for St. Edmund of
Abingdon. This and other editions indicate the hold that the Abingdon
preacher had taken on the minds of Englishmen. In the English envoy
of the printer it professes to be ' rudely endited ', ' that ye reders leve
not the fruytfull sentence of within for the curious fable of without.'

In memory of St. Edmund in 1288, Edmund, Earl of Cornwall,
founded St. Edmund's Chapel in the parish of St. Helen's at Abingdon,
near St. Edmund's reputed birthplace. The maintenance of the
Chapel and its two priests was undertaken by the Abbot of Abingdon,
who was patron and rector of St. Helen's. The measurements of the

St. Ed-
mund's
Chapel.

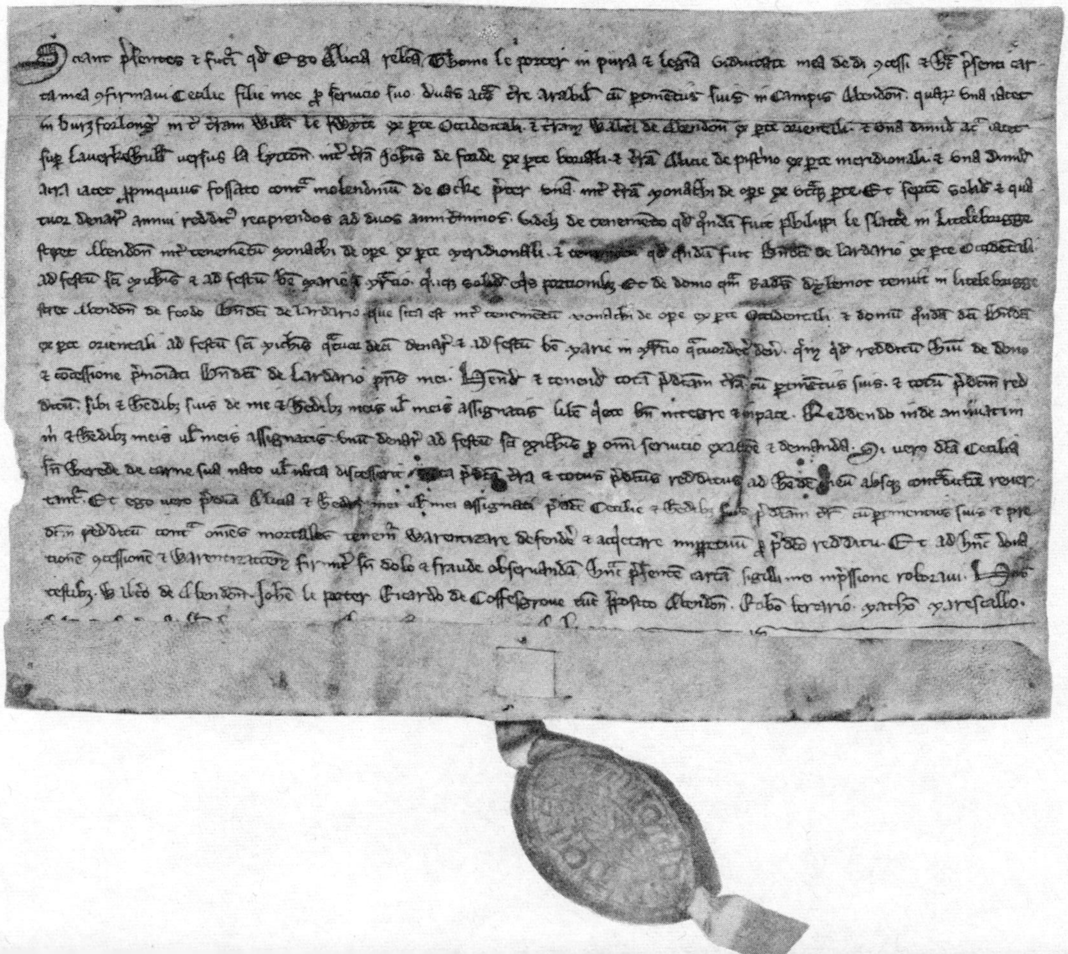

Chapel were 88×60 feet. The buildings comprised chapel, hall, pantry, buttery, kitchen, upper chamber, and dormitory. The Chapel appears frequently in the accounts of the Chapel Wardens.[1] The site of the house and garden now known as the Old Vicarage, lying between St. Edmund's Lane and West St. Helen's Street, seems to suit the various references as well as any other that has been suggested.[2]

Among the Corporation treasures is a Henry VI map of Abingdon, 9×1½ feet, which was for centuries in the possession of the Verneys of Buckinghamshire. This great oil painting of the middle of the fifteenth century gives the course of the river very clearly, and the positions of buildings from Radley to Barton, the great Abbey, and the market-place. Its colouring is very vivid ; the handwriting of local names is late Elizabethan in its careless style. The Abbey buildings seem to have been partly erased, perhaps to bring it up to date. On the left of this map is a chapel with windows in two storeys, and a round tower at the south-west corner. This has been accepted as a symbol of St. Helen's Church. But this would be carrying the artistic licence too far, as the lines and junction of East and West St. Helen's Streets are clearly defined, and this chapel stands not near the river, but half-way up West St. Helen's Street on the west side. In fact the building fits in so well with the description and traditional position of St. Edmund's Chapel that it is difficult not to identify it as such. In that case we must account for the absence of St. Helen's Church from the map by an erasure of that corner of the map.

Most of the tenements belonging to the Chapel were bequeathed Porter by one John Porter, for the souls of whom and of his wife daily prayer family. was said. Among the documents presented by Sir Edmund Verney to the Corporation is a beautifully written little Latin parchment— 8 × 6 inches—with a nice seal, undated, of the thirteenth century.[3] It is a deed of gift of Alice, relict of Thomas le Porter, in pure and lawful widowhood, to her daughter Cecilia, of land and tenements :— one acre in the ' burgh forlong ' between the lands of William le Fwyte and of Walter de Abendon ; half an acre on Lauerkehulle—Larkhill— towards la Lyttone between the lands of John de Forde and of Alice of the Bakery ; half an acre near the ditch against Ock Mill ; besides an

---

[1] Cp. Kirk, *Account Rolls of the Obedientiars*, Introduction and Index. There are six Accounts, 1404–79.

[2] Lysons, however, gives the traditional site as west of St. Edmund's Lane.

[3] See Plate III.

acre between the land of the Monk of Work on either side.   Also rents
from a tenement in Litelebrigge stret, formerly belonging to Philip le
Slatter, between the tenements of the Monk of Work and of Benedict
of the Larder ; and from the house which Ralph Dylemot held in
Littlebrigge stret from the fee of Benedict of the Larder.   This rent
Alice le Porter had inherited from Benedict of the Larder, her father.
This is witnessed by Walter of Abendon, John le Porter, Richard of
Coffesgrove, then provost of Abendon, Robert the herdsman, Matthew
the Smith, John de Forde, William the Porter, and many others.

The Porters were evidently people of substance at the end of the
thirteenth century.   John the Porter, who witnesses this deed, may
well have been the benefactor of St. Edmund's Chapel.[1]

[1] The 'monk of work'—*monachus de opere*—may have been the officer
in charge of the Abbey buildings. The Abingdon Consuetudinary uses 'operarius'
in that sense.   James I's charter (1609) mentions a Monk of the Works as lately
owning ninety-two acres of land in Abingdon fields, part of the Manor of Nore-
cotte.   Benedictus de Lardario would also be an Abbey officer.

CHAPTER IV

THE THIRTEENTH AND FOURTEENTH CENTURIES

1189–1416

THE itinerary of King John shows that he was constantly in this neighbourhood in his visits to Woodstock, Faringdon, &c. In the course of his rapid journeys he was at ' Abbedun ' on December 2, 1200 ; again on April 21, 1203 ; on February 6–8, 1205 ; on March 29, 1205 ; and lastly, on July 15, 1215, just a month after signing the Magna Carta—which must have made him a pleasant guest.[1] *King John.*

Matthew Paris, who has been described as the greatest and last of our monastic historians, quotes a letter addressed in 1216 by the Pope to the Abbot of Abingdon to excommunicate the refractory barons. This was published by the Abbot, but received contumaciously. It speaks of John as ' the most illustrious King of England, signed with the cross, and the vassal of the Church of Rome '.[2]

When the friars first came to England from the Continent about the year 1221, they were brought into early contact with the Abbey of Abingdon or its dependents. The story appears in J. R. Green's *Short History*, but the authority is not given. *Henry III. The Friars.*

' The Black Friars of Dominic, the Grey Friars of Francis, were received with the same delight (by the neglected towns). As the older orders had chosen the country, the friars chose the town. They had hardly landed at Dover before they made straight for London and Oxford. In their ignorance of the road the two first Grey Brothers lost their way in the woods between Oxford and Baldon, and, fearful of night and of the floods, turned aside to a grange of the monks of Abingdon. Their ragged clothes and foreign gestures, as they prayed for hospitality, led the porter to take them for jongleurs, the jesters and jugglers of the day, and the news of this break in the monotony of their lives brought prior, sacrist, and cellarer to the door to welcome them and witness their tricks. Their disappointment was too much for the temper of the monks, and the brothers were kicked roughly

---

[1] *Archaeologia*, 1829, xxii. 131.
[2] *Chronica Majora*, Rolls Series, ii. 642.

from the gate to find their night's lodging under the tree. But the welcome
of the townsmen made up everywhere for the ill will and opposition of both
clergy and monks.'

It is beyond the range of this book to speak of the work done by
the friars in the slums of the mediaeval cities as well as in the schools
of Oxford in contrast with the rural seclusion of the great seats of
monachism. But perhaps the fourteenth rather than the thirteenth
century might be taken as the point at which monachism began to
get out of touch with the main stream of national life, content to live
in rural backwaters, sometimes beneficently, sometimes harmlessly,
sometimes in luxurious sloth.

**Langland
on Monks
and Friars.** William Langland, in *Piers the Plowman* (1362–99), compares the
monks and the friars to the advantage of the latter, taking Abingdon
as the type of the monastic life.

> And thanne freres in here freitoure shall fynden a keye
> Of Costantynes coffres in which is the catel
> That Gregories god-children haue yuel dispended,
> And thanne shall the Abbot of Abyndoun and alle his issu for euere
> Haue a knocke of a kynge and incurable the wound.[1]

The general sense is that some day the poor friars will not have
to beg their bread, but will find their food in a refectory at the expense
of the wasteful monks, the god-children of Pope Gregory, who sent
Augustine. The prophecy was curiously fulfilled two centuries later
when the Abbot and monks of Abingdon had 'a knock of a king' from
Henry VIII on their tonsured crowns. Abingdon Abbey is justly
taken as representative of English monachism. When Ingoldsby
centuries later writes his rollicking legends, the phrase 'the fat Abbot
of Abingdon' seems to come naturally into his alliterative verse.

In 1222 the Abbot of Abingdon presented a full set of vestments and a cope to the Cathedral of Salisbury, which was then
being built.[2]

A transcript in the same register gives a summary of privileges
granted c. 1224 to the Abbot of Abingdon, as against the church of
Sarum, by Honorius, Bishop of Rome : freedom from certain tithes,
and from episcopal control except in cases of evident necessity, and
the free enjoyment of ancient liberties and approved customs. Honorius

---

[1] Skeat's *Edition, B. Pass.,* x. 326.
[2] *Reg. S. Osmundi,* Rolls Series, 1883, *ad an.*

speaks of the Abbot as ' from the din of this age retiring in cloistral seclusion, contemplating the charm of peace.' [1]

In 1232 a curious leave was granted by the Pope to the monks of Abingdon to wear caps at divine offices, ' the cold of those parts being vehement.' [2]   Henry III.

In 1239 the Abbey Church was rededicated by Robert of Salisbury about the same time as the church of Wells.[3]   In June, 1249, Abingdon was devastated by a flood, which swept away crops and sheep, and even mills and bridges.[4]

Matthew Paris is our chief authority for this reign, and his friend-ship with Henry III did not bias his independent and patriotic attitude. From him we learn that in 1248 the living of St. Helen's at Abingdon, a rich and famous church estimated at 100 marks,[5] was demanded by the Pope of the Abbot, John de Blomevil, for a certain Roman, and by Henry III for Ethelmar his half-brother, who already had so many livings that he knew neither their number nor their worth. The per-plexed Abbot gave it to the King's brother under promise of protection against the Pope. But, alas ! deserted by the King, he had to travel in age and sickness to the Roman court at Lyons, where he was harassed and heavily fined. This same Ethelmar, when he became Bishop of Winchester, so starved and ill-treated the monks of Winchester, that in 1254 they took refuge at Abingdon and other monasteries of the black order.[6]   Ethelmar.

In 1256 the monks of Abingdon, foreseeing the end of their aged and now paralytic Abbot, sent a deputation to bargain with Henry III for a licence to elect a successor. Henry, not knowing the facts about the Abbot's hopeless condition, let them have this for 500 marks. The Abbot died within a fortnight of the monks' return—to the wrath of Henry, that he had not exacted more.[7]

Many royal visits of Henry III to Abingdon, during his struggle with the barons, are recorded : for instance, on his return from Gascony in 1258 he was present at a grand procession at the Abbey. In 1260 he was honourably entertained at the Abbey after Michaelmas, and he came again the year following at the Feast of St. Barnabas. In   Visits of Henry III.

---

[1] *Reg. S. Osmundi*, Rolls Series, 1883, *ad an.*   [2] *Cal. Pap., Letters.*
[3] *Chronica Majora*, iii. 638.   [4] Ibid., v. 75.
[5] ' Ecclesia nobilis et opulenta.'   *Chronica Majora*, v. 38.
[6] *Chronica Majora*, v. 468.
[7] Ibid., v. 567. Henry expresses himself regally, ' O pro capite dei, qualiter fallor ! '

1262, on St. Leonard's Day, he marched from Oxford to Abingdon with his whole army with banners flying.[1]

In 1257, Boniface, Archbishop of Canterbury, came to Abingdon in visitation.[2] In 1258 the Abbot was involved in a dispute with the Pope about the appointment to Sutton Church, and forced to accept the Italian candidate in place of the English. In that year the Abbey had bought Sutton Church for 110 marks.[3] In 1260–1 a deputation from the Abbey brought back from Rome many privileges—at the price of 600 marks—including the grant of the churches of Kensington, Sutton, and of St. Helen's, Abingdon, to their own use, and the privilege

Edward I. of the mitre.[4] In 1285 the Archbishop of Canterbury visited Abingdon. A general chapter was held at the Abbey at St. Matthew's Feast.[5]

In 1297 this chronicler gives a hint of the declining popularity of the clergy. Under the year 1297 he says that rectors of churches and other clergy wore close garments, when they rode, that they might not be recognized, and so might travel in security.[6]

Visits of Visits of Edward I to Abingdon are also upon record : for instance,
Edward I. in 1276 on November 12 and November 20–4 ; in 1281 on March 2–3 ; in 1290 on February 18.[7]

In 1301 the Abbot of Abingdon was ordered by Edward I to search his house for historical matter relating to Scotland,[8] doubtless with a view to establishing the English claim to the crown, or at least the overlordship of Scotland. It is curious that two centuries and a half later, in the reign of Edward VI, Sir John Mason, a distinguished Abingdonian, was engaged in searching the public records for the same purpose.

Lotorium. In the Verney Papers (Camden Society) is quoted in the Latin an Indulgence, dated 1308, to all, who, being penitent and having confessed, should help to erect the ' Lotorium '—probably a building for ablutions in the church—or should do other needful work in the Church of St. Mary, Abingdon ; or should leave a legacy to the same, or procure the leaving thereof ; or should say the Lord's Prayer and Angelical Salutation thrice with a pious mind for the souls of the faithful there resting in Christ.

---

[1] Chronicle of Abingdon Monastery, *ad annum*. This Cambridge MS. published by the Berks Ashmolean Society, 1844, covers the years 1218–1304.
[2] Cambridge MS., *ad annum*.   [3] Ibid.   [4] Ibid.
[5] Ibid.   [6] Ibid.
[7] *Brit. Arch. Soc. Collect.*, 1863, ii. 115–36.   [8] Parliamentary Rolls.

On July 27, 1315, the Abbot of Abingdon with three monks and two sailors was drowned in the Thames near the Abbey in returning from the hospitality of a certain knight in the neighbourhood.[1]

Abbot drowned.

In 1327 a fierce attack was made upon the Abbey by the townsmen of Abingdon, supported by people from Oxford. Anthony Wood gives the following spirited account of the affair : [2]

Great Riot of 1327.

1327. This year I find a most bloody outrage to have been committed by the Scholars and Townsmen of Oxford, joined with the Townsmen of Abendon, on the Monks of the Abbey at that place. The particulars of which being mostly beyond my purpose, yet because the Oxonians had a hand in it, I shall in order set them down.

On Monday next following the Octaves of the Passover, a little after nine of the clock of the night, all the Township of Abendon, great and small, unanimously met together, at the tolling of the common bell, in St. Helen's Church ; and taking counsell together about the ordination of the Mercat, and Stalls, which time out of mind belonged to the Abbey, concluded among themselves, that by their authority the Stalls should be removed, and disposed, as they thought fit. Then the chief Speakers among them laying open to the company the unreasonable dealings (as they termed them) of the Abbat and Convent in relation to the said Mercat, they all unanimously thundred out divers menaces of spoil and death to the Abbey and Monks thereof : which meeting being broken up, the Monks had intelligence of their proceedings by some there present that bore them good will.

The wednesday following, they all met together at the tolling of the bell in the same church of St. Helen about the middle of the night to counsel together how they might execute their malice on the Monastery. At length having concluded what to do, and each captain with his party appointed what part to act, they went at the breaking of the day to the New house, called the Gild hall, situated in the middle of the Town, which having been lately built by the Abbey because the Town and Mercat was theirs, they burnt and totally destroyed. From thence (having intentions to commit an outrage on the Abbey) they went to the church of St. Nicholas, which joineth to the entrance into the said Abbey, and the Gate of that church they forthwith burnt. But while they were in doing it, certain Seculars, who were deputed for the defence of the Monastery, sallied out of the Gate, and violently falling on the said Malefactors, killed two of them, and putting the rest to flight took of them John Bolter, John Bishop, William Poeny, Mr. Maurice, and others; all which they put in the Abbey prison, as Malefactors to be tried by the King's Justices itinerant. Soon after the Monks made proclamation in the King's name in the middle of the Town, that if any of the Malefactors that had committed the outrage and escaped their

---

[1] *Chronicles, Edw. I and II*, Rolls Series, 1882, i. 278.
[2] Anthony Wood's *History of Oxford*, i. 412-19.

hands, would render themselves up, they should be saved harmless etc. with other invitations for stopping of more bloodshed. Soon after many came in, and were with the imprisoned Malefactors set free by the Abbat John de Kannyngs, then newly returned from the country.

But the Abendonians taking these things very grievously, resolved among themselves to be revenged for this bloodshed committed by them. Wherefore they sending privately to the Commonalty of Oxford their complaints of the matter, with great aggravations tending to the disgrace of the Monks, desired their speedy help for satisfaction. This errand the generality of them did willingly receive, and expressed themselves ready to do them service, and the rather because the quarrel was against men of the Clergy ; for they having to do with such people at home, and fighting continually with them (whereby such an innate hatred was ingendred among them, that it was become natural, and is to this day so, as being transmitted from father to son and from man to man), were very sensible of the condition of the Abendonians, and did not know to the contrary, but that they might make use of their help at the next quarrel with the Clerks. Wherefore on the Lord's day following, being the morrow after St. Mark's day the Evangelist, came in the middle of the night the whole Commonalty of Oxford, the Mayor and other Burghers, accompanied (as 'tis said) with a multitude of Scholars, such I suppose that were of a desperate condition, and were glad of any diversion, rather than to study, These I say being all armed, and guided in their way with burning torches, came first to the Manor of Northcote belonging to the Abbey, distant on this side of Abendon about half a mile, and all the houses there that were inhabited by the Tenants they straightway burnt and plucked down. Then entering the Town of Abendon they made a dismal shout to the terror of all the neighbourhood, and going forthwith to the Abbey gate, insultingly cried aloud, gave base and aggravating language, threw stones, shot arrows, and put fire to the Gate, besides other enormities.

At the same time another party went to the gate of St. John's Hospital, hoping there to have entrance, but those that were within stoutly resisted them till the rising of the sun. Soon after they went to the Church of St. Nicholas (while others to the manor of Berton belonging to the said Abbey, which they burnt) through which and the Pietanciary these ministers of Satan entered into the Abbey, and the first thing they did was the freeing of those Malefactors that the Abbat by his authority did detain, then the burning the outer and inner gate of the Abbey, to the end that the diabolical rabble might enter in. These things being done, Edmund de la Beche the captain, favourer and prime ringleader of these malefactors, enters the Church with certain of his followers, and there finding some of the Monks at prayers at the high altar, ready to receive the fatal blow, they dragged them thence, and the head and arm of one of the senior Monks he almost cut off, and so that place by the shedding of blood was polluted. In the mean time the

Abbat and rest of the Monks consulting flight, venture over the river behind the Abbey, and so (except some that were drowned) escaped.

Afterwards the said Malefactors entred into the Treasury of the Church, and there all vestments, copes, chalices, books, and all ornaments of the said church, they sacrilegiously took away. The box also wherein the holy Eucharist was with great devotion reposed, these devils did not fear to lay hands on, use it scornfully, and to throw it among other things to be conveyed away. Then they went to the Treasury of the Abbat, and there all the muniments, charters, obligations, defeisances, rolls of accompts, and of courts, and other evidences of the Monastery which they could find, they consumed them publickly in a fire made for the purpose in the Abbat's court or yard ; nay, those ancient muniments or writings of Noblemen which were merely reposed there for security and safety sake in the times of war among the Saxons, these confounded varlets did with the rest of the Charters most wickedly burn, to the great grief of the Convent, and greater of those that had a respect for venerable antiquity. All the locks in the Dormitory, Infirmary, Kitchin of the Abbat and that of the Convent, with the Larder, Offices of the Obedientiaries, they broke open, and whatsoever they found of any value, they took away, besides the Caxcolae in the Cloister ; all their horses also they led away, and whatsoever was moveable, they left not untouched.

The next day being Monday, the Commonalties of Abendon and Oxford to the number almost of three thousand, for the most part armed, gathered together by the authority of Sir Philip at Bech, or de la Bech, John and Edmund at Bech, in Bagley wood, which is a mile or more distant from Abendon toward Oxford : and after some consultation had among them, they sent for the Prior and those few Monks that remained in the Abbey, to the end that they might treat of peace and concord. After they had received summons for appearance, went to the fatal wood Robert de Haulton the Prior, Reynold de Okke the Chantor, and Thomas de Hakebourne one of the Monks, who being smitten with overmuch fear, were ready to do anything to please the said Malefactors, and to answer to those things they should urge or command. At length several things were demanded of them ; viz. first, a release of all right which the Abbot and Convent were wont to hold and possess in the Town of Abendon by the King's donation beyond the memory of man. Secondly, a release and quiet claim of all action, injury, demands or obligation that should arise from their spoiling the said Abbey, with other things that should be performed with a corporal oath.

All which being proposed, or rather demanded, and the Malefactors protesting in public, that unless they and the Brethren at home would conclude to these things and confirm them, they would cut off their heads, burn the church, Abbey, and all the Mannors belonging thereunto. To these the Prior and Monks humbly answered, that they would grant all these things as much as in them lay, and likewise persuade all the Brethren at home

TOWNSEND

or abroad to do the like, and confirm them. The next day being Tuesday, certain persons of the said Commonalties that were in a special manner deputed for this purpose, came with their Public Notary into the Chapter House of the said Monastery, and the Articles aforesaid with other matters being read before the Prior and rest of the Brethren, whether protest or not protest, did swear to them with their hands laid upon the holy Bible, that none of them or any in their names ' vel procurationem contra dictam conventionem verbo vel facto veniret seu venirent quovis modo, nec super jure eorum seu injuria in curia regali vel aliunde ad eorum remedium aliquid impetrarent etc.' Which being done, a Notary then present was required to make a public instrument in perpetual memory of the thing being done, and afterwards having got the common seal of the Abbey forced the Prior to seal with it, and to three bonds of a thousand pounds apiece not to molest, vex, or call them in question for what they had done.

In the meantime many affronts and troubles were done by the men of Abendon and Oxford to the Monastery, Monks thereof and their tenants.

Fifteen days after, the Bishop of St. David's came, at the instance of the Prior, to the Abbey, and there reconciled the Church, and restored it (after many enormities and bloodshed had been committed therein) to its former state. But the Abbat John de Kannyngs who was forced to fly, as I have before told you, having heard all the passages of this outrage by certain messengers sent for that purpose, made haste to the King, and telling him all the particulars of the desolation of his Abbey, humbly desired that he would provide some course, that the Church, which is subject to his patronage, might be righted for the injuries done thereunto, according to the laws of the kingdom. Wherefore the King in presence of many of his Nobles promised the Abbat that he by the deliberation of his Council would fulfill what he desired. Soon after the King sent letters of protection, to be proclaimed in the counties of Oxford and Berks, to the Sheriff of them, and other faithful subjects, that is a protection of those that had been injured, vexed, plundred, beaten, wounded, etc. Which proclamation being made several times at Oxford, and especially at Abendon by the Sheriff, accompanied with a numerous train, a great terror possessed the hearts of the Malefactors, and lessned immediately their malice.

The Sunday next going before the feast of St. Simon and Jude the same year, the Abbat by the King's command returned to his Monastery, accompanied with many Nobles especially deputed for his protection, besides many Esquires of the counties of Berks, Oxford and Wilts, with a great multitude of Archers from the forests of Windsor, Bernwood, Shotover and Chilterne. All which having before met the Abbat at Offuncton, honourably conducted him to his Monastery with great solemnity, state and triumph. At whose appearance many Malefactors fled from the Town, while others hid themselves in obscure places, but several Officers attaching them carried them to Wallingford Castle, and there kept them in safe custody. Soon after one of the King's Justices sitting there in judgment, he condemned twelve of the said Malefactors, and were forthwith hanged. There were also three-score more cast, and being upon the point of condemnation, the Abbat sent Giles de Pagham his Esquire with a supersedeas to hinder it, and so the matter at that time rested.

As to the losses which the said Monastery suffered by the aforesaid Malefactors, of which little or nothing I conceive could be recovered for the present, were very great. Among them were an hundred Psalters, forty Missals, a hundred Graduals, twelve Codes, ten Decretals, ten Chalices, twenty white Vestments called Surplices, sixty Copes, forty Casulae, or sacred Garments, a Censer and Candlestick of silver, sixty little Cups or Goblets of Gold, forty silver Cups, a hundred silver pieces of Plate, forty silver spoons, two hundred Dishes or Platters, a hundred carcasses of Beif, a thousand carcasses of Mutton, three hundred Hoggs, linnen and wollen Cloth to the value of a thousand pound, besides the goods and chattels of the House, Church and Abbat, which amounted to the value of a thousand pound more, etc. In another place tis said that all the losses of the Abbey came to ten thousand pound, and in a certain Writ sent from the King to certain Justices to examine this matter at Oxon tis said that the losses of the Abbat and Convent amounted to forty thousand pounds.

Soon after the process was ended at Wallingford, the King commanded John Mautravers Junior, John de Stonore, Robert de Aston, John Loveday, and Robert de Hungerford, Justices, to go to Oxford, and that any four, three or two of them make enquiry into the transgressions of Peter de Ewe, William de Wells, etc., of the same place, made against the Abbat and Convent of Abendon, and determine according to the law of the kingdom. In obedience to which command they came and by a Jury found very many guilty, but whether they found the Mayor John de Docklyngton guilty of such crimes, who is said to be present in that grand riot I cannot tell ; sure I am that some of the most notorious felons (not Peter de Ewe) suffered. It must also be noted, that before or after the said Justices came, one William de Shareshull was sent to make peace between the Abbat of Abendon and Commonalty of Oxford, but he hearing that the Scholars lay in wait to do him mischief, was guarded into the Town to Mauger Hall, where he lodged during the time of treaty. There was also a strict examination made concerning such Scholars that were associats with the Burghers of Abendon, and many being found guilty, 'tis not to be doubted but that some suffered : Others that were less guilty had their names (if excommunicated) returned to the respective Prelates of the Nation, to the end that when any of them were about to obtain Rectories, Prebendships, or other preferments, might be stopped till such time they were absolved by the Chancellor of the University.

Soon after John de Kannyngs, Abbat of Abendon, a person of a meek spirit, died, and in his place was elected and confirmed one Robert de Gareford, who being quite of another temper, bestirred himself much in obtaining reparations of the men of Abendon for the great losses that the Abbey suffered by them. Those in the first place that he prosecuted were John the son of Richard Bishop and William his brother, Ingelram le Spycer, Hugh de Culneham, Roger the son of Gilbert le Chaundler, William de Harewell Cook, John le Spycer, and Robert de Knyghton of Oxford. After which he prosecuted others, and at length some of the Laics of Oxon ; from most of whom he got reparation, or at least the goods that they took away.'

Wood's account is based upon Brian Twyne, the Oxford antiquarian. They had access to documents which we do not possess.[1] The account is supported by state papers of Edward III and by the *Calendar of Papal Letters*, ii. 218, &c. The Provincial Council at St. Paul's excommunicated those who had robbed Abingdon Abbey or had committed sacrilege.[2] It was not merely an attack upon the Church as such, but also an attempt to secure the control of the Abbot's Monday market, holding the fairs outside the Abbot's jurisdiction in the Hundred of Sutton and Ock, and to secure the right of electing annually the provost and bailiffs. Leland speaks of it as a 'ple for Fraunchese.'[3]

The troubles did not subside immediately. In May, 1330, a writ of aid was issued to Robert Marye and Richard Peper in conveying to Windsor Robert le Spicer and five others for felonies at Abingdon Abbey.[4]

We naturally reflect on the change that had taken place in a couple of centuries, since the successors of Faricius were the champions of the town against Wallingford and Oxford.

Account-rolls of the Abbey. Much light has been thrown on the highly complex life of the Monastery in the fourteenth and fifteenth centuries by the Account-rolls of the Obedientiars of Abingdon Monastery,[5] of which twenty-six have been preserved, dating from 1322 to 1479. These parchments were discovered in the great wainscoted room in the roof of Claydon House, Bucks, the seat of the Verneys. They were taken there by the little daughter of John Blacknall with a mass of title-deeds, for she was a great heiress. The originals of monastic account-books are exceedingly rare, and these give the most interesting details of the

---

[1] 'Chron. Rot. Monasterii Abendon MS., et in quodam Fasciculo Chartarum de rebus diversis in Chartophylac. Civit. Oxon.' Also 'Reg. Abendon quod dividitur in particulas.'

[2] *Chron. Edw. I and II*, Rolls Series, i. 345 ; cp. i. 332.

[3] *Itinerary*, vol. vii. [4] Edward III, Pat. Rolls.

[5] Camden Soc., 1892, with a valuable introduction by R. E. G. Kirk.

income and expenditure of the monks, and recall the flavour of the manners of the time.

The Obedientiarii were monks who were heads of departments, and among the accounts preserved are accounts of the Pittancer, Infirmarer, Lignar, Gardener, Treasurers, Kitchener, Sacristan, Chamberlain, Refectorer, Trinity Warden, Chapel-Wardens of St. Edmund and Common Chest.

Unhappily the Almoner's and the Cellarer's accounts are missing, and the Abbot was accountable to no man, so that a great part of the revenue has left no record of its varying use or abuse. Consequently there are few entries of almsgiving except an occasional bequest to the poor, such as that of Abbot Nicholas. All inferences from these accounts must be qualified then by the fact that only part of the rolls have survived, and still more by the fact that the Abbot received and spent at pleasure his lion's share without issuing an account at all.

The accounts of the Chapel-Wardens have been already drawn upon in the Chapter on St. Edmund, and the accounts of the Trinity Warden are reserved for the chapter on the early history of Abingdon School.

In the Accounts of the Treasurers of the Convent there are records of substantial quantities of malt sold to the Cellarer to brew for the convent—'ad braciandum pro conventu.' There are entries for wine and beer—cervisia—especially for the festivities of the autumn ; for instance, for twenty-six gallons of wine at fivepence a gallon consumed at the Feast of St. Edward the King, and for similar amounts on the obits of King Edgar and Abbot John or Hugh. There were beer-drinkings on the Feast of St. Luke and the obits of the Abbots Luke and Roger. However, it is not to be supposed that these liquors were all consumed by the Abbot, prior, sub-prior, third prior, twenty-one monk-priests and ten monk novices.[1] There was also the army of retainers, artificers and servants. Doubtless the tenants had their share of jollity after harvest, and probably many of the poor found the monks their most hospitable neighbours. The greater part of the Treasurers' income was spent in building operations, notably upon the ' old work ' and the ' new work ' in St. Mary's Church, which early writers mention as one of the glories of English architecture. There are many entries for a costly dovecote. An interesting ' gift of courtesy '

[1] These are the numbers given in the Chamberlain's Account of 1417-18. Kirk, p. 86.

is recorded ' to Brother Nicholas Drayton for the care he took about the writing in the cloister windows '.[1]

The Treasurers maintained two students at Oxford, a small number for so great an Abbey, and probably only sufficient to fill the gaps in the diminished society.

The Refectorer's Account reveals many secrets. Every brother had his napronys or table-napkin, pewder or pot, maser or wooden bowl and spoon. Also there were in the stores of this department two pelves of ' tyn', i. e. ewers for washing at table before the age of forks, eleven salt-cellars, a ' tyn ' dish-spoon, and three ' twell ' or towels for carrying the cheese.

The wages paid in various accounts illustrate the steady change in the value of money. In some cases these wages may have been supplemented by board or board and lodging. The tailor received 12s. a year, the lavendarius or laundryman and needleman 12s., the cordubanarius or shoemaker 12s., the cartorius 6s. 8d., the valettus 10s. For shaving the brethren three barbers were paid 30s. a year. In one year tunics, cowls and sandals cost 13s. 4d., the repair of vestments 22s. 4d., the femoralia or monks' breeches 6s. 10d., mending the same 22d., stockings of woollen cloth 28s. 6d. There are indications of money-payments to the brethren four times a year in proportion to their ranks—this was contrary to the earlier rule of St. Benedict.

In 1417–18 the Chamberlain paid to the King ' an entire tenth ' of £6. 10s. 2d. for Berks, and 3s. 6d. for Oxon. The Infirmary Account is small, as it was evidently not a public hospital. Among the entries are :—for gathering herbs 7d., surgery 8s. 10d., making waters 12d., cummin and liquory-stick 8d., aniseed 4½d., 8 lbs. of sugar 10s. 8d.

The Kitchener handled large sums of money. He received about £300 a year from the Pittancer, as well as the rents of the mills and the stallage at the fairs. In his accounts he receives corn, malt, mixtillion and wax as rent, and pays stipends in kind to millers, bailiff, smith, gardener, &c. There are large payments for every kind of meat, eels from the weir, oysters, salmon, probably local, sugar and spices. There is little doubt that at this time the brethren had learnt to live uncommonly well.

In the Sacristan's Accounts are large entries for wax for the tapers, and particularly for the great Easter taper.

[1] Kirk, 46 ' In j pelle cordiban' empta pro Fratre Nicholao Drayton', pro sollicitudine facta circa scripturam que est in fenestris claustri, ex curialitate, ijs.'

The Pittancer's Account of 1322-3, the only roll that survived the great riot of 1327, has two interesting payments of 9s. 6d. and 2s. 2d. for stocking and feeding the new fishpond, which we take to be the one at Daisy Bank on the Radley Road.[1] To these may be added an expenditure by the Kitchener of 8d. on cleaning the fishpond about the year 1377.

The sale and purchase of fish between the departments of the Abbey show that the fisheries of the Thames, the moat and the fishpond were very valuable.

Frequent entries in the Accounts of the Gardener and the Pittancer show that the monks cultivated the vine, perhaps in the quarter that still bears the name of the Vineyard, and made wine in the fourteenth century : e. g. payments for vines and alleys 7s. 11½d., for vine-props 4s. 6d., for gathering of grapes 4s. 4d. ; and receipts for the sale of wine 13s. 4d., for the sale of grapes 20s. 0½d. The year 1412 was a bad grape-year, so that the Gardener had to buy figs in London and in the town of Abingdon, especially during Advent and Lent, the grapes being only fit to make verjuice. The vine-culture seems to have been abandoned about that date.[2]

Among the payments from the Common Chest is an item of 66s. 8d. given in rewards to Oxford scholars and various townsmen remaining with the Lord Abbot to defend him in the field of Drayton Wike in the collecting of a certain portion there. This suggests that he was gathering his tithes from reluctant yeomen.[3]

A number of references to Welford in the Chamberlain's Account-rolls show that it was a favourite resort of the Abbot and monks. The Chamberlain records that he spent 3s. 6d. in 1428 in riding on three occasions to Welford with his servants to bring back trouts to Abingdon.[4] Welford was conveniently placed as a half-way house between the Abbey and the cathedral city of Salisbury.

The right of the Borough to send one member to Parliament commenced with the charter of 1555. But Willis in his *Notitia Parliamen-* Representation in Parliament, 1337.

---

[1] ' In pisce empto ad vivarium instaurandum ix⁸ vjᵈ.'
  ' Pro piscibus pascendis ij⁸ ijᵈ.'
  ' Item pro vivario mundando viijᵈ.' Kirk, p. 3, 40.
[2] Kirk, Introd. xxxiv. and Index.
[3] Kirk, p. 90 ' Item in rewardis datis scolaribus Oxon' et diuersis hominibus de villa existentibus cum Domino ad defendendum eum in camp' de Drayton. Wike pro quadam porcione ibidem colligenda lxvj⁸. viijᵈ.'
  Kirk, 106 : ' . . . et portantibus trough' tes usque Abendon', iij⁸. vjᵈ.'

taria (1715) quotes a curious isolated instance of representation in the Council at Westminster :

> ' Co. Berks. Abingdon. This, as a town of great Trade, sent once, upon a peremptory summons, to a Council, Anno 11 Edw. 3, though it never was made a Borough, till by Charter Anno 3 and 4 Phil. and Mar., when it was allowed to have one Burgess in Parliament.'

The members sent were John Bishop, Thomas Wateby and John de Berewyk.

Hundred Years' War. This important Parliament of 1337 supported Edward III's claim to the crown of France, which was the ostensible cause of the Hundred Years' War. The underlying reasons were the fear that French domination on the Continent would shut us out of the wool-markets of the Netherlands, and that French help to Scotland would prevent the union of the island of Great Britain under one government.

In connexion with the same great war the Abbot was required on May 13, 1342, to furnish men for service in the Isle of Wight against France.[1]

Black Death. In 1348 the Black Death, which swept off such an enormous proportion of the population of England, did not spare Abingdon. For the Abbot was forced to petition the Pope to allow thirty priests to be ordained at the youthful age of twenty.[2] A glance at the list of vicars and rectors of St. Nicholas' and St. Helen's Churches in the Appendix will suggest that preferment was very frequent at that time. It may be assumed that death was not busy with one class of society only.

Peasants' Rising. On the other hand the great peasants' rising, associated with the name of Wat Tyler, appears to have been felt only slightly in Berkshire.

Cemetery dispute. A prolonged dispute about the rights of burial disturbed Abingdon at the end of the fourteenth century. Leland, quoted in *Monasticon*, says : ' In old time many of the villages about Abbingdon had but Chapelles of Ease, and Abingdon Abbay was their Mother Chirch, and there they buried.'[3] This right of the Abbey was challenged by St. Helen's Church, but the Abbey triumphed in the end.[4]

Henry IV. Some of the troubles that followed the deposition of Richard II in favour of Henry IV affected the district of Abingdon. In January, 1400, Queen Isabel with her brother-in-law the Earl of Kent and other Earls, set off to Wallingford and Abingdon. Capgrave[5] relates that

---

[1] Prynne on the *Institutes*, p. 212: ' 16 Edward III, De Abbate de Abbydon iii homines ad arma.'　　　[2] *Cal. Papal Letters.*　　　[3] Leland, ii. 13.
[4] See Chap. VII.　　　[5] *Chronicle of England, ad annum.*

' in the secund yere of this King, the Erl of Kent' tries to raise men in favour of Richard II at 'Wyndesore, Radyngis, Wallingforth, Abyngdon, and Cicetir'. The movement was checked by Henry IV at Maidenhead, and the result of the zeal of the 'Erlis' was the sudden death of Richard at Pontefract Castle.

Henry IV and his queen spent Christmas, 1403, at Abingdon, as is shown by letters and papers dated from there December 23–9.[1]

In 1405 more rebels passed through Abingdon on the way to Cardiff, to join Glendower and the Percies, with Lady le Depenser and the young Mortimers, who had been smuggled out of Windsor. But the rebellion was crushed at Shrewsbury.

The building of Abingdon Bridge in 1416 is dealt with in the chapter on the Guild of the Holy Cross (Chap. VI).

[1] J. H. Wylie, *Henry IV*, ad annum.

CHAPTER V

THE FIFTEENTH CENTURY AND THE DISSOLUTION

1431–1538

Henry VI.
Rising of
Jack
Sharpe.

IN 1431 a certain William Mandevill, a weaver and bailiff of Abingdon, hatched a conspiracy among 'certain lewd persons under pretence of religious-minded men' at Abingdon against the Church and against the government of the Protector, Humphrey, Duke of Gloucester. Mandevill took the name of Jack Sharpe, of Wigmer's Land in Wales.[1] Duke Humphrey came down to Abingdon in person to crush the rising. There is a lively account of the affair in the *Chronicles of London* : [2]

'In the same yere bytweene Ester and Whitsontyde the duke of Gloucestre had wytyng that ther was gadered a meyne of rysers at Abyngton, ageynst men of holy chirche, for they seyde they wolde have thre prestes heedes for a peny. And the name of her chyveteyn was Jakke Sharpe. And thanne anone in alle haste the Duke of Gloucestre and his meyne redyn to Abyngton; and ther was takyn Jakke Sharpe, and other men; and they were found deffettyf and therfore they were done to deth; and on the fryday in Whitsonweke the hedde of Jakke Sharpe was brought to London, and hit was sette on London Brigge, and alle the remnant of his felisship that myht be takyn weren putte to deth at Abyngton.'

Gregory's *Chronicle* (*ad annum*) gives the details rather differently :

'Jacke Sharpe makes a rising in the cytte of London : taken at Oxford 19th of May, drawyd, hangyde and quarteryde, and hys hede set on London Brygge, and hys quarterys i-sent to dyvers townys of Ingelonde, as to Oxford, Abyngdon, and to moo othyr.' [3]

Thomas
Bekynton.

The Journal of Thomas Bekynton, who held the living of Sutton, and was afterwards Bishop of Wells, records a visit to Abingdon in 1442, on his leisurely journey to take up an embassy in France :

---

[1] Little, p. 25.   [2] Ed. Kingsford, 1905, *ad annum*.
[3] Gregory then passes on abruptly to the tragedy of Joan of Arc at Rouen : 'And on the xxiii of May the Pusylle was brent at Rone, and that was pon Corpus Christi evyn.'

' Wednesday. Rode as far as Sutton.

Thursday, June 7. Lunched at Abyndon with the Lord Abbot, where was the Bishop of Salisbury.' [1]

Some episodes of the Wars of the Roses were connected with Abingdon. Margaret of Anjou was at Abingdon with her court in 1458. The *Chronicle of Brute* (*ad annum*) reads :

Wars of the Roses.

' The xxxvi yere of kyng Harry in the moneth of January, dyed the erle of Deuynshire in the Abbey of Abyngdoun poysened, as men sayde, and being there at that tyme with quene Margarete.'

The Earl of Devon was a serious loss to Margaret's cause.

William of Worcester says that Henry VI was betrayed in his hiding-place in Lancashire by an Abingdon monk, and brought to London with his feet tied to the stirrups.[2]

In a later stage of the wars Edward IV halted with his army at Abingdon from Saturday to Monday, April 27–9, 1471, on his march to the battlefield of Tewkesbury.[3]

Hall [4] relates that :

' With such an arraye as he—Edward—had gotten about London, he set forward into Oxford shyre, and there sekynge a place apt and mete to pitch hys tentes, was conducted to Abyngdon, where he encamped hym selfe, comaunding all men appoynted for the warre, with all celeritie to folow hym to that place.'

In Little [5] we read that some of the Fraternity of the Holy Cross assisted the host of Richard III at Bosworth Field in 1485, but the Fraternity afterwards obtained pardon of Henry VII.

The rebellion of Lambert Simnel—the son of an Oxford joiner—made an echo in this neighbourhood. After the battle of Stoke-upon-Trent in 1487, ' Homfrey Stafford also hearying of this mischaunce happened to the lord Louell, in a great dolor and agony, and for feare, in lyke manner fled and tooke sanctuary in a village called Culnaham, two miles from Abyndon.' [6] But the King's Bench decided that this sanctuary was not a sufficient defence for traitors.

---

[1] *Journal of Thomas Bekynton to Bordeaux*, Rolls Series, *ad annum.*

' Die Mercurii. Equitavit usque Sutton.

Die Jovis, vii. In prandio apud Abyndon cum domino Abbate, ubi fuit episcopus Sarisburiensis.'

[2] *Wars of the English*, &c., Rolls Series, ed. J. Stevenson, vol. ii, pt. ii. 785.

[3] Ramsay, *Lancaster and York, ad annum.*

[4] Hall's *Chronicle*, 1548, p. 299.   [5] p. 28.   [6] Hall's *Chronicle*, p. 419.

In 1488 the Lord Abbot John Sante of Abingdon penned an interesting letter from Sittingbourne on the Dover road—he was going on an embassy to Charles VIII of France, and had been employed in similar embassies in 1474 and 1479—to a friend at Canterbury to borrow ' an honest horse ', as the Rochester hackneys were unworthy to appear amid the estates or dignitaries at Canterbury.

' John Abbot of Abingdon to Dom. Raynold Goldstone a monk of Ch. Ch.

Rigth wurschipfull brothyr, y recommend me unto yow and pray you that, with licence of my Fader and youris, ye wyll send me an honest horse for myselfe unto the town is end. Y am looth to ryde into the cytey among all these asstatis with Rochestyr hakeneyys. All so y pray yow recommend me unto my Father and youris.

Fro Sidyngbourne the xii day of April.

The Lord Abbot John of Abindon unto my rygth well belovyd brother Dan. Raynold Goldstone, Batcheler of Divinyte, and brother of Crystischurch in Canterbury.' [1]

The next year under the reign of this same Abbot a writ of capias was issued for the arrest ' of Richard Norwiche and Thomas Foweler, brethren of the monastery of Abendon, who have sacrilegiously despoiled the monastery of many goods, and now wander from county to county '—to be delivered to the Abbot for punishment, according to the rules of the order, July 25, 1489.[2]

This Abbot John Sante with his three predecessors was one of the great builders, and the Abbey as seen by Leland after the dissolution must have been largely the late perpendicular work of the fifteenth century. Leland[3] says that the tower in the centre, the western towers, and the body of the church, as he saw it, were built by the four abbots immediately preceding the last four : i. e. A. D. 1427–95 Leland compares the buildings to Wells, but gives us few definite architectural details :

' At the west end of the area wheryn the Abbay Church stondith is a Charnel Chapelle, to the which is given the profite of a chapelle at Bayworth by Bagley Wood.' 'On the south side of the area is al the Abbate and Conventes Lodging.'

' Again this (S. Nicolas Church) on the other side withoute thabbay Gate is a Chirch dedicate to S. John and there is an Hospital having 6 Almose menne.'

[1] *Christ Church Letters*, Camden Soc., 1877.
[2] *Materials for Reign of Henry VII*, Rolls Series, 1877, *ad annum*.
[3] *Itinerary*, ii. 13.

Some of these buildings were still stately ruins when Camden wrote in James I's reign, and the ruined battlements were visible from the town in 1641.[1]

William of Worcester [2] gives some details of the Abbey Church, which correspond remarkably with the proportions of Westminster, also Benedictine, before the erection of Henry VII's Chapel.

Dimensions of Abbey Church.

Length of Nave	180 feet
Width of Church with two aisles . .	72 ,,
Length of Chapel of the Blessed Mary .	36 ,,
Width of Choir with aisles . . .	72 ,,
Transepts from east to west . .	69 ,,
(on double columns with chapels).	
Length of choir with chapel . .	192 ,,
Transepts north to south . .	174 ,,
Tower in middle of transepts, square .	36 ,,
Circumference of columns in nave . .	15 ,,
Thickness of walls	6 ,,
Width of aisle of nave . . .	18 ,,
,, ,, choir . . .	15 ,,
Height of new tower on west . .	100 ,,
Width of ditto, either way . . .	14 ,,

There were twelve columns and twelve arches on either side of the nave.

Perhaps it is not out of place to print here one of the tales of the exuberant Skelton (1460–1529), which couples Oxford and Abingdon before the Reformation, as they have often been coupled since. It is in ' Certayne merye tales of Skelton, Poet Lauriat '.[3]

Skelton.

' How Skelton came late home to Oxford from Abington. Tale i.

Skelton was an Englysheman borne as Skogyn was, and hee was educated and broughte up in Oxfoorde : and there was he made a poete lauriat. And on a tyme he had been at Abbington to make mery, wher that he had eate salte meates, and hee did com late home to Oxforde, and he did lye in an ine named ye Tabere whyche is now the Angell,[4] and hee dyd drynke, and went to bed. About midnight he was so thyrstie or drye that hee was constrained to call to the tapster for drynke, and the tapster harde him not. Then hee cryed to hys oste and hys ostes, and to the ostler, for drinke ; and no man wold here hym. Alacke, sayd Skelton, I shall peryshe for lacke of drynke ! what reamedye ? At the last he dyd crie out and sayd : Fyer, fyer, fyer ! when Skelton hard every man bustle hymselfe upward,

[1] Hearne, *Remains*, ii. 294.   [3] Quoted in Dugdale.
[2] Printed in 1575, and probably earlier.   [4] In Cornmarket.

and some of them were naked and some were halfe asleepe and amased, and Skelton dyd crye : Fier, fier ! styll, that everye man knewe not whether to resorte. Skelton did go to bed, and the oste and ostis, and the tapster with the ostler, dyd runne to Skelton's chamber with candles lyghted in theyr handes, saying : where, where, where is the fyer : Here, here, here, said Skelton, and poynted hys fynger to hys moouth, saying : fetch me some drynke to quenche the fyer and the heate and the drinesse in my mouthe : and so they dyd. Wherfore it is good for everye man to helpe hys owne selfe in tyme of neede wythe some policie or crafte, so bee it there be no deceit nor falshed used.'

Skelton was not the last Oxonian to visit the little neighbour town.

A seventeenth-century letter quoted in Quiller-Couch's *Reminiscences of Oxford* suggests that two centuries later Laud and the Puritans were alike unable to repress the undergraduate in his visits to Abingdon, which have become a tradition with later generations.

For ' the horse growing resty he must have leave to ride to Abingdon once every week to look out of the tavern windows and see the maids sell turnips.'

But Abingdon is not justified in claiming the ' Miller of Abingdon ' as part of her literature. This is one of the stories founded on the same original as the Reve's Tale of Chaucer, and it refers to Abington, a place seven miles distant from Cambridge and from Trumpington.[1] But Porter's *Two Angry Women of Abington* (1599) has its setting in Berkshire.

Dissolution of the Abbey.
The reign of Henry VIII brings this history to the close of its first half with the dissolution of the Abbey, closely followed in the reign of Edward VI by the dissolution of the Fraternity of the Holy Cross.

In the spring of 1518 Henry VIII made a prolonged stay at Abingdon from fear of the sweating sickness, which was raging in London. He told Pace that the Abingdon folk did not come continually and tell him of deaths, as the people at London did. At this time he established relays of posts every seven hours between himself and Wolsey, and read ' every word of all the letters ' sent to him by his minister.[2]

Little states[3] that during a visit of the King to the Abbey in the twenty-third year of his reign conferences were held there between ' the best-learned scholars ' in the University of Oxford and members of the Privy Council, such as Sir Thomas More. This seems to have been a trial of wits to amuse the King. There are other instances of

---

[1] A black-letter quarto: 'A mery Jest of the Mylner of Abyngton with his Wyfe and his Daughter, and the two poore scholers of Cambridge.'

[2] Pollard, *Henry VIII*, Illustrated Ed., p. 95.   [3] pp. 34, 35.

friendly relations between the King and the Abbey. But the Abbey was doomed. Financially it was not flourishing. It was persecuted by Thomas Cromwell and harassed by lawsuits with its tenants—notably by a prolonged lawsuit with John Audelett, steward of the Abbey lands, and Katherine his wife and widow.[1]

The notorious Dr. Layton visited the Abbey in 1535, and the report of Leigh and Layton blackened the character of the Abbot and monks. In 1536 the smaller monastic houses were confiscated. An entry in Thomas Cromwell's notes of 1537 indicates what was coming : ' Item, the suppression of Abingdon.' [2] On July 17, 1536, the Abbot voted in person in the House of Lords—for the last time.

In the Parliamentary lists of April 28, 1539, his name is missing. For on February 9, 1538, the Abbot and twenty-four monks were induced to sign a ' voluntary ' surrender of their privileges and estates to the Crown, anticipating the compulsory closing of the greater monasteries in the following year. To facilitate this surrender £600 was spent. The Abbot, Thomas Rowland, alias Pentecost, received the manor-house of Cumnor with a pension of £200 a year—a sum at least equivalent at the present day to the pension of an ex-cabinet minister. The monks from the prior downwards received handsome pensions varying from £22 to £5. Of these pensions some thirteen were still being paid in 1553 to these men or their assigns—three being dead and one married of the thirteen.[3] The value of the Abbey revenues at the dissolution is given by Dugdale as £1,876. 10s. 9d. a year—which has been reckoned as roughly the equivalent of £37,000 of modern money. It is generally admitted that the Abbey had ceased to correspond with the needs of the age, but the grant of these considerable pensions is generally accepted as weighty evidence that the Abbot and Monks were regarded by the King and his advisers as innocent of the more scandalous charges brought against them. The last Abbot of Reading chose the more heroic course. With two of his monks he denied sturdily the King's supremacy and was hanged, drawn and quartered. One monk at Abingdon was of the same metal. He told his colleagues that those who set knife and pen to the book to scrape out the Pope's name in favour of the King were cursed. So Shaxton of Salisbury kept him safe in prison.[4]

[1] Gasquet, *Henry VIII and the Monasteries*, ii. 293-5 ; cp. *Victoria History*, Berks.   [2] Gasquet.
[3] Willis, *Mitred and Parliamentary Abbies*, 1718 ; cp. Dugdale.
[4] Gasquet.

On February 22, 1538, Sir Richard Rich reported upon the Abbey buildings as being in great decay, and the site unsuitable for a royal park : 'I think a great part thereof may be defaced, and sufficient left to the King's contentation.'

Abbey buildings. The spoils of the Abbey were gathered into the royal treasure-house. Two mitres were purchased by Sir Thomas Pope. A silver-gilt cross with two pontifical rings was preserved for the King's own use.[1] The Abbey buildings were stripped and plundered by all and sundry. The site of the Abbey was granted to Sir T. Seymour, afterwards to Sir T. Wroth. It passed soon into the Blacknall family, who treated it with scant respect. For instance, among the Corporation deeds is a transfer, dated 1615, of the right ' to digge rubble and small stones ' in the gate of the late Abbey. A quantity of Abbey papers passed with the heiress of the Blacknalls into the Verney family.

Of the remains of the famous buildings little is left. There is the gatehouse (fifteenth century) used for a long time as a prison, but now more worthily as part of the Corporation buildings. Also a line of buildings running east and west on the south or river-side of the Abbey precincts. The west end is in the basement a fine piece of early thirteenth-century work with stone vaulting. In the upper storey this is supplemented by Decorated work and there is a fine fireplace. Eastward this continues in a long open timber and brick building of the fourteenth or fifteenth century, apparently a refectory or parlour, and a dormitory with a corridor. East of that the line of buildings connected doubtless with the chapter-house and south transept of the great church. These buildings were used for more than a century as a brewery store, but were acquired and restored by the corporation in 1895. From the bridge may be seen a fine hooded chimney, of the thirteenth to fourteenth centuries, belonging to the great fireplace in the prior's room. It is built of stone, the quoins and other masonry worked, rubblestone elsewhere. Not open at the top, it terminates with quaintly pretty gables, in each of which are three lancet-headed piercings for the smoke to pass through. Much interesting stonework may be traced in Thames Street, in the Abbey Lane and elsewhere in Abingdon.

The arms of the Abbey were Argent, a cross fleury between four martlets sable.

A strange doubt has been expressed locally as to whether the mitred

Gasquet.

Abbot of Abingdon was entitled to a writ to attend Parliament. Two Abbot in Parliament. or three casual instances are sufficient to show that he always enjoyed this privilege—with industry these instances could be indefinitely multiplied. In 1225 the Third Charter of Henry III was witnessed by the Abbot of Abingdon among others at the Council of Westminster.[1] In 1276 he was present at a Council at Westminster on November 12 ; and he received his writ to attend Edward I's famous Parliament of 1295, the model of representative government in England.[2] In 1483 he was summoned to Parliament with twenty-two other Benedictine abbots. By that time the smaller abbeys and priories had begun to seek devices to renounce the burdensome privilege.[3]

People will regard the work of the Abbey with varying degrees of Work of the Abbey. sympathy and severity, but there can be no question as to the magnitude of the gap it left to be filled. It is significant that in Abingdon, as elsewhere, the commencement of poor relief and the establishment of a workhouse became necessary. Thorold Rogers, who was a stern critic of monachism, has pointed out that the foundation of schools throughout England after the Reformation of 1547 was not due so much to a new zeal for a new learning, but that it was a fresh and very inadequate supply of that which had been so suddenly and disastrously extinguished. He points out that the monks of the Middle Ages comprised practically the whole of the professional classes—men of letters, jurists, philosophers, physicians, students of nature. As builders of course their claim to our admiration is unchallenged—to take the humble instance of the thirteenth-century tithe-barn at Northcourt, what stonework, what timber! The great barn at Barton has now gone ; so also the great barn of Cholsey.[4]

J. R. Green [5] sums up the proceedings of Henry VIII and Thomas Cromwell:

' In the general carelessness which prevailed as to the spiritual objects of their trust, in the wasteful management of their estates, in the indolence and self-indulgence, which for the most part characterized them, the monastic houses simply exhibited the faults of all corporate bodies which have out-lived the work which they were created to perform. But they were no more unpopular than such corporate bodies generally are. The Lollard cry for their suppression had died away.'

---

[1] ' Hiis testibus . . . Abbate de Abendon . . .'   Stubbs, *Select Charters.*
[2] *Parl. Rolls.*   [3] Stubbs, *Constit. History.*
[4] This last was 303 feet long, by 54 wide, by 51 high. A print of it is in the *Gentleman's Magazine*, Feb., 1816.   [5] *Short History*, p. 339.

TOWNSEND

Again, in speaking of the ' Black Book ' :

' It was acknowledged that about one-third of the religious houses, including the bulk of the larger abbeys, were fairly and decently conducted.'

With regard to the charges against the rest he says there is ' little doubt that the charges were grossly exaggerated '.   Lastly, as to the suppression :

' But from the enslavement of the clergy, from the gagging of the pulpits, from the suppression of the monasteries, the bulk of the nation stood aloof. It is only through stray depositions of royal spies that we catch a glimpse of the wrath and hate, which lay seething under the silence of a whole people.   For the silence was a silence of terror.'

He proceeds to compare the rule of Thomas Cromwell to the Reign of Terror, associated with the name of Robespierre.

Transcriptū ē de verbo in verbum verum exemplar omniū
singlor libertatio cartaz scriptoz et mūnimētoz oīm cha-
rtoz terraz et tenementoz pīoz paļ pastur Reddituū serviē.
et provenc ffraternitate sue gilde scē crucis Abendon in com
Berk fundate Incipit cū dei laude Amen. et tpīmo de mayno
de Seintelenes.

Sciant psentes et futuri qd ego philippus filius et heres
Willmi de Seynt eleyne dedi concessi et hac psenti carta mea cōfirmavi Gillmo de aydebourn ppetuo vicar ecłie
scē elene de Abendon. Rico Belle pbo parochiali ecłie sd nicholai et Johām Bulthup oēs terre et tenemēta mea que hēn in uie
hereditar in villa de Suttone. Suttonwyk. Drephemwyk.
et in villa de Abendon una cū reddicibz a molendinis homa-
giis libertatibz liberoz hoīm serviē. Ward et eleins estachis
villenagiis villanis. villenagia illa tenentibz. cū coz catallis
et sequelis pīis pastuis pastur a moris haijs sepalibz et comun
et omnibz ubiq ptin suis sine aliquo retenemēto q in et hered
meis accidere poīnt aliquorum Dedi etiā et cōcessi pdcās Gillmo
Rico Johī unū denaz annui reddituos ppicieñ de mayno de ffry-
lesford una cū reversione eiusdm mayñm et cū omibz ptiñ suis
quandis acciderit. quod quidem maīnum Edmūdus de Seynt
eleyne frater meus tenet de me ad tminū vite sue tīm. et Un-
reversio ad me spettat post morte dīa Edmūdi. Hñd et tenend
pdcas Willmo Rico et Johī et coz hered et assīgn oēs terras et
tenementa pdcā cū oibz ptiñ suis pdcīt libere qēte iure
hereditar inppetuū. ffaciend inde capitilibz dnis feodi ił
oīa serviū que ad terras et tenemēta illa ptinet p cū futuro
sēculari exaccōe et demanda. Et ego dcūs philippus et heres
mei oēs terras et tenemēt pdcīt unacū reddicibz homa-
giis libertatibz siue reuōnibz et omnibz alijs pertinētys

CHAPTER VI

THE FRATERNITY OF THE HOLY CROSS

THE most interesting institution in Abingdon before the Reformation—always excepting the Abbey—is the Guild or Fraternity of the Holy Cross, which built Abingdon Bridge in 1416, and in which centred the growth of civic life during the three centuries preceding its dissolution in 1547. It is of more than antiquarian interest, for its work continues under altered conditions to the present day.

The historian of the Guild is Francis Little, whose manuscript history, brought down to 1627, is preserved among the archives of Christ's Hospital, Abingdon.[1] Francis Little, alias Brooke or Brooker, was not perhaps a very critical historian, but he was touched with the enthusiasm of history, and deserves our gratitude for preserving a mass of valuable matter in his delightful book. He was for thirty-eight years a governor and twice master of Christ's Hospital; three times Mayor of the town;[2] and in 1597 Member of Parliament for the borough. His name appears among the visitors of the Grammar School, who examined and admonished the scholars in 1604.[3]

In the Churchwardens' Accounts of 1619 it appears that Francis Little was among those fined 12d. for non-attendance on Sundays, and other offences—but we record with a sigh of relief that it was not for himself but for his man. His death occurred in January, 1630, but there is a curious doubt as to his place of burial. For in the register of St. Nicholas' there is the entry : 'Mr Francis Littell allast Brooker was Beried the xth of Janewary 1630.' On the other hand in St. Helen's Churchwardens' Accounts for the same year there is the entry: 'Item for the grave of Mr Little xs.' As he could not be buried in both parishes, we incline towards St. Helen's, for there are several entries

Francis Little.

---

[1] *A Monument of Christian Munificence*, printed in 1872, ed. by the Rev. C. D. Cobham.

[2] Borough Records. In 1598, 1606, and 1617. His name appears on the beautiful title-page of the Register of Acts of the Corporation, 1599.

[3] Borough Records.

of the burials of his wife and family at that church, of which he was churchwarden 1590-3.

The Incorporation of the Guild by Letters Patent dates from 1441,[1] but it had long been in active existence and in possession of considerable property. Mr. G. W. Wallace[2] finds indications of its existence in the cartulary and the original deeds at the Hall of Christ's Hospital as far back as the reign of Edward III, and states that the rental shows that the Fraternity was in possession of a considerable extent of land about Abingdon, including the site of some of the Almshouses of Christ's Hospital, in the year 1383-4, 7 Richard II. Little (p. 2) tells us that the Fraternity set up a stately cross or rood in St. Helen's Church, and two of the brethren were yearly chosen as proctors to collect alms and maintain the ceremonies of worship. He states that these proctors were in existence at least as early as 1388-9, 12 Richard II.

In 1416 the Brotherhood set on foot a great civic undertaking, namely, the building of the bridges at Burford or Borough-ford and Culham Hithe or Ferry with the connecting causeway. These bridges placed Abingdon on a main route from London to the west, and left Wallingford with her dozen churches to dwindle on a superseded road. The work was at once the result and the cause of a great development of trade, particularly of the cloth-trade. The old fords and ferries were often very dangerous. About twenty years ago, in some dredging operations, the old elm-timbers of the borough ford were discovered in the river-bed near St. Helen's in a fairly good state of preservation. Accordingly, Henry V, whom Little describes as ' a president of zeal to God ', granted a licence for the work to John Hutchion and John Brite or Bret and the commons of Abingdon. John Hutchion and John Banberie, ' two of the chiefest of the Fraternity,' compounded with the Abbot and Convent for Culham Ferry and a strip of land fourscore feet wide leading thence to Abingdon at the price of £115. Neither the Account-rolls of the Abbey nor the accounts of the Guild suggest that the Abbey contributed to this public work. Henry V was formerly commemorated in a window at St. Helen's with figures of himself and his brothers, of whom Humphrey of Gloucester visited Abingdon in the next reign. The window bore the following inscription :

> Henricus quintus quarto fundaverat anno
> Rex pontem Burford super undas atque Culhamford.

[1] Oct. 20, 20 Hen. VI.   [2] *Charity Com. Report*, 1908, p. 77.

The work is described in a lengthy poem, chiefly in old English, written in 1457–8 by Richard Forman or Fannande, ironmonger. These lines may serve as a specimen :

> Many moo myscheves there weren I say.
> Culham hithe hath causid many a curse.
> I blyssed be our helpers we have a better waye,
> Withoute any peny for cart and for horse.[1]

Little records that Sir Peter Besils of Besilsleigh helped on the work, furnishing stone from his quarries at Sandford and Besilsleigh. He left by will in 1424 his lands and properties in Abingdon towards the perpetual maintenance of the bridges. Also Geoffrey Barbour, a Bristol merchant and former bailiff of that city, who had retired to Abingdon, gave 1,000 marks towards the bridges. At his death in 1417 he left by his will of the previous October legacies to various churches and charities, particularly to the Fraternity. At the dissolution of the Abbey his remains were removed from there to St. Helen's Church. His brass, in which he is figured in monk's dress, is now on the western wall of St. Katherine's aisle. In the *Calendar of Papal Letters* for 1414 is a record of indults to the following to choose their confessor, who may grant them absolution and enjoin a salutary penance : 'Geoffrey Barbour of Abyndon merchant of the diocese of Salisbury.' *(margin: Benefactors of the Guild.)*

William Hales, citizen and mercer of London, and in 1437 sheriff of that city, a feoffee of the Guild, built three new stone arches at the south end of Abingdon bridge to carry off the flood-water at his own costs. This work was finished by Maud Hales, his widow, after whom the pool there was named Maud Hales' Pool. Adjacent cottages still bear her name. William and Maud Hales were commemorated in the glass at the east end of St. Katherine's Chancel at St. Helen's, ' where it is likely that he and his wife lieth buried.' [2]

In the great riot of 1327 there is no mention of the Fraternity of the Cross, although it is evident that St. Helen's Church was the centre of the discontent. *(margin: Procession at St. Helen's.)*

[1] MS. in Christ's Hospital Hall, printed at end of Little. It winds up with the ' Rebus ' :—
R. A. B. I. N. D. O. N. R. F. I.
Take the first letter of youre foure fader with A, the worker of Wex, & I and N, the colore of an Asse; set them togeder, & tell me yf you can, what it is than. Richard Fannande Irenmonger hathe made this Tabul, & set it here in the yere of Kyng Herry the sexte xxxvi[te].
[2] Little, p. 24. Cp. *Charity Comm. Rep.*, p. 77.

An ordination of Bishop Neville of Salisbury in 1437, in dealing with points of dispute which are narrated in the chapter on St. Helen's, gives permission for the holding of a procession in that church on the feast of the Holy Cross in the month of May on behalf of the Fraternity of the same, with solemn mass on the Sunday following, and other ancient customs according to ancient use. Provided that the procession be held in a holy and devout manner, and that there be no men accompanying it of a carnal and diabolical countenance. This expression refers to the masks and dress of carnival.[1]

Formal Incorporation. So far the Guild had been content with an informal but active existence. In 1441 it obtained by Letters Patent its formal incorporation. It was now a considerable corporation, for it held the Barbour Almshouses, which were probably the Old Almshouses over the Water, and in 1434 John Golafre, Esq., afterwards Sir John Golafre, of Fyfield, had conveyed to the feoffees his manor of St. Elyne's and all lands lately belonging to Lady Alianora de Saint Amand in Sutton Courtney, Suttonwyke, Okke, Hanney and Abendon, upon a yearly payment of 20 marks during his life. There are other bequests before and after 1441, some of them attested by existing deeds and others vouched for by Little.[2]

To Sir John Golafre the Guild appears to owe the obtaining of its charter. Little states that ' he built at his own charges the great stone bridge, called New Bridge, in Oxfordshire '—surely Dorchester Bridge, a necessary link in the new road. He is called by Camden Sir John of St. Helen's, as the successor of that ancient family. He died in 1441.

In 1446 the Guild built the Long Alley Almshouse for thirteen people.[3]

At this period the members of the Guild spent much of their increasing wealth in beautifying St. Helen's Church.

The Exchequer. Little gives an interesting account of the life of the Guild, which we venture to summarize here. Their place of meeting for business was the Exchequer, a small chamber over the second north porch of St. Helen's, where the Master and Governors of the Hospital of Christ afterwards kept their charter, common seal and deeds, and continued to meet from time to time in the seventeenth century. It was tenanted

---

[1] Reg. Bishop Sarum, reg. Neville, fol. 109. We quote from an imperfect copy among Lempriere's transcripts.
[2] *Charity Comm. Rep.*, p. 78 ; Little, p. 16.
[3] Little, p. 18, calls this the New Almshouse, or Feat Almshouse.

until recently by a mass of interesting documents, going back to the reign of Edward III, and by a race of spiders of apparently similar dates. The documents are now in the strong room of the Hall of Christ's Hospital.

The allowance to the poor men and women was one penny a-piece weekly, and in 35 Henry VI 4s. a-piece every quarter. They were enjoined to pray for the Fraternity, for the souls of departed Brothers and Sisters, and for all Benefactors.

Two priests, who sang mass daily at St. Helen's, received a yearly pension each of £6 13s. 4d. at the audit : one was the rood priest, the other the bridge priest.

Upon the third day of May, the day of the Invention of the Holy Cross, was held a bountiful feast. They spent usually six calves, 2s. 2d. a-piece, sixteen lambs, 12d. a-piece, fourscore capons, 3d. a-piece, eight hundred eggs, 5d. the hundred, many marrow-bones, much fruit and spice, great quantity of milk, cream and flour—wheat was good cheap, being sold for 12d. a quarter—besides many gifts from tenants and from the brethren and sisters. **The Guild Feast.**

At these feasts they had twelve priests to sing a dirge, to whom they paid 4d. a-piece for their pains. They had twelve minstrels, some from Coventry and some from Maydenhyth, to make them merry, to whom they gave 2s. 3d. a-piece besides their diet and horse-meat. They held likewise ' in the tyme of Poperie ' a solemn procession, pageants, plays and May-games.

They did not make these feasts without profit ; for those who sat at dinner paid one rate, those that did stand paid another.

These feasts were kept for a long time at Banbery Court in West St. Helen's. That house had been the mansion of John Banberie, the bridge-builder ; in 1585 it was occupied by Mr. Blacknall ; in 1627 it was the property of Richard Hide of Wick, Esquire. Afterwards the feasts were held at a house in East St. Helen's Street, given them by Mr. William Dier, Vicar of Bray, which in 1627 was in the tenure of William Eyston, gentleman.

Besides the stately rood which they set up in St. Helen's Church, they built in the time of Henry VI the Cross in the Market-place. It bore the coat of arms of Sir John Golafre. There is a faded picture of it on the wall of the Long Alley towards the Thames. It was copied about 1543 in the Cross Cheeping at Coventry, which was pulled down in the eighteenth century as not up to date. Hearne gives the specifica- **The Cross.**

tion of the Coventry Cross. It was to be 'after the manner, form, fashion, and due proportion of the Cross at Abington'; to be 45 feet above the highest step 'or higher if the said Crosse in Abington be higher'. The Abingdon Cross had eight steps, the Coventry Cross was to have four. The Abingdon Cross had eight panes in the first storey, six in the second, 'to the deformitie of the said Crosse'. Coventry stipulated for six panes throughout.[1]

It was repaired, gilt and garnished in 1605 in the mayoralty of Thomas Mayott by the benevolence of the gentry of Berks and the inhabitants of this town and neighbouring villages. Mr. Little himself provided more than thirty pounds and had the pains and travail of collecting the rest. Leland describes it as 'a right goodly cross of stone with faire degrees and imagerie'. A century later, in 1641, the people sang the 106th Psalm at the Cross. Three years later it was sawn down by Waller as 'a superstitious edifice'.

Thomas Chaucer, perhaps the son of the poet, Speaker of the Commons, and connected with Ewelme and Oxford, is mentioned by Rimer and Lysons as an early member of the Brethren of the Holy Cross. It is supposed that he was concerned in designing the Cross in the Market-place.

Later history. To pass on, in 1483 Richard III granted a fresh charter to the Fraternity on account of the devotion he bore to 'the most blessed Helen, being the inventor of the most victorious cross of Christ'. At Bosworth Field the Fraternity assisted Richard against Richmond, who, as Henry VII, had the clemency to pardon them. In speaking of Richard, Little speaks 'only of his works of piety'.

In 1520 Henry VIII granted to the Fraternity one fair to be holden yearly upon the feast-day of St. Andrew the Apostle, the eve and morrow after, with profit of pickage, stallage and tolls, as lords of the fair.

Dissolution by Edward VI. In 1547, nine years after the dissolution of the Abbey, Edward VI dissolved the Fraternity and confiscated their possessions. The income was certified by the Chantry Commissioners to be £81 13s. 10d. a year.[2]

In 1553 among the pensions to chantries are given : 'St. Mary's Chantry, to William Abendon, Incumb. £6. To John Crystall, late deceased incumbent of Parish Church Chantry £1 13s. 4d. Ibid. St. Crosse's Fraternity. To James Bell, one of the priests, £5.' The Account-rolls of Abingdon Abbey indicate that there was a St. Mary's

---

[1] Hearne, *Lib. Nig. Scacc.* Cp. Rimer's *Ancient Crosses.*
[2] *Charity Comm. Rep.*, p. 79.

Chantry in St. Helen's Church. Little describes this period as one of great distress in Abingdon.

A fly-leaf of the famous cartulary of the guild [1] gives a list of the The last twelve masters at the time of the suppression in 1547. Of these four Masters of survived to be placed on the new foundation of Christ's Hospital in the Guild. 1553. A fifth, William Kelynge, died between the erection of the new foundation and its confirmation.

This interesting list, in the Elizabethan hand of William Braunch, who was a governor from 1557 to 1601, may be compared with the lists in Little, p. 30 and Appendix.

'The names off the Twellve maysters off the fraternitie off the hollye Cross lyvyng Att the Tyme off Suppreston of ye Same

Thomas Read Esquier	who wear for the most pt de-
Lyonell Wodward gent	ceased before the last Erecon
Thomas Hyde gent	only these Mr. Thomas Read
Nicholas Hewatt gent	Rycds Mayott Hmfray Bos-
Rycds Braynche	tock Jhon Shene and Wyllm
Gilbert Freman	Kelynge who also deseaced
Humffray Bostock	before the same was fullye
Wyllm Kelynge	confermyd.
Rycds Mayott	Wyllm Braunche.'
Jhon Shene	
Adam Pope	
& Thomas Earle	

[1] In the Hall of Christ's Hospital.

CHAPTER VII

ST. HELEN'S CHURCH

Architec-
ture.

ST. HELEN'S is generally esteemed the finest Perpendicular parish church in Berkshire. Structurally it consists of five separately gabled aisles of seven bays. A peculiar effect is produced, especially inside the building, from the fact that the breadth exceeds the length.[1] The two north aisles are narrower than the others ; all are of approximately equal length, if we add the low-roofed, narrow vestry to the last south aisle. At the north-east angle rises the elegant Early English parapetted tower, to which a Perpendicular spire was added probably in the fifteenth century, and rebuilt in Charles I's reign.[2] It is an octagonal spire, supported by tiny flying buttresses springing from crocketted turrets on the angles.[3] Above the ornamental band the spire becomes less steep. The tower, with the fine porch at its base, forms the earliest part of the church which is visible to-day, and appears to belong to the early thirteenth century. The ironwork of the doors is older than the oak. In the north—Jesus—aisle are further traces of Early English among the Decorated and Perpendicular work. Above the second north porch is the tiny Exchequer Chamber of the Fraternity of the Holy Cross. This was restored in 1873 together with the figures of the exterior by Christ's Hospital, as part of their property, and the entrance was diverted from the interior to the exterior of the church.

The three-
aisled
church.

Until the Reformation, the church appears to have consisted of the three northernmost aisles, named in order from the north the Jesus aisle, Our Lady's aisle, and St. Helen's aisle. Of these, Our Lady's aisle formed the nave with the high altar in the present Lady Chapel. The arcading of these aisles dates from the middle of the

---

[1] Length 97 feet, not including porch ; breadth 108 feet, not including tower or porches. The area forms a rough rectangle, but the west wall is longer than the east, the south wall than the north.

[2] The earliest definite mention of the spire that I remember to have come across is in the churchwardens' accounts for 1595.

[3] Cp. J. H. Parker, *Ecclesiastical Topography : Berks*, 1849.

fifteenth century. At that period the Brethren of the Holy Cross found an outlet for their artistic and religious aspirations in redecorating and practically rebuilding the church, which they regarded as preeminently their own. For instance, the rich timbered roof of Our Lady's aisle and chancel with its catalogue of the house of Jesse was ceiled by Nicholas and Amie Gold, c. 1442. Little gives the inscription in a crest in the ceiling : ' In the worship of our Lady, pray for Nicholas Gold and Amie.'

But the roof appears older than this date, and in fact older than the present stone arcades and piers that support it. This impression is strengthened by the following Latin verses which run round under the cornice. They were deciphered by Mr. J. Parker, of Oxford, in 1873. Their meaning in brief is that William Beve founded and endowed the chapel to the glory of the Virgin, that Henry Bernyngtone furnished it with vestments, that William Cholsley repaired the roof, and that Boniface IX—his date is 1389 to 1404—granted an indulgence to all who support or repair this chapel.

SOUTH SIDE
1. Virgo maris stella ducens ad celica mella
2. Post mundi bella quibus haec [est] facta capella
3. Nomina servorum sistunt subscripta tuorum
4. Mentes fer quorum clemens ad regna polorum.

5. Istam fundavit Wilhelmus Beve capellam
6. Quam bene dotavit tenementis, ac quasi cellam
7. Virginis ad laudem fieri quam fecerat iste
8. Hic ut quaque die memoretur mors sua. Amen.

NORTH SIDE
9. Henricus dictus Bernyngtone praebet amictus
10. Sacros qui[bu]s bissus dat materiamque colorem :
11. Argentique crucem dat ad omnipotentis honorem.

12. Wilhelmus Cholsley laris istius reparari
13. Tectum per proprios sumptus fecitque novari.
14. Quatuor attribuit veniae Bonifatius annos
15. Nonus cum totidem quadragesimis sociatis
16. Omnibus hanc qui sustentant reparantve capellam.

It is curious that the lines of the timber do not correspond with the stone piers, which seem to have replaced older work. The arcading of the whole church is not regular in its lines.

The five-
aisled
church.

On the destruction of the Abbey Church further accommodation became necessary at St. Helen's Church, which succeeded St. Mary's as the ancient mother-church of the district. Accordingly, the two south aisles, named in order from the north St. Katherine's aisle and Holy Cross aisle, were added in 1539, in the rather thin style of that period.[1]

The south
aisles.

The difference between the Perpendicular work of the fifteenth century and of the sixteenth is marked. The roofs of the two south aisles are flatter, the arcading is more depressed, and the work generally is rougher and more rigid in design. The Holy Cross aisle is some-times called the Read aisle. Katherine Audelett, widow of John Audelett, tenant of Barton and steward of the Abbey lands, was the chief contributor to this work. In her will, dated November 27, 1539, she desired to be buried 'in the gild within the church of St. Eleynes which I have builded'. 'I. A.' and 'K. A.', the initials of Katherine and her late husband, alternate round the capitals of the aisle, together with the date, 1539. Katherine Audelett's heir was Thomas Read, of Barton, her nephew. The Guild of the Holy Cross appears to have had some part in the work before its dissolution in 1547.

It is possible that the present vestry at the south-east angle of the church was in existence before the Reformation as a chantry, standing detached from the three-aisled church.

The
modern
restoration.

The great modern restoration took place in 1873. Something had already been done in the middle of the nineteenth century : in 1845 the present clock was erected ; in 1848 the high pews were cut down, and about the same time the pulpit was moved to its present position from the west end of the nave ; still more important, the eight bar-barous galleries that had grown up with the strange taste of the seven-teenth and eighteenth centuries were swept away. These galleries destroyed the acoustic excellence of the church. It had been the custom for the successive churchwardens to paint their pews in the gallery some vivid colour, and the layers of crimson, green, scarlet and purple were applied to the neighbouring portion of the stone pillars. The last of these galleries survived in the Lady aisle until 1873. Behind it the Jesus aisle was boarded off as a sort of desolate corridor.

In 1873 about £7,000 was raised to restore what has been described

[1] In the absence of a clear record we assign St. Katherine's aisle to the same period as the St. Cross aisle.

as a 'comparative heap of dingy ruins'. The vicar resisted the suggestions that it would be better to build a new church. The present nave was heightened, but the Perpendicular windows of the clerestory were preserved as before, with the addition of the new internal hood arches.

The east end of the chancel was rebuilt with a good Decorated window, the reredos being removed to the north wall of the church, and the picture of Christ bearing the Cross to the vestry.

The west wall of the nave was entirely rebuilt. The chancel received its present handsome ceiling of oak, and the nave its present high-pitched open roof of oak and pitch pine. This raising of the roof and gables of the central aisle may have added to the internal dignity of the structure, but it has sadly broken the picturesque line of gables, as viewed from the churchyard. The new oak screen with the great cross was placed between the nave and chancel—there is no chancel arch. The stone and oak screens to the north of the chancel belong to the same date. New bases were put to all the shafts throughout the church. The church was reseated with pews of yellow deal. The old carving of the Corporation pews was retained on the new seats. The old pulpit was remounted on a fresh stone base. All the monuments were restored, particularly the canopied tomb of John Roysse, near the baptistry.[1] A new font was added. In levelling the floor of the south aisle the restorers discovered some old foundations of earlier buildings, perhaps of a porch or baptistry.

In 1886 the four porches were restored ; and the spire, condemned as leaning at a dangerous angle, was rebuilt from the tower. It was feared at the time that it would be necessary to rebuild also the tower, but this was happily averted.

The handsome reredos of carved wood, gilt and coloured, was erected behind the high altar in 1897. Its only fault is that it obscures the modern tracery and glass of the Decorated east window.

The light oak screen of the Lady Chapel dates from 1907.

Among the interesting treasures of the church may be noted the six fine brass candelabra, particularly the great candelabrum in the nave, dated 1710,[2] and the sixteenth-century candelabrum in the Lady Chapel with the mitred heads, which perhaps had an earlier home at the Abbey.

---

[1] At the expense of members of the Grammar School.
[2] It is figured in Cox's *English Church Furniture.*

There is a fine brass, dated 1417, of Geoffrey Barbour, the bridge-builder, in a monk's dress. It was removed from the Abbey, and is now on the west wall of St. Katherine's aisle. A brass of William Heyward, S.T.D., vicar. ob. 1501, at the other end of that aisle. A brass of Thomas Mayott, ob. 1627, with the three boars' heads impaled with the arms of the Lydalls.

The glass is modern, with the exception of a few scraps ; it is of varying merit.

The Jacobean pulpit is encircled with the verse, ' Ad haec idoneus quis,' and the date 1636. The door of the second north porch bears the date 1637.

In that decade much work was done in the church, besides the re-building of the spire, and we would assign to it the building of the gateway of the churchyard.

Bells.   The bells give a peal of great sweetness. Their history goes back to very early times. For instance, they were rehung and the great bell recast in 1590. In 1619 the churchwardens' accounts give a list of five bells, with the weights—the great bell, fourth bell, third bell, second bell and treble. These were conveyed by barge to Reading in that year, and recast as six bells, of approximately the same total weight of 77 cwts. 03 qrs. 09 lbs. The smallest, or churchwardens' bell, bears the date ' 1641, churchwardens W. C. and R. B.' Other bells are dated ' 1764, Lester & Packer of London ', at which date the peal of six was increased to eight. In 1886 the peal was increased to ten.

Organ.   In 1719 a resolution was passed by the Town Council, by which any member failing to ' subscribe to the charge of erecting Organs within the parish of St. Hellen's within this Borough, shall not have any benefitt of selling goodes or be imployed in any profitable worke belonging to this Corporacion ', nor have ' any benefitt of the sealing fees upon the granting of Leases by this Corporacion to any person whatsoever '—a bit of compulsion sadly missed now by collectors for laudable objects. Again, in 1725, the Council voted £50 ' toward the erecting of a Good and Sufficient organ in St. Hellen's Church '.[1] This organ was built by Jordan of London, and set up in the new gallery at the west end of the nave in 1726.[2]

[1] Borough Records.
[2] In 1724 the Corporation contributed £10 ' toward ye Erecting a Gallary in the Midle Isle in St. Hellen's Church '. Borough Records.

The churchwardens' accounts yield many references :

1726. Jan. 1. ' To William Snow for half a years sallery for Bellows Blower to the Organ £1 0 0.'

Feb. 24. ' pd Mr. Jorden's man as is Customory when an Organ is set up £0 10 6.'

' for a chear in the gallery for Ye organést £0 2 0.'

1727. Inventory—' Item an Organ.'

April 10. ' To Mr. Wheeler for half a year's sallery for playing the Organ due at a Ladyday last £10 0 0.'

' William Snow for half year's sallery for blowing the organ Bellows £1 0 0.'

1728. ' To Mr. Munday Organest for three-quarter year's sallery £15 0 0.'

' To William Snow Bellows Blower a year's sallery £2 0 0.'

There reposes in Bodley a copy of the *Sermon at St. Helen's, Ap. 2. 1726 on the occasion of Opening an Organ,* by Joseph Stockwell, B.D., Fellow of Trinity, Oxon. It justifies the lawfulness and propriety of church music, but its interest is homiletic rather than historical. The Faculty says that the Minister, Churchwardens, Mayor, Master of the Free School and Principal Inhabitants set up this organ without charge to the parishioners.

Another grant of £50 was made by the Corporation in 1779 towards a new organ.[1] This was the present organ, built by Byfield, England & Russell. Some of the dates cut on the fine, old organ-case are older than 1779. It is uncertain whether these panels are part of the earlier organ-case, or whether, if the tradition that part of the organ came from Salisbury is correct, these dates and initials were cut by artistic choir-boys at Salisbury.

In 1849 this organ, with the fine figure of King David and his harp, was brought down from the gallery at the west of the nave, which it had occupied with the choir, and was placed by the south door. In 1873 it was entirely rebuilt in its present position in St. Katherine's aisle, south of the chancel.

The documentary evidence takes the history of St. Helen's much further back than does its architecture. There is an early reference, A.D. 995, in the Chronicle of Abingdon Abbey to St. Helen's Church as a place of sanctuary. It occurs in a charter of King Adelred, who explains somewhat discursively how the grant came into his hands : Three brothers dwelling in a certain inn, the man of one of these, by name Leofric, the devil instigating him, stole a bit or bridle. This

Documentary history.

Earliest mention.

1 Borough Records.

being found in his bosom, the owners engaged in battle the three brothers, who defended their man. Two brothers, Ælfnoth and Ælfric, were slain ; and the third, Athelwine, barely escaped with the thief, by entering St. Helen's Church.[1]

St. Helen's Church next appears in the *De Consuetudinibus*, c. 1154–89 A.D., as paying three marks' rent to the infirmary of the Abbey.[2] For it is not mentioned in the Domesday Survey, but the same is the case with other churches of Berkshire, known to have then been in existence.

About A.D. 1225 comes an interesting notice : 'Robert by the divine pity humble minister of the monastery of Abbendon' disclaims acquiring any fresh right in the church of St. Helen, which the Abbey had received to farm from Stephen de Columna, subdeacon of the Lord Pope.[3]

In 1245 an indult was granted to Master Roger, rector of St. Helen's, to hold an additional benefice.[4] These two references indicate that the Abbey had not acquired the rectorship of St. Helen's in the first part of the thirteenth century. This acquisition was made in 1261.[5]

Ethelmar.

In 1248 the living of St. Helen's, then rich and famous, was a matter of dispute in high places. It was demanded by the Pope for a certain Roman, and by Henry III for his half-brother Ethelmar—the greatest of all pluralists, having already so many livings that he knew neither their number nor their worth. The perplexed Abbot, who was the patron, gave the living to the King's brother, under promise of protection against the Pope. Deserted by the King, he had to travel in age and sickness to the Papal Court, where he was harassed and heavily fined. Ethelmar or Athelmar was also made Bishop of Winchester. He died in 1261.[6]

A most important document [7] states that John de Cliford has been

---

[1] Stevenson, i. 394 ' Sanctae Helenae intrans ecclesiam.'

[2] Ibid., ii. 328.

[3] 'Carta de ecclesia Sanctae Elenae Abendon.'   Printed in *Salisbury Charters*, p. 168, Rolls Series, 1891.   [4] *Cal. Papal Letters*, i. 213.

[5] *Cambridge Chronicle of Abingdon*, p. 12.

[6] Matthew Paris, *Chron. Majora.*

[7] It is preserved in an imperfect copy among Lempriere's transcripts of a copy, dated 1594, stated to be in 1801 in the Registry of the Archdeacon of Berks, the original belonging to the Hon. Lord Henry Norris, Baron Ricott. It is a decree of Master John de Burton ' officiarius a sede Cant., Decano & Capitulo Sarum sede vacante institutus ' : this fixes the date as 1284, for John de Burton, precentor at Salisbury from 1272, was official of Sarum in 1284, the see being vacant. Le Neve, ii. 641. In the copy the transcriber has underlined as illegible most of the contractions, but only one or two words are obscure.

presented to the official for the vicarage of St. Helen's by the religious men, the Abbot and Convent of Abingdon, and proceeds to settle the income of the church according to the advice of the precentor of Sarum and others. The vicar of St. Helen's was to receive all the oblations and obventions of the altar of St. Helen's, and all the lambs, wool, flax and all the small tithes of the altarage of St. Helen's in the town of Abingdon. Further, he was to take all the traders' tithes in Abingdon. Also the oblations and small tithes of the chapels of Radley, Drayton, Shippon and Dry Sandford,[1] except the tithes of lambs, wool and cheese, which the Abbey was to have entire in these chapels. The living in 1284.

It provided that in cases where the number of lambs was not great enough for one lamb to be given as tithes, the money in lieu of this should be assigned to the portion of the vicarage. Similarly, in cases where in the house of any parishioner cheese could not be made from the small quantity of milk.

Further, it assigned to the vicar as hay-tithe of certain parishioners according to an old arrangement all the hay of the meadow called Dunnemore, or forty shillings from the Abbey, as the Vicar should prefer.

Also, the houses in Abingdon belonging to the rector of St. Helen's. Also, the house with the croft, where the chaplains serving Radley were wont to abide.

It proceeded to settle the vicar's duties. He was to provide that St. Helen's Church was served by two fit chaplains, of whom he himself might be one ; that the chapel of Radley was served by one chaplain, Drayton by a second, and the chapels of Shippon and Sandford by a third, and by other fit ministers. The vicar was to maintain in the mother-church and in the chapels books, ornaments and lights. He was to support, according to his portion, episcopal and archidiaconal ornaments, and all other ornaments, ordinary and extraordinary.

The Abbey was to take the tithes of sheaves in fields and gardens, the tithes of hay belonging to St. Helen's and the chapels, except the hay already assigned to the vicar ; also all the tithes in meadows, and all the pastures belonging to St. Helen's and the chapels. Also to the Abbey were assigned all tenants, homages and dues, with all rights of ' escaet '. Also all mortuaries throughout the parish. Also the

---

[1] ' de Radeleia, Dratton, de Scupen, de Samford.'

tithes of lambs, of wool and of all cheese of Radley, Drayton, Shippon, and Sandford.

This document exhibits a large and fully organized parish, whose complex life and arrangements explain many matters of our own day.

The account of the great riot of 1327 indicates that St. Helen's Church was the centre of disaffection, and that her bell gave the signal.

Account-rolls. The Account-rolls of the Abbey have references to St. Helen's in the fourteenth and fifteenth centuries. For instance, in 1322 and in 1369 the church paid the Pittancer lxvi^s. viij^d. In 1404 and 1422 the Chapelwardens pay the vicar of St. Helen's 5^s., and in other years to the Kitchener on behalf of the vicar.[1] In 1356 the Infirmarer receives as rent or tithe of the tenement of Littlefeld in Abingdon nothing ' for the part occupied by the Chaplain and proctors of the Chantry of the Blessed Mary in St. Helen's Church '. In 1417 and 1428 the Chamberlain records a payment of xiiij^d as rent to the Warden of the Chapel of the Blessed Mary of St. Helen's for the Barbour tenement.

Cemetery dispute. At the end of the fourteenth century St. Helen's engaged in a prolonged struggle to wrest from the Abbey the rights of a cemetery. In 1391 the Pope, Boniface IX, issued a mandate to license a cemetery for the parish of St. Helen's, upon the petition of Henry Bryt, vicar, and of his parishioners. The petitioners alleged that the tumult caused by the funerals within the grounds of the monastery disturbed the monks. Further, that when the vicar had celebrated the office of the dead, the monks sometimes kept the body waiting three days for burial. Also that pigs were allowed to do damage in the cemetery. Lastly, that costly tombstones that had been erected were sold irregularly. They stated that the proposed cemetery adjoined the parish church, and was enclosed with a stone wall. The Abbot complained to Rome of this decision, and in 1392 the Pope called in the case to himself. In 1396 the litigation was still proceeding under the elaborate forms of ecclesiastical law, and in the evidence is given a list of sixty-seven people who had already been buried in the new cemetery. Finally, the Abbey won the appeal, and recovered all its burial rights.[2]

[1] Kirk, 140 'Et eidem Coquinario nomine Vicarii Sancte Elene pro oblacione Sancti Edmundi per annum v^s.'

[2] Vide *Cal. Papal Letters*, v. 5, and see Index.

The list of persons buried at this cemetery between 1391 and 1396, when it was closed, seems of sufficient local interest to print in full. It includes the name of John Kent, which has persisted in Abingdon down to the nineteenth century.

The cemetery of St. Helen is mentioned as a landmark, as well as the chapel of St. Helen's, in the account-roll of the Treasurers of the Abbey in 1440.

PERSONS BURIED AT ST. HELEN'S CEMETERY

Wᵐ atte Grene, priest
Wᵐ Mullewarde
Wᵐ Shakul
Robert Poreman
John Carroway
Wᵐ Tylare of Bristol
Rd and Iulian Symonis
Jota or Joca Johannis
John Kent
Robert son of Walter Sawyare
Peter son of Wᵐ Shakul
Wᵐ and John sons of John Couper
brothers
Simon son of John Spane
John son of John Masoun
Wᵐ son of John Batteshore
John son of Thos Bakere
Robert son of Thomas Hakebourne
Julian, Hy and John sons of Simon
Harwe
John son of Robert Liford
John son of Thomas Smyth
Denis and Wᵐ sons of Matthew
Couper
John son of Thomas Payntour
Wᵐ son of John Bouchére
Rd son of David Werkman
John son of Thomas Wolmonger
Rd son of John Cardmakere
John son of Rd Proute.
laymen.

Emma Townshende and Agnes
Stotardi

Cecily daughter of Thomas Hake-
burne
Agnes and Alice d. of Simon
Harwe
Margaret d. of Robert Clerk
Alice d. of Rd Lambhurde
Margery d. of Thomas Hambur-
makere
Alice d. of Matthew Fotere
Matilda d. of John Grym, Spiser,
Matilda d. of Rd Horseman
Elizabeth d. of John London
Agnes d. of Wᵐ Northcote
Cristina d. of James Grey
Elizabeth d. of Robert Northcote
Matilda d. of John Blockley
Matilda d. of John Shakul
Margery d. of Thomas Hul
Cristina d. John Webbe
Beatrice d. of Elizabeth, Matmaker
Edith wife of Patrick Warkman
Eve w. of David Werkman
Emma w. of Rd atte Water
Alice w. of Rd Rokkynne
Denise w. of John Ponche Boch
Isabella, Alice and Cristina hand-
maids of Adam Taylour, John
Shakul and Adam Taylour
respectively parishioners of /
sd parish.

These two exhumed
John son of Rd Proute and Edith
wife of Patrick Werkman.

A dispensation was granted in 1414 to Richard Beel, perpetual
vicar of St. Helen's, to hold for ten years, with the said vicarage of
value not exceeding 50 marks, one other benefice with cure of souls.
Within the ten years he is to exchange one of the two for a benefice
compatible with the remaining one. And the next year a further
dispensation allowed him to receive the stipend during ten years
while studying or residing in the Roman Court or any honest
place.

Bishop Neville's Ordination.   An ordination of Bishop Neville concerning a dispute in 1437
between the vicar and parishioners of St. Helen's about the bells, is
addressed by Robert by the divine permission Bishop of Sarum to our
beloved son in Christ Master Richard Mey, vicar of the parish church
of St. Helen of Abendon.[1]

The Bishop ordered that the ringing of the bells, except in the
divine office, should be at the discretion of the churchwardens, and
proceeded to give detailed directions as to the ringing of the 'Day-
bell' and the little 'Toll-bell', and as to the services. The procession
of the Fraternity of the Holy Cross is allowed.[2] A celebration at the
Purification of the Blessed Mary is ordered, either by the vicar or by
a suitable chaplain. The vicar is ordered to show tact in encouraging
gifts of copes and church ornaments by the living and by the dead,
and to carry out faithfully the wills of the testators and donors as to
masses for the dead, &c., that the popular devotion may be the more
aroused.[3] Mention is made of the assistance of the vicar by priests
and chantry chaplains celebrating in the said church. The vicar was
ordered to pay 3s. a year towards the repair of the three minor bells,
and of the little toll-bell.

The fif-teenth century poor in material.   There are no churchwardens' accounts extant prior to the Reformation, and literary history becomes more and more scanty with respect
to matters ecclesiastical and political as we advance from the thirteenth
to the fifteenth century. So we have practically nothing to add to the
account of the church, as recorded in her stones and timbers. These
have already told us something of the work of the Fraternity of the
Holy Cross in these centuries.

The union of the vicarage of St. Nicholas' with the vicarage of
St. Helen's, in 1508, is discussed in the chapter on St. Nicholas'.

---

[1] Sarum Reg. Neville, fol. 109. The date 1437 is fixed by the words ' nostrae
consecrationis anno decimo '.
[2] See Chapter VI.   [3] ' ut popularis devocio maius excitetur.'

The Reformation brings us into another period, and to fresh sources of information. Leland, writing about 1541, speaks of St. Helen's—now a five-aisled church—as ' the great resorte of all the Towne '. He adds that ' In S. Ethelwolde's tyme wer straunge Thinges and Tumbes found yn digging ' near St. Helen's.

The register of St. Helen's, dating from 1538, and the churchwardens' accounts, from 1555, afford a mass of valuable and sometimes racy information about the events and manners of the times. We give a few typical extracts from the early register :

1557. ' buried the xxv day of August Wm Simpson and Maud his wife both in one day and was first town clark after the towne was incorporated.'

1558. ' buried the thyrd day Aprell Richard Large Highbyrgis.'

1568. ' buried the same day—xiiii January—Thomason Hide gent. from banburie curte.'

1588. ' Sir Wyllyam Wyntter knight came the xi day of Marche to the new inn and there laye all the nyght and goyng in the morning into his owne country to be buryed. And had . . . . three peales with all the bells one at his comeing and two at his departure and gave the Ringers vs.'

1589. ' The xxii day of Aprell the Erle of Wisseter being dead passing to his owne manor to be buried stayying heere all nyght payd to the Ringers xiis.'

1655. ' 7 Aperill buried Francis Will. Whitt Skoolmaster and Mary his wife.'

We give also a few early extracts from the churchwardens' accounts.[1]

The churchwardens appear to have made many payments under the Tudors, which would now be regarded as outside their liability. In 1555, or 1 and 2 of Philip and Mary, 21d was expended for twelve tapers at the ' yeres mynde of maister John Hyde ', i. e. for the mass for the rest of his soul upon the anniversary of his death. Similar entries occur for the ' monethes mynde ' of various people, the expense

---

[1] The first batch, 1555–91, are taken from *Archaeologia*, vol. i. 11–23, where it is stated that the originals were then—in 1770—in the possession of the Rev. Mr. G. Benson, and edited with observations by J. Ward. The only Rev. Mr. G. Benson that I have yet traced in the history of Abingdon in that century is the distinguished Presbyterian and Independent minister there from 1723 to 1729, who died in 1762. He was a Doctor of Divinity, who had the habit of brightening his discourses with Greek and Hebrew quotations of two or three minutes in length.

varying according to their station and purse. Then comes a payment of 8^d ' to the sextin for watching the sepulter two nights '. It was the custom to build a Holy Sepulchre and place in it the Host, which was watched from Good Friday to Easter morning. Another entry of somewhat more liberal payment : ' To the Suffrigan for halowing the churchyard and other implements of the church 30^s 0^d.' Again, ' for wast of the paschall, and for holye yoyle 5^s 10^d.' In 1559 an entry of 20^d ' for taking down the altere ' marks the end of Mary's counter-Reformation. The following year a communion table was put in its place. There are various entries for the rood, the rood-lights, the rood Mary and John and the patron, the rood-loft, &c., until in 1561 there are payments for taking down the rood-loft. The rood or image came to mean the same as the rood-cross, rood-beam, or rood-tree, which stood in the rood-loft over the entrance from the nave into the chancel. It was natural that Mary and John should be associated with the emblem of the Crucifixion, as well as St. Helen, the finder of the Holy Rood. Apparently it was found politic to tone down the severities of the Reformation in Abingdon, for in 1560 1^s 0^d was paid ' for two dossin of Morres belles ', and in 1566, ' payde for setting up Robin Hoodes bower 18^d.' These entries are explained by a sermon of Bishop Latimer, quoted in *Sports and Pastimes*, in which he relates how on a certain holiday-ride he was unable to enter a certain church on account of some rowdy May sports going on there :

' I thought my rochet would be regarded, but it would not serve, it was faine to give place to Robin Hood's men.' The procession of the Fraternity of the Holy Cross at St. Helen's on May 3 goes back beyond 1437—probably into Saxon times.

There are several entries for books : ' Anno MDLXIII or 6 of Elizabeth payde for one boke of Wendsdayes fasting, which contaynes omellies 6^d.' In the previous year 10^s 0 was spent ' for a bybill for the church '. This would be the popular Geneva quarto, while Archbishop Parker's great folio Bible of 1568 was bought in 1576 for 40^s 0. The entry in 1565 of 6^d ' payde for two bokes of common prayer agaynste invading of the Turke ', recalls the great struggle going on in Malta and in Hungary between the Cross and the Crescent. In 1564 was paid 5^s 2^d ' for the reparations of the cross in the market-place '. In 1591, ' payde for an houre glass for the pilpitt 4^d.' Men found that they had not time to fight the Armada and listen in the same century to sermons without a time-limit.

To these may be added a few more typical extracts from the originals preserved at St. Helen's :

1587. 'Itm. Re. of Thomas Webb for arrerage of Rent for ye house over the Churchegate viij^s.'

'Itm. Re. of Mr. Lee and Mr. Orpwodd in parte of payments of the iij^{li}. ix^s. xj^d. then owed on their accompte and thother xx^s. then accepte as paid for that Mr. Smyth paid xx^s. of the parishes debte. Re. ij^{li}. ix^s. xj^d.'

'Itm. (The Churchwardens) charge themselves with monie receaved at the Comunion table that is to saye at Easter 1587. the Wyne and bredd being discharged as followeth the som of xxxiij^s.'

1590. 'In primis receaved for Hobbe childes knyll vj^d.'

'Itm. ye bell for a straunger wh. died at the kinge heade viij^d.'

'Im. for his grave j^s. viij^d.'

'Itm. of goodwife Ryder for seate with Lyonell Welford in the midell Ile ij^s.'

'Itm. to Wyll. for his wages for a whole yere at Michaelmas 1587, for settinge the clock vj^s. viij^d.'

'Itm. paide for a Communion Booke iij^s. iiij^d.'

'Itm. for Ironwork when the bells were haunged and for great bolte that went throughe the crose beames xxx^s. viij^d.'

'Itm. to Mother Dyers for one great bolte of Iron to hange the Thirde Bell viij^d.'

'Itm. to Sansom the Smithe for his work ix^s.'

'Itm. paide to the Goyle at Readinge viij^s. viij^d.'

'Itm. paide to the Parriter of Saulsbery for his fees iij^s. iiij^d.'

There are constant payments under the Stuarts for bell-ropes and costly repairs to the bells, payments to the gaol at Reading, to the Parriter of the Bishop of Salisbury, payments for the ringers at the Assizes and on the Fifth of November, and payments for the washing of the napery ; while the rent of the seats was a steady source of income. There was an organized system of taxations to pay for the repairs of the church.

1590–3. 'Itm. for the knyll of one White that was prest to death[1] at thassises viij^d.'

'Itm. paide to Jones the Joyner for the wainscott on the pulpitt. xij^s. iiij^d.'

---

[1] If the prisoner refused to plead, he was condemned to the 'peine forte et dure ', i. e., to have iron laid upon him as much as he could bear and more. If he died thus without pleading 'By God and my country ', no forfeiture took place, and the property was preserved for his heir. Stephen's *Criminal Law*, i. 298.

' Itm. paide unto Mr. Carter the Belfounder of Reading for the newe
casting of the greate Bell and for 500 waighte of metell put more
into the same bell   xx^{li}. xj^s. vj^d.'
' Itm. paide for mending the Dyall by the Almes house   ij^s.'

1595.   There is a reference to ' the wedinge porche ', i. e. one of the
north porches.

' Itm. to Billson for warninge us to appeare before the Commissioners   j^d.'
' payed more to Billson for bringing of the booke of Artickles   j^d.'
' Itm. payed for a booke of prayers contayninge the good suceses of
the fleete   iij^d.'
This is a reference to the war of which the Spanish Armada was the
most striking episode.

1603.   ' Rec. of goodman Yate for the knill for his Daughter Mr. Dunches
mayd that was slayne with the cart   xviij^d.'
1607.   ' Itm. pd for franckencence and cole and viniger at the tyme of the
plague and at other tymes this present yeare   ij^s.'
1611.   There is a mention of ' the high chauncell newly built '.
1612.   ' pd. to old Butler the slatter for ii daies a peece for his neveu and
him selfe for pointing the chincks uppon the leads and slatting
the end of the chauncell   iij^s. iiij^d.'
1612.   ' pd to Bartholomew for his yeres wages for whipping doggs out of
the Churche   xij^d.'

There are similar entries to this last in other years, and Scott has
something of the sort in *Woodstock*.

1610.   An entry which gives the date of the removal of the high
altar from the Lady Chapel to the central aisle :

' Item Received of Mr. William Bostock for his seate and his wives seate
at the upper ende in the Chauncell in our Ladie Ile next the high Chauncel
newlie built and set upp at the Coste and Charge of the said Mr. Bostock as
well the som of vj^s. viij^d. as also the surrender of his wive's seat in the Middle
Ile where Mr. Peeter Probie's wife hath nowe placed and seated hir selfe.'

1615.   The churchwardens ask an allowance of xx^s for a payment
to Thomas Clempson

' in respect of a fayer green Carpett of broad cloth imbrodered with greene
sylk and bordered with a greene sylk frindg and is in length 3 yards and alf.
The farther charge whereof is bestowed by the sayd Thomas Clempson out
of his owne benevolence in addysshon unto his Brothers the sayd Rychard
Clempsons aforesayd gyft which delivers to his accompt for the parish.'

In 1619 in the inventory of the church goods is mentioned a Bible bought in 1612. This Bible, with its chain, may be seen near the organ.

1619. 'Fines levied upon divers persons for not being at Church on Sondaies at Divine Service and not shutting their windows and selling commodities.'

In the list appears the blameless Francis Little, fined xij^d for his man.

1630. 'Item pd to the Chymers for to Chyme the Bell when the Bishope of Salsberry came to visitt xij^d.'

In 1632 a large 'taxe' was raised towards the rebuilding of the steeple and extensive work was done in the church in the years following. There are entries in many years for ridding away the filth outside the porch.

1638. 'Itm. for lookinge unto the unruelye boys 8^s. 8^{1}.'
'Itm. pd for a hower glasse 7^d.'
'Itm. pd for guildinge the hower glasse 3^s. o.'

One more extract will illustrate the duties of the churchwardens and the style of their accounts.

The churchwardens of 1667 devoted a whole page of their accounts to the items of payments for apprenticing an Abingdon lad in London —to take one of many instances during that century. They paid Francis Trewlock 3s. 7d. for carrying Winsmore's boy to London and for victuals on the way; 9d. for his dinner and supper in London; 2s. 6d. for two pairs of stockings; 2s. 6d. for one pair of shoes; 6s. od. for a suit (doublet and hose only); 1os. od. for three shirts, + 6d. more; 2s. od. for a pair of 'lynings'; 6d. for mending his shoes; £3 for his apprenticeship; 8s. 4d. for indentures; 6d. given to the boy; £1 1os. od. for a new suit at London; and 5s. to the master to lay out for the boy. Total, £6 12s. 2d.

Of course from the time of the dissolution of the Abbey the poor relief lay chiefly in their hands, though from time to time they acted 'by order of Mr. Mayor'.

These accounts are almost continuous during the interlude in Church history of the Civil War and Commonwealth, during which St. Helen's was 'the great meeting-house' served by Puritan preachers. We have drawn largely on these accounts for the general history of Abingdon in this and the later periods.

TOWNSEND L

After the Restoration.

The period from the Restoration to the nineteenth century is perhaps the dullest in the history of St. Helen's. It coincides with the great growth of Protestant dissent. It is an age of pluralism. Vicar and parish entertained rather material views of their relationship. In that period the outlying chapels were grossly neglected. B. Willis speaks of Sandford and Shippon chapels as in ruins in 1733.[1] Some interesting figures stand out : for instance, a future primate of Ireland was born at St. Helen's vicarage in 1729. Vicar and parish engaged in many disputes and controversies, due largely to an ignorance of the history of the earlier centuries. From 1700 to 1800 the appointment of one churchwarden by the vicar was allowed and disputed intermittently, until Lempriere, that prince of litigants, at last relinquished the struggle.[2] In the nineteenth century tithes were still being computed in kind.

Vicarage House.

The question of a vicar's house in the parish of St. Helen's is rather interesting. A document quoted in the chapter on St. Nicholas', c. 1230–40, suggests that the rector of St. Helen's had a house. In later history there is no trace of a vicarage house until the present vicarage in the Park was built in 1874. In 1699 the Rev. Anthony Addison received £20 in lieu of rent, ' the parish not having provided a house for him.' In 1753 the salary for house-rent was stopped. In 1757 the parish allowed the new vicar £6 10s. for a house. In 1783 Cleoburey explained to the Bishop that there had never been a vicar's house. In 1800 the question of a house or equivalent payments was raised by Lempriere. During Mr. Dodson's pastorate there was no vicarage house.

The house in St. Helen's which bears the name of the Old Vicarage seems to have acquired that title from being rented and inhabited by some vicar, it being attached to a garden that was from time immemorial in ecclesiastical hands.

Cleoburey's answers to the Bishop.

The following answers sent by Mr. Cleoburey, the vicar, to queries proposed by Bishop Barrington to his clergy, preserve some valuable information.[3]

MAY 20, 1783. ST. HELEN'S, ABINGDON.

Query 1. How often, and at what hours upon the Lord's Day, is divine service, both prayers and preaching, performed in your church ? If divine service be not performed twice every Lord's Day, what is the reason ?

[1] *Parochiale Anglicanum.*
[2] Cp. Vestry Book, *ad annum*, 1704, 1720, 1753, &c.; also Lempriere's notebook.   [3] From a manuscript book at the Vicarage.

Answer. Twice each, the service in the morning beginning at half past ten, and in the afternoon at half past three, except during the winter quarter, when the latter commences at half after two. The morning discourse is preached by the vicar, that in the evening by the lecturer.

Q. 2. Is divine service performed in your church upon any week days, holidays, or festivals that happen on week days ?

A. On Wednesdays and Fridays in Lent, and on all holidays and festivals in St. Helen's : and in St. Nicholas' morning and evening daily throughout the year.

Q. 3. Do you perform divine service as Incumbent or as Curate of your parish ?

A. As Incumbent.

Q. 4. Do you serve any other cure ? If so, what cure, and how many, and at what distance are the cures you serve from one another ? Are you duly licenced to the cure you serve ?

A. None.

Q. 5. How often in the year is the holy Sacrament of the Lord's Supper administered in your Church, and at what times of the year ?

A. The first Sunday in every month ; on Good Friday, Christmas, Easter, and Whitsuntide at St. Helen's, and on the Sundays following each of the three preceeding festivals at St. Nicholas'.

Q. 6. What number of communicants have you generally in your parish ? In particular what was the number which communicated at Easter last ? Was it greater or less than usual ?

A. The number of communicants in this parish are (communibus annis) about one hundred and eighty, but the exact number which communicated at Easter last I do not now recollect, but believe it to be much as usual.

Q. 7. Are there any reputed papists in your parish, &c. ?

A. One only old and poor.

Q. 8. Are there any presbyterians, independents, anabaptists, or quakers in your parish ? And how many of each sect, and of what rank ? Are there any other places made use of for divine worship than such as are used by the above mentioned sects ? What are the names of their teachers, and are they all licenced as the law directs ? Is their number greater or less of late years than formerly, according to your observation, and by what means ? Are there any persons in your parish who profess to disregard religion, or who commonly absent themselves from all public worship of God ?

A. But few quakers, and independents, without any regular teacher, anabaptists and presbyterians more than can be conveniently numbered, and some of the first rank and property in the place. The name of the teacher of the former sect is Daniel Turner, that of the latter John Lake. Of late years the anabaptists have rather increased owing to their indefatigable pains in making converts, with this view employing and trafficking with those of their own persuasion in preference to the members of the established church, and impressing the same notions on their followers and dependants, and when there is a religion attended with instant temporal gain, the consequence especially amongst the lower class of the people is easily deducible.

Q. 9.　Do your parishioners duly send their children and servants, who have not learnt their catechism, to be instructed by you ?　And do you either expound to them yourself, or make use of some printed exposition, and what is it ?　At what particular seasons of the year, and in what language are the young persons of your parish catechised ?

A.　Children are duly instructed in their catechism, generally on the Wednesdays and Fridays during Lent, when I have occasionally expounded to them, but find they make quicker progress in the knowledge of their duties by an attentive perusal of Lewis's exposition of the catechism, which I have sometimes distributed with success.

Q. 10.　Have you a register-book of births and burials duly kept, and in good preservation ?　And do you regularly make your returns of births and burials into the Registrar's office, as the canon requires ?　How far back does your register of births and burials go ?

A.　The returns of births and burials are regularly made into the registrar's office, and the register-book is duly kept, which goes as far back as the year 1653.　We have indeed some registers of a more ancient date but they are so obliterated by time and defaced by mice, as to be but in very few places legible.

Q. 11.　Is there a register-book duly kept according to the directions of the Act of Parliament against clandestine marriages ?

A.　There is.

Q. 12.　Are there any chapels of ease in your parish ?　What are the names of them ?　How often are there prayers and sermons in them ? Have they any estates or funds particularly appropriated to their maintenance ?　How far distant are they from the parish church ?　By whom are they served ?　Have you any ruinated chapels in which there is no divine service performed ?

A.　To this vicarage are annexed the chapels of Drayton and Radley. The parishioners have usually provided themselves with an officiating minister for the former, and the Stonhouse family do by custom nominate a clerk to fill the cure of the latter.　And altho' the vicar of St. Helen's is presented, instituted and inducted to both, he thereby enjoys at present no other advantage than the trifling annual acknowledgment of the sum of 3*s*. 4*d*. for the one and 5*s*. for the other.　The reputed distance of each from the mother church is three miles.

Q. 13.　Have you a true and perfect account and terrier of all houses, lands, tythes, pensions, and profits which belong to you as minister of your parish ?　Hath a duplicate thereof been laid up in the bishop's registry ? Hath there been, since that was done, any augmentation made of your living ? And hath an account of such an augmentation been transmitted thither also ?

A. I have been at some trouble and expence in searching your Lordship's and the archdeacon's registry for the original endowment terrier or any other materials from which to frame a terrier of the profits of this vicarage of St. Helen's, but hitherto without success. Some friends likewise are now examining for me the records in Westminster, the Tower, etc., with the same view, and should I be so fortunate as to find any of the aforesaid instruments, I shall not fail to transmit duplicates thereof to be preserved in your Lordship's registry. But an imperfect account (and such only am I at present enabled to form) by specifying too little or too much might hereafter tend only to injure and mislead the incumbent or his parishioners.

Q. 14. Is there any free school, almshouse, hospital, or other charitable endowment in your parish ? And for how many, and for what sort of persons ? Who was the founder, and who are the governors or trustees ? What are the revenues of it ? Are they carefully preserved and employed as they ought to be ? Are the statutes and orders made concerning it well observed ? Have any lands or tenements been left for the repair of your church or for any other pious uses ? Who has the direction and management of such benefactions, and who takes an account of and conducts them ?

A. The only charity of which the minister and churchwardens are the guardians is that of the late Charles Twitty of Westminster Esqr., who gave by his will the sum of 1700£ for building and perpetually endowing an hospital for maintaining in meat, drink and apparel, and all other necessaries of life, three poor aged men, and the like number of poor aged women, not receiving the common alms, the interest of which sum has been and continues to be faithfully applied to the above purposes. There are besides numerous and various charitable endowments, but which being by royal grant chiefly under the direction of the corporation are here omitted, as presuming them not to be the immediate objects of your Lordship's enquiry.

Q. 15. Are the churchwardens in your parish chosen every year in the easter week ? How are they chosen ? By the minister or parishioners together, or one by the minister, and the other by the parishioners ?

A. The churchwardens are annually chosen in the easter week, formerly one by the minister, the other by the parishioners, but about the year 1754, to answer some election purposes, the minister was arbitrarily deprived of his right, and the parishioners then for the first time chose both, and now modestly claim custom for continuing so to do.

Q. 16. Is there or has there been founded any public school in your parish ? Is there any charity school in your parish ? How is it supported ? By voluntary subscription, or by a settled endowment ? Is it for boys or girls, and for how many ? What are the children taught ? More particularly is care taken to instruct them in the principles of the Christian religion, and to bring them regularly to church ? And are they also lodged, fed and clothed ? And how are they disposed of when they leave school ? Does your school flourish, and if not, for what reasons ?

A. There is a free grammar school, which was founded by John Royse of London, mercer, in the year of our Lord 1563, and in the same school is founded an ushership by Thomas Teasdale, for an additional number of boys, who are designed by the founder for Pembroke College in Oxford, and this school is the seminary for that college. It is not supported by contributions, but is endowed with certain specific salaries arising from houses and lands. Care is taken to instruct the children in the principles of the Christian religion, as well as in Classical learning. The foundation boys, six in number, called Bennet's Scholars, are never sent to Pemb. College, from the inability of their friends to support them there, but on their leaving school, they are generally put out apprentices to some trade. Three pounds yearly is allowed to each to purchase books, for the space of six years, and 18£ at the expiration of that time to bind them apprentices.

Q. 17.   Do you constantly reside upon this cure, and in the house belonging to it ?   If not, where and at what distance from it is your usual place of residence ?   How long in each year are you absent ?   And what is the reason of such absence ?

A. I constantly reside upon my cure. But it is rather a singular circumstance that there neither is, nor can I discover the most distant traces that there ever has been a house belonging to it.

Q. 18.   By whom and to what uses is the money given at the offertory disposed of ?

A. One third by the Minister, the remainder by the Churchwardens, to the aged, sick and infirm, more particularly to those who constantly attend the church and the holy communion.

Q. 19.   Is there any other matter relating to your parish, of which it may be proper to give information ?

A. None that I know of.

Q. 20.   What is your place of residence, and the nearest post-town ?

A. Answered by the reply to Query the 17th.

The above queries answered by the Rev. John Cleoburey, M.A., ordained deacon Dec. 22nd, 1771, priest Dec. 19th, 1773, and instituted to the vicarage of St. Helen's, Abingdon, with the chapels of Radley and Drayton thereunto annexed Nov. 15th, 1775.

The Rev. Nathaniel Dodson.

Nathaniel Dodson's long incumbency through nearly half of the nineteenth century was marked by a revival in church life, and much valuable work was accomplished before Mr. Dodson was overtaken by age and blindness. He stands out with his successor as one of the great vicars of Abingdon. From his time the vicar has always been vicar of Abingdon and rector of St. Nicholas'. In 1836 Berks was transferred from the diocese of Sarum to the diocese of Oxford. The patronage of the living passed from the Crown to the Bishop of Oxford.

Sunday trading was repressed, the National Schools were built, the hamlets of Drayton, Shippon, Dry Sandford and Radley were separated from the vicarage of St. Helen's. To end the dispute about Radley, Mr. Dodson presented that living to Bishop Wilberforce. Drayton was separated in 1867. Shippon Church and Dry Sandford were built in 1855, and formed into ecclesiastical parishes, the former in 1865, the later in 1867. In 1867 St. Michael's Church was built as a chapel of ease to St. Helen's, at the cost of Mr. Dodson. In 1856 St. Helen's graveyard was ordered to be closed, and this was effected after some delay, putting an end to the interesting burials within and without the walls of the church.

Add to this that Mr. Dodson maintained a dispensary, relieved and doctored and lawyered his own poor, and did much in restoring the fabric of the church. He celebrated weddings before breakfast in his busy days, and worked the parish for a time without a curate. A tale is told in his daughter's biography of him [1] of one old parishioner, who refused to give up his gallery-seat to facilitate the removal of the galleries. When the man walked in to service as usual, he found his gallery gone, all but one seat, with a ladder attached to it. He decided that the vicar 'somehow always do get his own way'. At that period morning service on Sunday was from 10.30 to 12.30, followed by communion service, once a month, lasting until 1.30—previously communion had been celebrated once a quarter. Afternoon service was at 3.0, followed by christenings and funerals ; evening service at 6.30. Mr. Dodson lived in the newer house, known as Lacie Court : this house, now pulled down, was built by Mr. Bowles.

Mr. Dodson was prebend of Lincoln, rural dean of Abingdon, chairman of the county magistrates, chairman of the new workhouse, and governor of the lunatic asylum. His activities were so manifold that, although he often excited fierce opposition, Abingdon may be glad that owing to the death of Lord Liverpool he missed the deanery of Chichester, so that the 'little gossiping country-town' proved not a stepping-stone, but the scene of his life's work.[2]

Archdeacon Pott succeeded to the vicarage of St. Helen's at a critical time, and in seven years accomplished work of great value, in bringing the church schools up to date after the first great Education **Archdeacon Pott.**

[1] *Glimpses of the Life of my Father*, by Emma Hessey, 1905.
[2] Of Dodson's three immediate predecessors, Sumner became Bishop of Winchester, Pearson Dean of Sarum, and Turner Bishop of Calcutta.

Act, in reorganizing the church services, in substituting the voluntary offertory for pew-rents and the abolished church rates, and in effecting the great restoration of the fabric of a great church. Under him the parish magazine began, the surplice was used in preaching, Easter offerings ceased to be claimed as a legal due from reluctant parishioners, and the registers of the two parishes were carefully repaired and rebound. His reforms were accepted even by opponents of reform on account of the respect which he won by his great business capacity, by his authority as a scholar, and by the tact and vigour of his character.

It is too early to appreciate historically the work of his successors, and this record may well conclude with the impressive ordination of deacons and priests that was held in September, 1909, by Bishop Paget, in the ancient mother-church of St. Helen's.[1]

---

[1] The writer has not attempted to collect all the distinguished visitors who have preached in St. Helen's Church, but two must not be left out : in 1587 John Prime, ' a noted Puritanical preacher,' delivered a course on the Galatians every other week ; and in 1604 William Laud, afterwards the great archbishop, preached in St. Helen's.

CHAPTER VIII

ST. NICHOLAS' CHURCH

St. Nicholas' Church consists of a small aisle-less nave and Architecture. chancel, with a small western tower projecting within the nave, flanked to half its breadth by a narrow upper chamber on the north side. The church is attached on the south side to the Abbey Gatehouse, whose building at the junction of the nave and chancel obscured the head of the window behind the pulpit. It is a church on which successive restorers have laid a heavy hand. Its oldest visible portion is the Norman doorway—the central arch is recessed in fourteen mouldings— under the tower at the west end. Above this doorway are traces of five Early English lancet windows, of which four were cut away to make place for the present Perpendicular western window. There are two Early English windows on the north side of the nave, and one under the Gatehouse. The Norman work must be a century earlier than 1280, the approximate date to which Leland assigns the building of the church by Abbot Nicholas. The rest of the building is in the Perpendicular style—except two Decorated windows on the south side of the nave.

The Perpendicular doorway on the south-west flank of the nave has an enriched parapet, and an enriched parapet runs all along the south side. The most modern restoration took place in 1881, when the roof of stainless red tiles was imposed on the church.

Inside the western door at the base of the tower is a rare example of a stone lantern, with a stone funnel. Above is a minstrels' gallery. On the north wall of the nave is a rough stone cross that was formerly plastered over. The Jacobean pulpit has lost two storeys of its height. A fine Jacobean monument of John Blacknall (1625) stands in the curious quasi-transept window on the north side. In this window is some interesting glass, and the glass behind the pulpit is also old, although it was placed in this church in modern times. Unlike St. Helen's, St. Nicholas' has a distinct chancel arch. The chancel has some pleasing glass, an east window by Clayton, and three windows by Kempe.

TOWNSEND   M

Under the nave runs the Stert. If we take the Stert as at this point the boundary of the parishes, then the tower and part of the nave of St. Nicholas' will be in the parish of St. Helen's—an arrangement in keeping with the complex history of St. Nicholas'.

Documentary history. Leland suggests that in early times St. Nicholas' was a more important church than St. Helen's. But we have found no evidence in favour of this view, and much against it. The following references exhibit it as always the minor church of Abingdon. It presents many puzzles and complications, which have been fruitful in disputes at all periods of its history.

First mention. The chaplain of St. Nicholas' was entitled c. 1154–89 to receive two 'crowned' loaves and one mess of food and ale from the Abbot's cellar, according to the Chronicle of Abingdon Abbey.[1] This entry is among the allowances and fees due to officers and servants of the Abbey. Also the chapel of St. Nicholas 'in Abbendonia' appears at the same period in *De Consuetudinibus Abbendoniae* as paying rent to the almoner, the amount due being erased in the MS.

Bodley Charters. Among the charters in Bodley there are some early references to St. Nicholas' Church, Abingdon. We quote from the Calendar of Charters in Bodley :

' Ch. 14. c. 1230 A.D. Robert, the abbot, and convent of Abendon and Benjamin the rector of the church of St. Nicholas, Abbendon grant and confirm to God and the blessed Virgin and the church of St. Nicholas of Sanford all the tithes in Baywrth of the demesne of Hugh de Sanford which they have by gift of Thomas de Sanford.

Witnesses—John de St. Helen, Matthew de Bicstrop, Ralph de Sanford, Alan de Farnham, James, rector of Wittenham etc.'

' Ch. 25. c. 1230–40 A.D. Benjamin, formerly rector of the church of St. Nicholas of Abbendon, grants to the church of St. Nicholas, Littlemor, for the health of his soul, and for the souls of his father and mother, and all the faithful deceased in frankalmoigne, one messuage in the village of Abbendon, situated between the gate of master R. rector of the church of St. Helen's, and the house of Hubert la Withe, paying to the abbot of Abbendon 8ᵈ at the feast of St. Michael and 1ᵈ at Chergeschet.

Witnesses Sir Alan de Fernham, Henry de Baywith etc.'

' Ch. 294. 1234–5 A.D. Certificate of the pronouncing of a sentence of suspension "ab ingressu ecclesiae" for contumacy and of a citation to appear on the morrow of St. Gregory in the chapel of St. Nicholas, Abbendon, to answer concerning the will of John de St. John.'

---

[1] Stevenson, ii. 238, and ii. 327 ' Capellanus de Sancto Nicholao, ii coronatos, et i ferculum, et cervisiam de cellario abbatis.'

In 1372 there was a dispute between Richard Clayvill, rector, and John Ydesdale, vicar of St. Nicholas', and Richard Donnyngton, vicar of St. Helen's, as to the right of ministering to certain parishioners of St. Nicholas', the Abbey officials, the master of the grammar scholars of Abingdon, &c. Robert Wyvill, the Bishop of Sarum, decided in favour of St. Nicholas' as to the parochial dues and the receiving of the sacraments.[1]

In 1386 the Archdeacon of Berks reported to Ralph Erghum, the Bishop of Sarum, on his visitation, that the vicarage of St. Nicholas', Abingdon, had been wont to receive all the oblations and obventions of the altar, the tithes of lambs, wool, linen, flax, whether of field or garden, milk, cheese, honey, artificers' work, calves, geese, pigeons, eggs and apples ; also certain other small tithes, and a corrody in Abingdon Abbey. All these barely amounted to £5 a year, and were insufficient for the vicar. Therefore the Bishop endorsed an agreement between the Abbot's proctors and the vicar, that in future the vicar, John Gray, and his successors should have the great tithes of wheat and hay in the township of Sugworth ; also that he should have for his dwelling, as had been wont, a hall adjoining the church, with two adjacent rooms and a kitchen. The Abbot was to pay for the chancel repairs, as well as the royal tenth and the pension of 14s. a year to St. John's Hospital. This re-ordination of the vicarage was confirmed by Pope Boniface in 1400, at the petition of John Russell, when he succeeded John Gray as vicar.[2]

In 1408 Bishop Hallam held an ordination in St. Nicholas', Abingdon ; and in 1414 in the chapel or oratory of the hospice.[3]

At the beginning of the fifteenth century the rector and vicar, who from 1310, and probably from earlier times, had been distinct persons, were apparently identified, doubtless on account of the poverty of the livings. The last distinct vicar was instituted in 1407.[4] In the fourteenth century the rector was presented to the Bishop of Sarum for institution by the religious men the Abbot and Convent of Abingdon : the rector appointed the vicar. There was an exception in 1361, when the rector was presented by Edward, King of England.

[1] Exemplification of a Composition in the Verney Collection.
[2] *Sarum Epis. Reg. Erghum,* 2nd Nos., fol. 80b ; and *Cal. Papal Let.* v. 275, both quoted in *Victoria County History ; Berks,* ii. 15.
[3] *Victoria County History ; Berks,* ii. 19.
[4] Cp. list in Appendix.

84 HISTORY OF ABINGDON

Account-rolls of the abbey. The Account-rolls of the Abbey have a few references to St. Nicholas' which fit in with the above account. In 1375 and in 1383 the vicar of St. Nicholas' received xii^d from the Treasurers' Account : in 1440 this payment was made to the rector. In 1412 the rector paid viii^d for a garden to the Gardener's Account, and in 1450 i^d as a year's rent for a chimney standing in the Lord's soil, and so demised by indenture for a term of years.[1]

Union of the vicarages in 1508. In 1508 came an important change. Edward, Bishop of Sarum, at the petition of the Abbot and Convent of Abingdon, who were patrons of the Rectory of St. Nicholas' and of the Vicarage of St. Helen's, and of Thomas Randalff, the Rector, and with the consent of Henry Leshman, Vicar of St. Helen's, decreed that the Vicarage of St. Nicholas' should be separated from the Rectorship and united with the Vicarage of St. Helen's. He discharged the rector of St. Nicholas' from the cure of souls, &c., so that from 1508 until the nineteenth century there was a sinecure rector of St. Nicholas', and a single vicar having charge ' in spiritualibus ' of the two parishes.[2]

In 1539 the question was again opened by John Lucas, rector of St. Nicholas', who produced the above decree in the King's Court, and claimed successfully a payment of sixty shillings yearly.[3]

The Blacknall tomb has already been mentioned : a note on that family seems to belong to St. Nicholas' Church.

The Blacknalls. The site of the dissolved Abbey, with its many buildings, soon passed by purchase from the Crown grantee to William Blacknall. He was at the time of the incorporation one of the first bailiffs and a principal burgess, and was afterwards twice mayor.

His son, William Blacknall, ' being bred up in learning, and a good estate left him by his father, lived in this town a private life, without intermeddling with the town's affairs.'[4]

His son, John Blacknall (1583–1625), was educated at the Free School, at Queen's College, Oxford, and at the Middle Temple, and was called to the Bar. He was a leading man in the county in wealth and position, and married a Blagrove of Bulmarsh. He and his wife died of the plague in 1625, at his house within the site of the Abbey, and his daughter Jane the next year. He left bequests to St. Nicholas'

---

[1] Cp. Kirk, Index. In the Appendix, p. 167, is printed a document, dated 1585, which mentions an ' orchard adjoining the Rectory of St. Nicholas' '.
[2] ' Unio vicariarum S. Nichi et S. Elene de ue de Abendon ' in the Bishop's Register at Sarum.   [3] Lempriere's Transcripts.   [4] Little.

and St. Helen's, to the school, to the poor of Abingdon, and to Queen's College. His surviving daughter, Marie (born 1615), a great heiress, is described by Little as 'a very towardly and hopeful young gentle-woman'. Three of the guardians, her kinsmen, endeavoured to marry her, a mere child, to a member of the family. 'The license was had, the wedding apparel bought, and the priest ready'; but Wiseman, the fourth guardian, defeated the plot, holding over the heads of his co-trustees a fine of £5,000, imposed by the King's Court. In 1629 she was married to Ralph (1613–96), heir of the Verneys of Claydon, taking into that family the possessions of the Blacknalls and a mass of valuable parchments. The *Verney Memoirs*, the *Verney Papers* (Camden Society), and the *Account Rolls of the Obedientiars of Abingdon Abbey* (Camden Society) furnish important additions to the history of Abingdon. A Verney letter of 1633 writes of 'the Ladie Verney the elder, the yonger the Lady Mairasse of Abingdon'. In the transept of St. Nicholas' is John Blacknall's monument, with effigies and a lengthy inscription. Upon this tomb are placed the loaves for distribution among the poor. One criticism may be allowed upon this family, common to them with their generation—that they did not pre-serve the architectural remains of the Abbey. Marie Verney, *née* Blacknall, died during the Commonwealth at Blois, where she had gone to convey a pardon to her husband in 1650.

In 1625 John Blacknall left money to endow a readership for daily prayer at St. Nicholas', that the church might be duly and orderly served by an honest, sober man, and not to attend wholly on the leisure of the vicar of St. Helen's. The Reader-ship en-dowed.

This readership that was thus placed upon a permanent foundation by Blacknall was already in existence, deriving a precarious support from the subsidies of the Corporation.[1] This is indicated by an entry in St. Nicholas' Burial Register of August 23, 1583, 'Jone the wief of John Smithe reder.' On February 17, 1620, Mr. Chr'ofer Capper was elected reader by the Corporation, as providing the allowance.

In 1628 the Corporation left to the Bishop of Sarum the appoint-ment of 'such parson as he shall thinck fitt', disclaiming all intention of making an allowance to future readers after the tenure of 'Mr. John Stone, the nowe reader', who was afterwards rector.[2] The decision

---

[1] Cp. John Blacknall's Will and Borough Records of 1620 and 1628; also *Char. Comm. Rep.*, 1908, p. 138.

[2] He signed the christenings as such in 1636.

of the Corporation is explained by Blacknall's will coming into force. Yet the payment of the £8 was continued until 1896, a virile instance of a threatened revenue.

Connexion with the school. In 1643 Mr. Anthony Huish, M.A., head master of the Grammar School, was admitted by the Bishop of Salisbury 'to officiate dayly prayer in Mr. Blacknall's donation'; and from that time until 1870 the reader has usually been the head master or the usher of the Grammar School.[1] For instance, Robert Payne, afterwards rector, whose name appears in the collections-accounts of 1661 as curate, was usher; as also the Rev. John Stevenson, rector 1764–75, reader 1762–83, was usher from 1762 until his death in 1783. The latter kept his own registers with exemplary neatness—his writing looks a century and a half more modern than the mediaeval scrawlings of the sextons in the same volumes. Stevenson's predecessor was Mr. Joseph Benet, the son of the Rev. Josiah Benet, vicar of Denchworth, lecturer of St. Helen's in Abingdon, and usher of the Free Grammar School, who was buried in the chancel of St. Nicholas', November 21, 1750.

Since 1870, when the school moved to its present buildings, the readership and deputy-readership have been held by the parochial clergy. Middle-aged men still remember Mr. Harper, the usher, leaving his class at ten o'clock to read prayers across the road.

Disputes in the eighteenth century. The period of the Commonwealth may be regarded as an interlude in church history, and it has been found convenient to treat the history of St. Nicholas' in the chapter on the Civil War and Commonwealth. The eighteenth century was a litigious age.

There is an entry in the churchwardens' book of a vestry held April 25, 1765:

'It is agreed to have the opinion of an able counsel to know wether the Reverend Mr. Portal is Vicker of St. Nicholas or not and that the churchwarden be authorized to procure a proper person to draw up the case on the behalf of the parish.'

The above order is signed, among others, by Mr. Bright (head master of the school), who, according to Lempriere, had some dispute with the vicar, from which no doubt arose this strange inquiry. The vicar promptly obtained from Mr. Thomas Frome, the Bishop's Registrar, some extracts from the decree of 1508, already quoted, which established the vicar's rights in St. Nicholas'.

---

[1] Transcript of Commonwealth documents among Lempriere's papers.

The question of St. Nicholas' continued to be a thorny one for the More dis- vicars of St. Helen's. On December 28, 1793, Messrs. G. Hawkins putes. and Bedwell, as deputies from the trustees of the Blacknall charity, applied to the Rev. J. Cleoburey to permit a weekly sermon at St. Nicholas', but he objected on the ground that the vicarages of the two parishes had been consolidated since 1508. He argued that 140 sermons a year were sufficient for the digestion of any moderate congregation, that the vicarial income of barely £120 a year would not allow of further decrease, and that the proposed change would detract from St. Helen's Church, where the accommodation was ample for the parishioners of St. Nicholas.'[1]

In December, 1796, the vestry of St. Nicholas' complained to Bishop Disputes Douglas of Salisbury that evening prayer was not read daily according with Lem- to Blacknall's will, and that Mr. Lempriere, the curate, omitted some- priere. times the prayers on Sunday morning, in order to serve his curacy at Radley. The total stipend paid to the reader at St. Nicholas' was £27 a year. They offered to pay half a guinea a Sunday for a sermon, and threatened to withhold payment of the salary. The vicar wrote defending Lempriere to the Bishop, pointing out that the work was underpaid, that there was no congregation in the afternoon. Mr. Stevenson, a former reader, 'charitable to the degree of weakness, dying poor man insolvent,' had attracted half a dozen paupers by his alms. These had vanished when Mr. Kennedy did not continue the alms. Stevenson had also held the lectureship of St. Helen's, and Mr. Kennedy had held another cure. Lastly, there was good accommodation at St. Helen's 'in a spacious and commodious gallery lately erected'. Lempriere also wrote in similar terms. The value of money had changed since 1622, and the stipend ought to be increased. He preferred the curacy of Radley, value £40 a year, presented by Sir George Bowyer 'in very handsome terms,' to an 'unsettled sermon of 10ˢ 6ᵈ a Sunday'. The Bishop replied, supporting Lempriere. He wrote from Windsor Castle, 'greatly afflicted with gout,' increased by the severity of the weather on Christmas Day, when he preached before his Majesty. The trustees then resolved to expel the reader by withdrawing his salary.

In December, 1799, Lempriere, failing to get his stipend, closed the church. The deadlock was solved by the death of Cleoburey in August,

---

[1] The three best family pews in St. Helen's were occupied by parishioners of St. Nicholas'—Messrs. Bowles, Child, and Harding.

1800, and the appointment of Lempriere to the vicarage of St. Helen's. After more correspondence it was decided that Lempriere had vacated the readership, and Mr. Smith succeeded him, and prayers were resumed in February, 1801.[1]

Rector versus Vicar.

Two entries in the registers of St. Nicholas' in 1803 indicate friction between the rector and the vicar: on Sunday, October 30, John Lempriere, Doctor of Divinity, vicar of the parish, 'chuses' a parish clerk. On December 23, Richard Bowles, as rector, protests against the above entry, and chooses another clerk. Some letters that passed between the Rev. William Smith and the Rev. N. Dodson in 1825 show that the dual control was still a cause of difficulty. After the death of Mr. Smith in 1845, Mr. Dodson and his successors have always been vicars of Abingdon and rectors of St. Nicholas'. But the dual control was not ended. For the Rev. Richard Bowles, B.D., formerly Fellow of Trinity College, Oxford, and late rector of St. Nicholas', left at his death in 1804 £2,000 4 per cent. stock to a Fellow of his college to found a Sunday lectureship.[2]

The Lectureship founded.

This has generally been held by the head master of the Grammar School as deputy-lecturer, in spite of an attempt made in the nineties to induce the Rev. Charles Gore[3] to appoint one of the parochial clergy. Mr. Gore took the view that the bequest was intended to give St. Nicholas' a Sunday lecturer other than and independent of the vicar, and appointed the Rev. T. Layng. The latest scheme of the Grammar School (1910) threatens to sever at a future date the old connexion between St. Nicholas' and the school—to the injury of both.

I believe that in 1836 the parish and church of St. Nicholas were never properly transferred from the diocese of Sarum to that of Oxon, and that, therefore, St. Nicholas' in ecclesiastical jurisdiction occupies a position that is the crown of its many anomalies.

The registers.

The registers of St. Nicholas' are inferior to those of St. Helen's, but are not devoid of valuable matter. Archdeacon Pott had them repaired and re-bound in 1869. The baptisms go back to 1603, burials to 1558, marriages to 1538. But there are clear indications that in parts these registers are old copies of the originals.[4]

---

[1] Correspondence quoted in Lempriere's transcripts. Cp. *Charity Comm. Report*, 1908, p. 138.

[2] Monument in St. Nicholas'.   [3] Now Bishop of Birmingham.

[4] e.g. in the christenings of 1681 there is a marginal note: 'Wonder not because eighty on is got before eighty it is right a nough ye falt is from ye former wrighter.'

The single churchwarden of St. Nicholas' dates from 1705. Until The single
the year 1704 there were usually two churchwardens, one new one church-
being elected each year. In 1704 the vicar appointed one and the warden.
parish elected one. After that there is one churchwarden elected by
the parish, with the consent of the vicar. It was a part of the churchwardens' duties at one time to apprentice poor boys of the parish.
For instance, in 1703 a churchwarden and the overseer 'placed and
putt forth' Richard Simms, an apprentice, with Thomas Geagle of
Abingdon, lamp-dresser and sackcloth-weaver, for eight years, 'with
him to dwell and lerne his secrets'. Geagle was 'to teach and inform
him and find and allow sufficient wholsome and competent meat
and drink, washing, lodging, and apparrell, double apparrell for Holy
dayes and for working dayes '.[1]

Miscellaneous entries in the registers and churchwardens' accounts Miscellane-
tell us that Abingdon was visited by plague in 1564 and 1607. Among ous entries .
the church collections for objects outside the parish the following occurs
in April, 1661 : 'Gathered in the parish of St. Nicholas in Abingdon in
the county of Berks by vertue of a Breife for John De Kraino Kranky Mr
in the kingdom of Lithuania the sume of seaventeene shillings.'

The Churchwarden's Accounts contain a copy of the original bill
of October 28, 1741, for six new bells, cast by Abel Hall, bellfounder,
of Gloucester. From the charge of £210 2s. 8½d., an allowance of
£140 0s. 10½d. was made for the five old bells.

On Wednesday night, August 25–6, 1785, St. Nicholas' was robbed
of its communion plate. The pieces given are :

A large silver flagon, the gift of the Rev. Thos. Woods ; a large silver
plate, the gift of Wm. More Esq. ; a small silver patten, the gift of the
Rev. J. Stevenson ; a gilded cup or chalice with cover.[2]

In 1820 a vestry was held in the church to consider the question of
large repairs to the roof, &c. It was summoned by ' the Churchwarden,
Surveyors of the Highways and Constables of the Parish '. The
adjourned meeting was held in the evening of June 28 at the George
Inn. A vestry room was built at the west (sic) end, instead of the one
then used. The chancel screen was set back against the east end. At
that date the communion table still stood between the chancel and
the nave.[3]

[1] Indenture at St. Nicholas'. It was approved by the mayor.
[2] Parish Register.   [3] Churchwarden's Accounts.
TOWNSEND

CHAPTER IX

ABINGDON SCHOOL

Its existence before the Reformation. UNTIL recently it was among Abingdonians an unchallenged article of faith that Abingdon Grammar School was founded by John Roysse in 1563. This view must be qualified in the light of evidence, which establishes clearly the existence of a grammar school in Abingdon at least as early as the fourteenth century. Roysse's work then appears to have been the refounding of the older institution, which had lost its local habitation in the troubles of the dissolution of the great monastery. The question has been discussed by Mr. A. F. Leach in the *Victoria County History of Berkshire*, and by Mr. G. W. Wallace in the *Charity Commissioners' Report* of 1908 on the charities of Abingdon.

Earliest mention. The earliest mention of this pre-Reformation grammar school occurs in a composition, dated June 17, 1372, in which Robert, Bishop of Sarum, settles a dispute between the incumbents of St. Helen's and St. Nicholas' as to the right to minister to certain parishioners of St. Nicholas', the officials of the Abbey and their servants, and, among others, 'to the master of the grammar school of Abendon and his servants and the scholars with him dwelling.'[1]

Connexion with the Abbey. This deed does not make it clear, but it leaves it probable that : (i) the schoolmaster was regarded as a servant of the Abbey ; (ii) he resided in the parish of St. Nicholas ; (iii) the scholars living with him were boarders, although this does not exclude the existence of other day scholars.

The Account-Rolls of the Obedientiars of Abingdon Abbey contain several references of interest to the master of the scholars, who apparently rode round the villages from time to time to select suitable pupils.[2]

For instance, the Treasurers' Account of 1375–6 has an entry of obscure import under the debitores : 'Ten' Scol maystur v^s viii^d.'

---

[1] *Charity Comm. Report*, p. 50. The deed is quoted from an exemplification, May 15, 1571, in the Verney Collection.

[2] Camden Society, 1892, ed. R. E. G. Kirk.

Again, the Treasurers' Account of 1383–4 gives two payments to the ' Instructor of the youths '.[1]

A deed, dated June 12, 1387, in the cartulary of the Fraternity of the Holy Cross, describes one Thomas Weston as ' magister scolarum ', master of the school of Abingdon.[2] This Thomas Weston is similarly described in the Trinity Warden's Account of the Abbey for 1414–15, and in some deeds between these dates he appears as ' clerk '. In the Treasurers' Account of 1440–1, Master John Maltby is given as instructor of the scholars.[3]

Mr. Leach associates these three masters with the same school, and regards them as the lineal predecessors of Godwyn and Woods. Mr. Wallace follows this view. Mr. Kirk, in his introduction, takes the view that the Abbey school received no outsiders, but only trained recruits for its own ranks. Accordingly he gives these references a different interpretation. It is possible that this Abbey, like others, had in fact three schools—a school of novices, a choir school and a town school.

The significant fact that Master Thomas Weston rented from the Abbey agrees with the natural policy of the Abbey—to keep under its control the schools even more jealously than it did the markets and hostelries of Abingdon. The fact that it was the Trinity Warden of the Abbey, who was the landlord, to whom the schoolmaster had to pay his rent of iii^d, suggests a reason why Roysse named his school the free school of the Blessed Trinity : he revived the old name.[4]

Mr. Wallace says that from this point ' there is no further mention of a school until 1558–9 '. But this is not so. For the Bishop of Sarum's decree for the union of the vicarages of St. Helen's and St. Nicholas', dated October 7, 1508, enumerates among the inhabitants of St. Nicholas' parish ' the master of the grammar scollers of Abingdon, and of all the scollers remayning and abiding with him '.[5]

It is beyond our purpose to lay claim, as has sometimes been done, to all the distinguished pupils of the Abbey as pupils of our school.

---

[1] Kirk, p. 44 'Instructori juvenum, l^s '; p. 51 'Johanni Brules, instructori juvenum, vii^{li} x^s.'

[2] *Charity Comm. Rep.*, p. 51.

[3] Kirk, p. 121 'Magistro Johanni Maltby, instructori scolarium, hoc anno xls.'

[4] Ibid., p. 78. Recepcio redditus : ' et iii^d de redditu Magistri Thome Weston ', Magistri Scolarium Abendon, solvendo tantum ad terminum Michaelis supra.'

[5] Bishop of Sarum's Reg. We quote from the English of Lempriere's copy of ' a deed in the chest in the vestry of St. Nicholas' '.

But we suggest that Sir John Mason, who was educated by his uncle, a monk of Abingdon, perhaps first showed his versatile abilities under the roof of the grammar school, for this would be the natural progress for a poor Abingdon lad, who enjoyed the patronage of the Abbey.

The school homeless at the Dissolution.

Another interval of half a century carries us past the fall of the great Abbey and of its dependent institutions. What happened to the grammar school in the years between 1538 and 1563 we do not precisely know. At all events it appears to have lost its home in an Abbey tenement, and probably it existed only in a humble and homeless condition.

In 1556 Thomas Read of Barton left in his will £10 ' to the ereccion of a free Scole ' in Abingdon.[1] This indicates that the need of a local school was present to more than one mind, as well it might have been, for, as Thorold Rogers has pointed out, the creation of grammar schools all over England in the middle of the sixteenth century was due, not so much to a new zeal for a new learning, as to a serious attempt to fill in some measure the disastrous gap made by the dissolution of the monasteries.

The Churchwardens' Accounts of St. Helen's for 1558–9 have an entry : ' At the burial of Richard Crosse, skolemaster, for 6 tapers 6ᵈ.'[2] The charter of Christ's Hospital (Abingdon) in 1553 directed the governors to apply their rents, among other things, ' ad sustentationem scholae grammaticae ibidem.' In the contemporary translations this is rendered, ' to the sustentation of a grammar school there.' Mr. Wallace would prefer to render it ' to the sustentation of the grammar school there '. We think it is better to adhere to the contemporary wording, but we agree with Mr. Wallace that the chain of evidence shows that it was intended to refound an old school, and not to inaugurate a new one.

The school refounded by John Roysse, 1563.

So far the history of the school has been an imperfect reconstruction from scanty evidence. From the early years of Queen Elizabeth dates its modern history. There are still difficulties : there is no light thrown upon the connexion of John Roysse, citizen and mercer of London, with Abingdon, and little contemporary evidence as to the exact steps taken to refound the old school by the various parties, namely, John Roysse, the Corporation and Christ's Hospital.[3]

---

[1] *Record of the Redes*, p. 8 : ' I give tenne pounds pc'll of the fourtie pounds Richard Beke oweth me, if it may be had, to the bayliffe of Abingdon towards the ereccion of a free Scole there in Abingdon.'

[2] *Archaeologia*, 1770.   [3] *Charity Comm. Rep.*, 1908, p. 50–52.

In 1561 the Corporation purchased, among other premises from William Blacknall, the premises of St. John's Hospital. In 1562 the masters of Christ's Hospital laid out moneys ' upon mayster Serjaunt Southcott when he came to vewe the house for the free skoole which Mr. Royse mynded to erecte within this Borough '. On January 31, 1563, Roysse executed a trust deed to establish ' a free grammar schole ' within the borough. In this it is stated that Roysse had delivered to the mayor, bailiffs and burgesses the sum of fifty pounds, to the intent that they should build or provide a convenient school-house to receive three score and thirteen scholars, and that this school, to be called ' the Free Schole of the Blessed Trinitie ', should be under the control of the Corporation. A month later Roysse conveyed to the Corporation for the endowment of the school the two properties known as the Bell and the Unicorn in Burching Lane, London, of the clear yearly value and rent of thirteen pounds, six shillings and eight pence.

The chamberlain's accounts for 1562-3 show a payment for the carriage of ' Mr. Royse's hogshead of wyne from London ', to celebrate the opening of the school. The ensuing years have entries for the cost of some of the work in the school-house.

In the ordinances attached to the first deed, Roysse ordained that there should be perpetually taught in the school three score and three children [1] of the borough of Abingdon, but one child of a house, and for lack of that number in the town, children from the country adjoining. Preference was given to the poor, to orphans and to widows' sons. He ordained that the mayor and principal burgesses should from time to time ' chuse an honest sadde and discreete man, vertuous in livynge, honest in his behavior, and charitable in his doyinges, as nere as they may, a learned man a priest or a wedded man, such as to them shall seme most mete, to be the scholemaster of the said free schole, and that he hath no cure or benefice '. The payments of the scholars were limited to one penny at first entry, unless the friends of a child should give more of their own free will. The Corporation were to survey every half year the school, schoolmaster and scholars, and in case of a breach of the articles and rules, ' for the first time warnying to be given, and the second time to expulse or put him out and speciallie for any things of the prayers prescribed.'

Roysse allowed further a larger number than these sixty-three, in-

Roysse's Ordinances.

---

[1] The number recalled the date and the founder's age, and is eternized in the ringing of the bell.

cluding ten private pupils to the schoolmaster, to be under the same rules, and of whom he ' shall take his advantage '.

The schoolmaster was not to license his scholars—under pain of fine —' to play above foure daies in the yere,' and that only at the request of the mayor and his brethren, when they came to view the school. But Sundays and holy days were not accompted.

The schoolmaster was thrice in the day to hear with a loud voice the children say upon their knees in English or Latin the prayers following : in the morning the Pater Noster, the Ave Maria and the Crede; at eleven, before dinner, the Deus in Nomine Tuo; and at night the De Profundis with the suffrages.   At the end of these prayers they were to say, ' Upon our founder John Roysse and all Christian people the Blessed Trynytye have mercy.'

School hours were fixed at six in the morning until five at night, but in winter at seven in the morning.   The schoolmaster was to teach his scholars ' as well nurtere as good maners, as lyterature and vertuous lyvynge and Christian auctors for their erudition '.   The school-house was to be swept and made clean every Saturday by some of the youngest scholars.   The scholars were to go to church to hear services and preachings, two and two, ' with their bokes in their hands, soberly and discreetly.'   The rules were to be exhibited in the school and in the Guildhall.   Examination by learned men was provided for.

Roysse provided further for a distribution of bread to twelve poor of the town upon Sundays after his death, ' the advantage loof of the dossen to be given to the scholemaster.'   At the annual sermon which he founded at St. Helen's Church—it is still preached on Founder's Day in July—he ordered that the schoolmasters and scholars should be present ; and he provided after the sermon for the mayor, principal burgesses, preacher and schoolmaster, for ' a potation or drinkinge twentie shillings ', as well as six shillings and eightpence to be given in bread, drink and cheese amongst the poor.

Finally, the mayor, bailiffs and burgesses were not to refuse admission to the school to ' any honest man gentleman or riche man's sonne or others ', subject to the same good rules, the master and usher being able to teach the number.   The fees were limited to six and eightpence a year.

These ordinances do not indicate, any more than do the accounts of the churchwardens of St. Helen's, that the Reformation had made progress in Abingdon.

In 1562 Roysse had obtained a grant of arms from the Heralds'
College, which he bequeathed to the Abingdon Corporation, evidently
as a record for the school arms : ' Gules, a griffin rampant and volant,
silver ' ; the ' difference ' was to be ' on the shoulder a rose of the field
seeded gold barbed vert.' [1]

Roysse's will, which was proved July 31, 1571, confirms these gifts,
and orders that his body should be buried in St. Helen's Church, ' near
unto the quior door in the midst of the church ' : ' And I will my great
stone in my arbor in my garden in London to be the upper stone of
my said tomb.' Roysse's
Will.

The next part of the will suggests a reason why Roysse looked for
his heirs in the generations of alumni of the free grammar school :

' for that my son hath marryed against my will another man's wife, as
doth appear in the spiritual court of record here in London ; and further,
for that he hath been associated and accompanyed with theives and
pyrates, ...'

The schoolhouse of that day continued to contain the school for
three centuries.   It may be seen in the school-yard outside the Abbey
Gatehouse—a long, narrow room, with the seats of the ' archidida-
scalus ' and the ' hypodidascalus ', the iron clasp for the great mace
on visitation days, the curious gallery for the library—with a way
into the schoolmaster's house—altogether a picturesque model of
antique discomfort.   What would be said to-day, if a minimum of
sixty-three boys were taught in that room, with the old apparatus and
the old staff ?   Yet it is a room with a distinguished record for success
in life and for breadth of learning, which justifies the motto over the
entrance, ' Ingredere ut proficias,' and that on the wooden gallery,
ἐὰν ᾖς φιλομαθὴς ἔσῃ πολυμαθής. The old
school-
house.

The old prints show the room peopled with boys and masters, and
adorned with the eagle, the clock, and the portraits.   The class-room
was added in 1809.   When the school was moved to its present home,
the old building was acquired by the Corporation, and is at present
used as a drill-hall.

Master Argall [2] was the first of a long line of Oxford men to hold
the office of schoolmaster in the refounded school.   The early head
masters were young men fresh from the University and remained only Early
school-
masters.

---

[1] *Vict. Hist. Berks*, ii. 264.
[2] For a list of the head masters see Appendix III.

a few years in the school, retiring usually within a decade, to take ecclesiastical preferment.

Of the early scholars mention may be made of Sir Thomas Smith (c. 1556–1609), who was born at Abingdon, the son of Thomas Smith, probably the mayor of 1584. From the school he proceeded to Christ Church, Oxford, becoming Public Orator in 1582, Proctor in 1584; then secretary to the second Earl of Essex, and clerk to the Privy Council in 1587. He was Member of Parliament for Cricklade in 1588–9, for Tamworth in 1593, for Aylesbury in 1597–8. In 1597 he succeeded as clerk of Parliament to Anthony Wyckes, *alias* Mason. In 1599 he was sent to summon Essex before the Privy Council. He was knighted by James I, and became the Latin secretary, master of requests, &c. He died at Fulham, where there is a monument to him, leaving bequests to Abingdon and to the Bodleian.[1]

Degorie Wheare.

In December, 1604, the mayor, the vicar and the leading magnates ' did repair to the freeschoole ' to examine the scholars and admonish the schoolmaster. Of the early head masters one of the best known is Degorie Wheare. His brief reign at Abingdon has left no history, but later on, after travelling abroad, he became the first Camden Professor of Ancient History and Principal of Gloucester Hall—a hall not unconnected with Abingdon in the days of the Abbey. A copy of his *Relectiones Hyemales* sleeps still in the school library.[2]

Dr. Godwyn.

The reign of the next head master, Thomas Godwyn, was long and important. It commenced in 1606, and appears to have ended about the time of his appointment as the first charter fellow of Pembroke in 1624. Some authorities suggest that he left the school in 1616, others that he continued in it until 1637. But Wood speaks of him as schoolmaster at Abingdon in 1624, and Mr. ' Heuishe ' is mentioned as schoolmaster in 1627.[3] He published a *Florilegium Phrasicon* and a *Romanae Historiae Anthologia*—both for the use of Abingdon School. Copies of both his *Posy* and his *Nosegay* still exhale their fragrance in the school library. Also a *Synopsis of Hebrew Antiquities, Civil and Ecclesiastical Rites*, and *Three Arguments to prove Election upon Foresight of Faith*.

' By his sedulous endeavours were many educated that were afterwards eminent in Church and State.' He became chaplain to the Bishop of Wells in 1616, and in 1636 was licensed to proceed in divinity. ' Before which time he being as 'twere broken or wearied out with the

---

[1] *Dict. Nat. Biog.*　　　　　　　　　　[2] Wood, *Fasti*, ii. 106.
[3] Minutes of Christ's Hospital, *ad annum*.

drudgery of a school had the Rectory of Brightwell near Wallingford in Berks confer'd upon him.' 'He was a Person of a grave and reverend aspect, and was a grace to his Profession.' He died in 1643.[1]

Among those educated in grammar learning under him at Abingdon was Sir Edward Turnour, who at the Restoration became Speaker of the Commons, Solicitor-General and Lord Chief Baron of the Exchequer.[2] The office of Speaker was filled also by 'Bolstrode Whitelocke', whose distinguished career is connected with Abingdon by his appointment as Recorder in 1632.[3]

An important development of the school took place under Godwyn by the benefactions of William Bennett of Fulham and Thomas Tesdale of Glympton. In 1608 William Bennett, who was brought up by Tesdale at Abingdon School, left lands at Blunsden, Wilts, to his uncle, Thomas Tesdale, for the benefit of six 'Bennett's Poor Scholars'. Besides the free education that these scholars received at the school provision was made for their 'placing and preferment' on leaving school. They continued to be distinguished by cap and gown 'of one coller and fashion' until 1868, when the distinction was dropped as invidious. In 1609–10 Thomas Tesdale endowed by his will a Tesdale ushership, which continued until 1868. That there had already been an usher is shown by a payment of £5 by the Corporation in 1600.[4]

Bennett and Tesdale's benefactions.

Tesdale made also a princely bequest of £5,000 to purchase lands for the maintenance of seven fellows and six scholars at Balliol College, Oxford, or, failing Balliol, at some other college. The trustees of this benefaction were George Abbott, Bishop of London, afterwards Archbishop of Canterbury, Sir John Bennett, Tesdale's nephew, and Dr. Henry Ayray, Provost of Queen's. In the election of fellows and scholars under this benefaction, preference was given to Abingdon School, and particularly to founder's kin and to Bennett's scholars. The somewhat intricate story of how this bequest came to be applied is discussed in Macleane's *History of Pembroke College*. It is enough to say here that negotiations were opened with Balliol, but that the people of Abingdon developed a laudable ambition to found a distinct college. And so after many delays and obstacles Pembroke College

Pembroke College.

---

[1] Wood, *Fasti*, ii. 28. [2] Wood, *Ath.* ii. 555.
[3] Borough Records, p. 141, and Macleane, p. 155.
[4] Borough Records. Mention is made of an usher in Roysse's ordinances of 1563.

was founded in 1624, with the aid of the Rev. Richard Wightwick of East Ilsley as co-founder, upon the ancient foundation of Broadgates Hall. The older hall occurs in the history of Abingdon Abbey, and within the precincts of Pembroke College is included a site known as Abingdon Chambers.[1]

Among the charter fellows were Thomas Godwyn, the veteran schoolmaster, who had twice married founder's kin ; Robert Payne, afterwards canon of Christ Church, and a victim of the Westminster Assembly ; Christopher Tesdale, afterwards a member of the Westminster Assembly ; and Nicholas Coxeter. Among the charter scholars are three well-known Abingdon names : John Lee, whose oration at the opening of the college followed that of the famous Thomas Browne ; William Reade ; and Richard Allen. Abingdon School has given seven masters to Pembroke—Dr. Langley, Dr. Radcliffe, Dr. Brickenden, Dr. Adams, Dr. Sergrove, Dr. Smith and Dr. G. W. Hall ; as well as four Heads to other Oxford houses—W. Walker, D.C.L., to St. John's ; John Clarke, D.D., to Oriel ; John Viscount Tracy, D.D., to All Souls ; and James Gerrard, D.D., to Wadham.[2]

Tesdale's career.   Thomas Tesdale deserves an ample record.[3] The grandfather, John Tesdale, is described as ' of the north '. The father, Thomas Tesdale, was brought south to Hanney and Stanford Deanley or Dingley, Berks, by his elder brother, John, who took the name of Cliffe on entering religion.[4]

Thomas Tesdale, the co-founder of Pembroke, was born at Stanford Dingley in October, 1547. When he was a child, his father moved to Fitzharris Farm at Abingdon, where he became a governor of Christ's Hospital, and was buried at St. Helen's in 1556. The father in his will charged Richard Tesdale, his brother, a sadler of Abingdon, and William Hopkyns of Abingdon, to bring up young Thomas in learning, and to

---

[1] Twyne thinks that the novices from Abingdon were educated at St. Aldate's Monastery early in the twelfth century. The parson of St. Aldate's was presented alternately by St. Frideswyde's Priory and Abingdon Abbey, the latter owning property to the south of the church. Abingdon Chambers fell into the hands of the Abbey probably in the twelfth century. Broadgates Hall paid rent for them in the second half of the fifteenth century.

[2] Macleane, p. 200. It is tempting to an *alumnus* of the daughter-college to divagate further into the fields of college history.

[3] For pedigree of Tesdales and Bennetts with their interesting marriage connexions, see Macleane, pp. 172-6.

[4] Buried April 28, 1540, being then ' Prior of the late dissolved Monastery of Abingdon, as by the Register of St. Nicholas' in Abingdon appeareth '.

apprentice him at London. When Tesdale was nearly sixteen, he was chosen and admitted by Roysse as the first scholar in the school. In his twentieth year he married Maud, the daughter of Reynold Stone of Henley and widow of Edward Little of Oxford and Abingdon, who had been a maid of honour to Queen Elizabeth. At Abingdon he 'traded in the making of malt, then a very gainful course there '.[1] He soon gained wealth and reputation, and held many offices in Abingdon. He was elected mayor in 1581, but ' was freed from serving that office by the payment of a fine ', on the ground that he had a little before left the town.

' And liking better of a country life, he dwelt the most part of his time at Glympton aforesaid, at which place and many others, in divers shires and countries, he traded in sowing and making of woad—used by dyers—, and was held to be the greatest dealer therein that was in the whole realm ; whereby, and by tillage for corn and by grazing of cattle, he attained to a great estate.' [2]

Fuller relates that he was clothier to the royal army and at one time an attendant at court. There is a fine alabaster monument to him and his wife in Glympton Church. There are portraits of both in the Hospital Hall at Abingdon and in Duke Humphrey's Library at the Bodleian, and a portrait of Tesdale at Pembroke.

Tesdale's coat of arms is—Argent, a chevron vert between three teazles proper. The teazles are a punning reference to his trade as clothier and to the pronunciation of his name.

To pass on to the later history, Anthony Huish, probably head master from c. 1624, was the first head master to hold the readership of St. Nicholas'. He figures in the history of the Commonwealth as the faithful minister of the persecuted church at St. Nicholas', supported by Heylyn. In October, 1653, he was ordered to ' amove himself ' in the following March for being remiss and negligent in attending to the free school. After the Restoration he received some compensation for his ' amovall '.

Anthony Huish.

After an interregnum of a couple of years under Robert Payne the usher,[3] Robert Jennings, a layman, became head master. He is mentioned in Vernon's *Life* as one of Heylyn's intimates at Abingdon. He

A fashionable boarding school under Robert Jennings.

---

[1] Francis Little, pp. 67–71, where a full life is given.
[2] Ibid., 69.
[3] Robert Payne the younger, one of the scholars expelled from Pembroke in 1648, and afterwards reader at St. Nicholas'.

appears to have made his fortune out of his fashionable boarding school.

' This person had before born Arms for his Majesty within the Garrison of Oxford, and being afterwards made chief Master of the Free School at Abingdon in Berks, continued there for many Years, got a plentiful Estate, and purchasing Lands in Oxfordshire near to Henley, was pricked and elected High Sheriff of that County in November 1694, but looking upon himself as too old to undergo that office, his Son James was Sheriff in his place.' [1]

The school library.

This period brings a mention of the school library, for the Borough Records of 1656 have the entry :

' Itt is ordered by the Comon Counceill, That One Le'ccicon, One Cooper's Dictionarie and one Rider's Dictionarie be pai'd for by the Chamber, and chayned in the Schoole, where is most convenient.'

There is a similar payment in 1662 of xls. to Mr. Jennens for shelves, chains, and books. The library contains still many ancient books, some the work, others the gift of distinguished masters and distinguished *alumni*. The oldest book is, I believe, a Vergil dated ' 1532, Parisiis ex officina Rob. Stephani ', with the signature of ' Stephanus Baluzius, Lutelensis ' ; it is also signed by J. P. Moreau, 1724. It bears in its binding the studs that once attached the chains. The oldest English-printed book is, I believe, the *Erasmus* with studded binding—the first tome of his ' paraphrase upon the newe testamente '. It is in Gothic type, and was ' Empriented at London in Fletestrete at the signe of the sunne by Edwarde Whitechurche the last daie of Januarie Anno Domini 1548 '.

Sir John Holt.

Of the boys of this period mention must be made of the son of Thomas Holt,[2] who, born in the town of Abingdon, became Recorder of London and Lord Chief Justice of England. Macaulay pays an emphatic tribute to his fairness and strength during the troubled politics of the times following the Great Revolution.

Connexion with St. Helen's Church.

The connexion of the school with St. Helen's Church continued down into modern times. In 1663 the Corporation directed the Chamberlain and others to erect seats in St. Helen's Church for the scholars.[3]

In 1671 ten scholars, including some Tesdales and a member of the Garbrand family, were ejected and expelled by the visitors for absenting themselves from their parish church.[4] The Accounts of the

[1] Wood, *Fasti*, ii. 60.
[2] Recorder of Abingdon, and Member for Abingdon in the Parliaments of 1654 and 1656.   [3] Borough Records.   [4] Ibid.

Churchwardens for 1723 indicate that the scholars had their places in the Lady Aisle. Until the restoration of St. Helen's the scholars sat in the gallery of the Lady Aisle, Dr. Strange's seat being near the Lady Chapel. Recent head masters, as deputy lecturers of St. Nicholas', have naturally taken their boarders there.

Of the eighteenth-century head masters Thomas Woods left a deep mark on the school. He became usher in 1711, and held the head-mastership from 1716 to 1753. An entry in the Borough Records for 1723 has been interpreted as suggesting that he also acted in the capacity of road surveyor. A school list of 1732 contains ninety boys, including a peer, two peers' sons, a baronet, and a large number of country gentlemen's sons; also Clement Saxton, afterwards High Sheriff of Berks, Thomas Head, afterwards knighted, Richard Graves, afterwards the author of the *Spiritual Quixote*, &c. — *Thomas Woods.*

Among Woods' pupils here was William Newcome, son of the vicar of St. Helen's and at the end of the century Archbishop of Armagh.[1] — *Archbishop Newcome.*

The year 1743 was marked by great activity in the school life. In that year the library was 'erected' upon a larger scale. In the 'Register of Benefactors of Abingdon School Library', which is preserved at the school, is a long and distinguished list of subscribers. The subscriptions amount to £186 4s. In addition Brazen Nose College gave the gilt wooden eagle, made in 1694, now standing in the modern chapel, and 'the Rev^d Mr. Woods gave ye Clock', which still marks the hours in the present schoolroom above the motto 'Pereunt et inputantur.' — *The school library.*

In the same year was apparently founded the Old Boys' Club with its annual dinner. In the same book is given a list of stewards from 1743 to 1822, with gaps from 1753 to 1758, and from 1775 to 1805. The list is headed: 'The Gentlemen Educated in Abingdon School met there August the 6th 1743 and made Choice of the Right Honourable the Lord Visc^t Wenman and the Honourable James Howe Esqr for Stewards for the Year 1744.' — *The Old Boys' Club.*

Woods' *Antiqua Silva* in the library has some references to 'Flogging Tom', added by an irreverent hand. There is a tablet to Woods in the chancel of St. Nicholas'.

Dr. John Abbot, who was head master from 1753 to 1758, is remembered as the father of a great Abingdonian, the first Lord Col- — *Lord Colchester.*

---

[1] The library contains a first edition of Pope's *Iliad*; it is stated, I do not know with what authority, that Alexander Pope, as well as Gregory Pope, had been a member of the school.

chester, Speaker of the Commons. Lord Colchester's portrait is in the Council Chamber.

School Motto.

The present school motto—'Misericordias Domini in aeternum cantabo'—is supposed to date from the reign of Dr. Bright, the author of *The Praxis*, a school book of hints for the composition of Latin and English. Dr. Johnson corresponded with him and sent him boys. An edition of Johnson's *Prayers* is properly in the library, for Johnson is known everywhere as an *alumnus* of the daughter-college.

French officers in Abingdon.

Of the eighteenth-century treasures in the library not the least striking are the little French books given for the use of the Free School by French officers in 1760. All of these were little pocket editions, chiefly of recent works, printed at Paris, Berne and Amsterdam, evidently the travelling companions of the donors, who may have thus recognized some courtesy that rendered less irksome their sojourn in Abingdon. Rousseau and the *Encyclopédie* were at that time new and potent influences upon the thought of Europe. The names of the officers seem to link the story of the school to the great struggle of the 'Seven Years' War': 'le Marquis de Chapuis, french officer.' 'M^r Le Chevalier de la Deveze, French King's officer.' 'Mr Deflotte, french officer.' 'Mr de Champelos formerly prisoner of war upon his parole at Abingdon as french officer in the anno of our Lord God 1760.'

The next head master, Andrew Portal, a translator of *Aeschines*, was one of many pluralists, for he was vicar of St. Helen's as well as head master, and had previously been lecturer of St. Helen's as well as usher.

The ushers as pluralists.

The ushers of that century were frequently pluralists, usually holding at least the readership of St. Nicholas'—except when it was held by the head master. To take an instance from St. Nicholas' Register : 'The Revd Mr. Josiah Benet Vicar of Denchworth, Lecturer of St. Helen's in Abingdon, and Usher of the Free Gramar School, was Buried in the Chancel of St. Nicholas' Novr 21. 1750.'

His son Joseph Benet succeeded him as usher, and was afterwards for forty-three years rector of Sunningwell, where is his tomb.

John Stevenson held during part of his ushership the rectorship and readership of St. Nicholas'. Stevenson's papers on the school and neighbourhood are in Bodley,[1] a wilderness of unsifted material.[2]

---

[1] Gough, Berks, 4–10.

[2] Mr. Falconer Madan, *MSS. in Bodley*, p. 186, says ' The writer has collected a good deal of material, but makes a very uncritical use of it '.

Stevenson was the donor of Tesdale's portrait in the Hospital Hall and of the portrait of Tesdale at the school in 1763 at the bicentenary. The fellow portrait of John Roysse at the school was given by Dr. Bright.

The last decade of the century brings the head mastership of Dr. John Lempriere, author of the famous *Classical Dictionary*. He was a born litigant and an obstinate pluralist. When he was head master he held also the readership of St. Nicholas' and the curacy of Radley. This gave rise naturally to disputes with the Corporation and with the parishioners of St. Nicholas'. During the second half of his eighteen years at the school he was vicar of St. Helen's. At the end of the eighteenth century the scholarships at Pembroke appear to have been captured by St. Paul's School, London.[1] The evidence in the appendix of the Charity Commissioners' Report of 1818 is full of striking evidence as to the condition of the school in the previous half century. In 1766 the school had been still full, with forty boarders and sixty-three day boys. But towards the end of Dr. Bright's time it began to decline, owing to a quarrel about a municipal election. The education, which had been broad, intelligent and successful upon a classical basis, degenerated into a narrow teaching of Greek and Latin, which was unpopular. Fees seem to have crept up for the benefit of the head master. Mr. Smith, who had been usher since 1793, and was also rector and reader of St. Nicholas', gave evidence that he taught the Bennett scholars separately, and chiefly in Greek and Latin ; further, that although he would assist in teaching other boys on request, he regarded himself as independent of the head master, endowed with the Upton tithes. The number of scholars on the foundation varied under Lempriere from two to zero ; under Nicholson it rose to twelve, only to sink again to three. Nicholson's two curacies obliged him to leave the school to itself for a somewhat generous week-end. Against this may be set the rebuilding of the ruinous schoolmaster's house in 1810, and the demand from the head master to the Corporation in the winter of 1819–20 for a stove to heat the school. The school hours were from seven to eight in winter, six to eight in summer, nine to eleven, and one to four. But the report suggests irregularities. The holidays are given as six weeks at Christmas and seven weeks at Midsummer.

Under Mr. Hewlett in 1829 there came a welcome revival in the

Dr. Lempriere. Decline of the school.

[1] Cp. Macdonnell's *History of St. Paul's School.*

numbers and life of the school, soon to be followed by a fresh decline.
The library contains peacefully bound into a single cover Tiptaft's
Christmas Sermon at St. Helen's in 1829, with Hewlett's counterblast
from the same pulpit on the Sunday following, together with the remarks on both by the 'Calm Observer'.

A printed account of the school with lists for 1830 is preserved at
the British Museum. At the visitation the following speeches were
recited :—Willis' *Absalom*, Livy's *L. Marcii Oratio*, Aeschylus' *Io's
Sufferings*, Cicero's *Orat. Pro Archia*, Byron's *Spain*, Virgil's *Footrace*,
Dryden's *Ditto*, and—as a crown of somnolence—Homer's *Nestoris
Oratio*.

The account speaks of founder's kin as wanting to fill the scholarships. It states that in 1818 the head master required twenty guineas
as a fee for private pupils coming to enter for these scholarships at
Pembroke within a year. In 1830 this practice had been abolished,
and two years' residence was required.

There were then fifty-four scholars, whose names are given. The
head master was the Rev. J. Hewlett, M.A. ; Tesdale's usher was the
Rev. W. Smith, M.A. ; the mathematical master, Mr. T. Walker.

The subjects were purely classical, if we may regard mathematics,
as taught until recently, as a counter-part of the classics. For instance,
Class I, the top form, had for its curriculum Greek—choruses by heart ;
Latin—the four books of the Odes by heart ; divinity, logic, mathematics.

The fees for boarders over fourteen were sixty guineas, under
fourteen fifty guineas ; for day scholars thirty guineas ; for free
boys four guineas for instruction in writing, arithmetic, or mathematics. If the value of money then and now is considered, these fees
must be regarded as indicating an expensive school. With regard to
the last item it is curious and significant that the free boys were taught
the classics gratis, but had to pay for instruction in the humble
preliminaries of education.[1]

Forty-four weeks out of the fifty-two were spent at school, there
being one month's holiday at Christmas, and the same in August.
The visitation was held in August.

---

[1] A parallel is furnished at Allhallows School, Honiton, where Latin, Greek,
German, Science are included in the school fees, and taught gratis to free boys,
but for instruction in French a yearly fee of four guineas is charged to all day
scholars.

During the mastership of Dr. Strange (1840–68) the school pros- Dr. Strange.
pered. William Alder Strange, the son of an Abingdon wine-merchant,
and a scholar of Christ's Hospital, London, qualified for a Tesdale
scholarship at Pembroke. He was Boden Sanskrit scholar in 1833.
Under him the numbers averaged over sixty—standing at the ter-
centenary at the founder's sacred number. On that occasion was
published the *Brief Memorial of Abingdon Free Grammar School*, which
contains rather a fulsome eulogy of Dr. Strange. He survives in living
tradition as a good master of the severe, caning order. The Doctor's
wrath was evoked at 'the unrighteous operation of the University
Reform Bill', under which in 1857–8 the Tesdale scholars ceased to
be elected at Abingdon—henceforth 'Abingdon Scholars' were elected
at Pembroke.

In 1866 the Schools Inquiry Commission reported unfavourably
on the buildings, and somewhat coldly on the classical and general
education.

In 1868–70 the present buildings were erected in the large playing Modern
fields near the new park, and the school was moved from its ancient buildings.
yard to an environment of grass and trees. During this period,
Mr. E. T. H. Harper, the last Tesdale usher, late Townsend scholar
of Pembroke, acted as headmaster in charge.[1]

Under the Rev. E. Summers (1870–83) the numbers rose from The Rev. E.
forty-five to nearly one hundred. In his time Roysse's tomb at Summers.
St. Helen's was restored (1871–3), the fives courts were built [2] (1873),
a large wing was added (1880), including studies, an infirmary, a common room and fine class-rooms, of which one was used as a chapel
for the boarders. The school games were fostered—on the river as
well as in the playing-fields. One criticism may be allowed : an
unfortunate impression existed that boarders received a more favourable reception in the school than day boys.

Under the Rev. W. H. Cam, an able scholar, the numbers for various The Rev.
reasons were not maintained, falling in 1893 to thirty-four. In that W. H. Cam.
period the *Abingdonian* was started (1890), and tentative steps were
taken towards the teaching of science.[3]

[1] At this time the old property in Birchin Lane was sold for £9,000.
[2] These had unfortunately to give place to the extended buildings eight
years ago.
[3] In the library Sanderson's *Compendium of Physical Science*, 1690, has
awaited in patient solitude for a couple of centuries the scientific development
of the curriculum : it conveys its science in the classical medium of Latin.

TOWNSEND   P

The present time.

Under the present head master, the Rev. T. Layng (1893), like Mr. Summers a Cambridge man in the long line of dark blue, the school has passed through the crisis that many old foundations have had to face. Its popularity and numbers indicate that it has done so with success.

The school modernized.

It has in fact been modernized. It is with regret that we see the encroachments of new subjects upon the older learning—so thorough, and sometimes so narrow. But as the age moves on, institutions must reform themselves, or cease to live.

The numbers have grown steadily—in spite of one serious setback, owing to the policy of the Board of Education—and in 1910 reached 122, with eight assistant masters. In 1893 a flourishing Old Boys' Club was founded. In 1895 the 'Young and Summers Scholarships' were founded for boarders in mathematics or science. In 1896-7 the Lodge was built to accommodate more resident assistant masters. In 1898 and 1910 two playing-fields, to the south of Park Road, acquired to protect the school from building-developments, were brought into the use of the school games. In 1900 Tesdale House was opened as a second boarding-house. In 1902 the school was re-admitted as a public school to the head masters' conference. In the same year was added, at a cost of about £6,000, a large block of buildings to the east, including a chapel, gymnasium, class-rooms, an art-room and laboratories. Quite recently a workshop has been added. The school music and games have been encouraged with success. The school has now adopted the policy of accepting grants from the Board of Education, the County Council and the town. These generally carry with them heavy burdens and responsibilities. The Roysse, Bennett and Blacknall Scholarships, re-organized in 1878, are now supplemented by County Council scholarships and an increased number of local scholarships and free places. Finally, the success of the old school in solving its modern problems of harmonizing the classical and modern sides in a mixed school of boarders and day boys is due partly to advisers like Mr. J. C. Clarke and Archdeacon Pott in 1870, partly to the strong body of partly representative governors, dating from 1878, and partly—perhaps chiefly—to the many gifts of the present head master.[1]

[1] Many omissions will be noticed in this sketch : in fact the school history would afford material for a separate volume. Much patient research was devoted to this subject by the late Mr. W. H. Richardson.

CHAPTER X

THE EARLY BOROUGH

1555-1640

WITH the charter of Christ's Hospital (1553) and the Incorporation of the Borough of Abingdon (1555) begins the second half of the local history. Apparently before then the townsmen had no voice in the election of the officers who managed the markets, fairs and government of the town. *Absence of civic life in early times.*

The provost (*prepositus*), bailiffs and chamberlain were appointed by the Abbot, who controlled the fairs and market. The famous riot of 1327, already described in the history of the Abbey, was partly an attempt on the part of the townsmen to obtain civic rights. The Lollard rising of 1431 was also a movement in the same direction. The relations of the town of Reading with Reading Abbey provide an interesting parallel, with important differences, for the Corporation of that town traces back to a charter from the time of Edward the Confessor. The great exception in the history of Abingdon is found in the Fraternity of the Holy Cross, into whose hands slipped a growing share of public usefulness in the period before the Reformation.

Since the Reformation there have been two civic authorities enthroned in Abingdon, for by the side of the mayor and corporation the master and governors of the Hospital of Christ have always kept their large powers.

The great Charter of Incorporation of 1555 is an interesting document in Latin, beautifully engrossed on great sheets of vellum. In the initial letter is worked in pen and ink a picture of Philip and Mary sitting upon their thrones.[1] *Charter of Incorporation, 1555.*

' Phillip and Mary, by the Grace of God King and Queen of England, Spain, France, of both Sicilyes, Jerusalem, and Ireland, Defenders of the

---

[1] We quote from the early official translation printed in Mr. Bromley Challenor's *Records of the Borough of Abingdon*, 1898, from which we quote freely in the succeeding chapters.

Faith, Arch Dukes of Austria, Dukes of Burgundy, Milan and Brabant, Earls of Hapspurge, Flanders and Tirol.'

This sonorous exordium is supported by a worthy seal. By this charter was granted a body corporate to this ancient and populous capital town of Berks, which was then fallen into ruin and decay. The town was henceforth a free borough, exempt from all hundreds, **Boundaries.** counties and shires.   The boundaries are defined as from the little bridge, built upon and over the Thames, called the Abbey Locks, upon the east to the Ock Bridge upon the west, and from the Stone Crosse on the New Bridge (i. e. over the Thames) on the south, to the Boundary and Meer Stone, marked with the leaden letter A, situate near unto a little hill called Barrow Hill, without the barrs of the publick Street of Barrow Street called the Bore Street Barrs, in the meeting of two public Ways, on the north.   Also from St. Helen's Bridge at the mouth of the Ock on the south-west to the meeting of two public ways without the Barres of the Wyneyard on the north-east.   From point to point the boundary followed the courses of the Thames and the Ock, includ- ing the whole of the river and the little stream.   From Ock Bridge it ran by the common way by Barrow Hill to Trynitie Closes, thence by the common way by Barrow Hill to the stone without the Barres of the Bore Street.   Thence it inclined towards the north ' untill you come to a certain Crooked little Ditch inclining towards the East ', including on the right Fitzharris Farm, Fitzharris Piece and Fitzharris Closes. Thence by another ditch, including Pykes Close, it reached the stone without the Barres of the Weyneyard.   From that point it followed another public way eastward towards the Thames, including a certain Conventuall Close called the Covent-Close, and one other little Close called the Pytenry, and so through the Thames to the Locks.   In this summary is preserved the spelling of proper names, as they occur in each place. These boundaries were to be perambulated from time to time.

The beating of the boundary continued as a somewhat rowdy per- formance until recent times. These boundaries were extended in 1890 to the line of the canal instead of the Ock on the south-west, to the line of Larkhill stream from the Marcham to the Faringdon and Wootton Roads and to Northcourt on the west and north.

Council.   The Council consisted of twelve principal burgesses and sixteen secondary burgesses, all to be of the better, honester and discreeter men. The officers of the Council were the Town Clerk, the Chamber-

lain, or treasurer, two 'Serjeants att Mace, for the executing of Pre-
cepts, Commands, Attachments, and other Processes', and the Clerk
of the Markett.

The Mayor, Bailiffs and Burgesses had the right and duty of elect- **Member of Parliament.**
ing a discreet and honest man of the borough to be 'a Burgesse of our
Parliament'.

The charter proceeded to nominate Richard Mayott to be first
Mayor, Richard Ely and William Blacknall to be first Bailiffs, Thomas
Medowes to be first Chamberlain, Wm. Sympson to be first Common
Clerk, and Richard Mayott, Richard Ely, William Blacknall, William
Mathew, Thomas Toules, James Fisher, Humphry Bostock, Thomas
Orpwood, Ralph Bostock, Thomas Jenyns, John Chaunterell, and
William Whytington to be first principal burgesses. It appointed the
Mayor for the time being Clerk of the Markett, a Justice of the Peace
and Coroner. Then follows provision for a Council House. In the
election of Mayor (he took office then on the Feast of St. Michael the **The Mayor.**
Archangel), 'the Secondary Burgesses and other the Burgesses and
Men of the Inferior sort in the said Borough, Inhabitants' nominated
at the Council House on the first of September two men of the more
grave and discreet principal burgesses, and the rest of the principal
burgesses elected one of those two as Mayor for the year. Penalties
of prison and fine were attached to an unreasonable refusal to take
office. Of the Bailiffs the Mayor elected one each year from the prin- **The Bailiffs.**
cipal and secondary burgesses, and the inhabitants elected the other
from the secondary burgesses.

When any burgess died or was removed from his place and office, **The Bur-**
his successor was appointed by the Mayor, Bailiffs and Principal **gesses.**
Burgesses, who also had the appointment of the Town Clerk and
Serjeants. The Council was granted the assize and assay of bread,
ale, &c., the control of weights and measures, a court leet and view
of frankpledge, the right and profit of market on Monday, and of five
fairs yearly, and the court of portrive and pye-powder.

The charter granted to the Corporation the reversion of the fulling **Grant of**
mill, which had been leased to William Blacknall by Edward VI, 'then **property.**
being wholly in ruin and decay in Abingdon, near unto three other
water mills there,' together with Cosener's Inne and Cosener's Close
(half an acre). Also of three water mills ' under one Roffe ' with the
ponds and pools and the whole of the fishery of the waters of Abingdon,
which had been leased by Henry VIII to John Wellisbourne, and by

Edward VI to William Blacknall.   All the above property had belonged
to the Abbey.   Also the reversion of Fitzharris Farm, formerly in the
tenure of Ralph Cradock, yeoman, and of Elizabeth, his wife, or of one
William Danield, and leased in the fifth year of King Edward VI to
Thomas Tesdale.   Also a large number of tenements, shops, cottages,
&c., belonging formerly to the Abbey, and situated in Burford Street
or Butcher Row, Sterte Street, West St. Hellen's Street, East
St. Hellen's Street, Lumbard Street, Little Bury Street, Boar Street,
Ock Street, the Bury, Brode Street, the Wineyard, Otwell Lane and
St. Edmund's Lane.   Also 'the house or Goale' in the middle of the
market.   Also Bushey or Thorne Close, measuring one acre in Bagley,
and Trinitie Close, measuring one rod, both lately belonging to the
Abbey.   Also certain properties of the late Chauntry of St. Mary the
Virgin in Abingdon.   Also certain properties in Abingdon, belonging
to the late St. Totte's Chauntry of Oxford, and certain lands in Wick
field, belonging to the late Fraternity of the Holy Cross.   A quit rent
was reserved to the Crown of £102 16s. 7d. ; a payment to the Vicar of
5s. yearly, and to six poor people of St. John's Hospital of £15 12s.

This summary will indicate that most of the names of the streets
and fields of Abingdon are of ancient date.   The method of the Tudors
in the dissolution of the monasteries has been compared to the method
of William at the Conquest : new tenants replaced the old, succeeding
to the old rights and duties of the properties.   The Chronicle of Abingdon
Abbey and the Charter of Incorporation illustrate this in local history.

Other charters.
There are nine later royal charters, which confirm and extend the
original charter, and may be more briefly treated.

Elizabeth.
A charter of Elizabeth in 1565 transferred the Court of Record
from the Bailiffs, as being often ' very unfit to decide the causes, complaints, and quarrells ', to the Mayor in a Court of Record to be held
every Tuesday except in the weeks of Whitsuntide, Christmas and
Easter.

James I.
The first charter of James I in 1609 granted to the Corporation, in
consideration of payment of the sum of £50 9s. 4d., divers properties
in Abingdon, at Drayton Wike and Sutton Wike.

The second charter of James I in 1609 made the Borough a Borough
of the Peace with a Recorder to be appointed by the Council.   Walter
Dayrell was nominated as the first by the charter.   It continued the
Mayor's weekly court and appointed three justices in addition to the
Mayor and ex-Mayor.   It granted two annual fairs at the feasts of

St. Mark and St. James, a Friday market for corn and victuals and a wool-market on Monday, the weights of the thread and wool to be the same as at New Woodstock. After 1836 the Recorder was appointed by the Crown.

The third charter of James I in 1620 dealt with market tolls.

The charter of Charles II in 1676 confirmed previous privileges, and enforced the corporal Oaths of Obedience and Supremacy. *Charles II.*

The charter of James II in 1686 described Abingdon as 'a very populous Burrough and the Cheife Towne of our County of Berks'. The twelve capital or principal burgesses appear under the name of aldermen. *James II.*

The charter of George II in 1739 granted a corn market on Tuesday, Wednesday, Thursday and Saturday, in addition to the market of Monday and Friday. *George II.*

The charter of George III in 1774 granted the Council powers to elect two additional justices annually. J. R. Green regards this charter as placing more power in the hands of a local oligarchy. *George III.*

The charter of William IV in 1836 granted a Court of Quarter Sessions to the reformed Borough. *William IV.*

The Reformed Borough, under the Municipal Act of 1835, had a Council of four aldermen and twelve councillors—the latter elected directly by the townsmen, the former elected by the Council. The Bailiffs disappear, the Chamberlain is replaced by the Treasurer, and the post of Coroner is separated from the Mayoralty. *The Reformed Borough.*

In the *Borough Records* are given lists of the Members of Parliament, mayors, members of the Town Council, &c.; in *Francis Little*, ed. Cobham, 1872, are lists of the masters and governors of Christ's Hospital.

The post of High Steward of the Borough was held in 1630 by the Earl of Banbury; in 1634 by the Earl of Holland; in 1661 by Edward Hyde, the great Earl of Clarendon; in 1675 by his son, the second Earl of Clarendon; since 1709 it has remained in the house of the Earls of Abingdon—the Norreys and the Montagu-Berties. It has been the custom of the High Stewards to allow the fees of their office to accumulate and to apply them to some public use. For instance, in 1811 the High Steward remitted £78 6s. 8d., and gave £100 more to build the gateway of the school-yard. A few years before he had remitted £93 6s. 8d. Again in 1823 the Corporation bought a pierglass with these fees.[1] *The High Stewards of the Borough.*

---

[1] Borough Records.

Sir John Mason (1503–66), to whose influence the town owes the charters both of Christ's Hospital and of the Borough, was the most famous Abingdonian since St. Edmund of Abingdon.[1]

He was born at Abingdon, the son of a cowherd and nephew of a monk, perhaps of Thomas, Abbot of Abingdon, who educated him. He graduated at Oxford in 1521, and was made a Fellow of All Souls. Then he became King's Scholar at Paris with an annual allowance of £3. 6s. 8d., which was afterwards doubled. In 1531 he was given the parish church of Kyngeston in the diocese of Salisbury. At this point he entered the diplomatic service, was present in 1532 at the meeting of Henry VIII and Francis I at Calais, and was sent on tour through France, Spain and Italy with a view to further diplomatic work. In 1534–5 he visited Spain, Padua and other towns of Italy, Corsica, Sardinia, the Lipari Islands, Sicily and Naples. He returned in 1536, and there is a tradition that at that time he saved the endowments of Oxford from confiscation. If that is so, Mason averted a national disaster with an incalculable train of consequence. In 1537 he was secretary to Sir Thomas Wyatt, the British envoy in Spain. In 1539 he was in the Netherlands reporting to the Government. In 1540 he was again with Wyatt. A shrewd judge said of him : 'None seeth further off than Sir John Mason.' In 1542 he became Clerk to the Privy Council, in 1544 Master of the Posts, and Secretary of the French Tongue. In December of that year he describes the proroguing in person of Henry VIII's last Parliament. In 1545 he was licensed to import French wares. In that year he visited Norfolk, 'Almaigne', and the court of Philip, Duke of Bavaria.

At the coronation of Edward VI he was dubbed Knight of the Carpet. About the same time he received £20 for searching the records for English claims upon Scotland. In 1549 he was made Dean of Winchester ; also a commissioner to negotiate the treaty with France, to which country he was appointed Ambassador in 1550. From this time his letters rank as important historical documents.

His health failing, he asked to be relieved of his post, and retired in 1551. He became Master of Requests and Clerk of Parliament. In 1552 he received grants of land in Middlesex, Berks and Kent. He was elected Member of Parliament for Reading, and afterwards for Taunton. From 1552 to 1556 he was Chancellor of Oxford University— perhaps as a reward for his services in 1536. He was a witness of

---

[1] *Dict. Nat. Biogr.* ; cp. Francis Little.

Edward VI's will : yet he joined the Lord Mayor in proclaiming Queen
Mary, and signed the Order in Council requesting Northumberland to
lay down his arms. Being high in Mary's favour in spite of his Protes-
tantism, he continued to hold his secular preferments. In 1554 he
was made Treasurer of the Chamber—the salary for this office and for
the Mastership of Posts is given as £240 a year and 12d. a day. In
that year he was Member of Parliament for Southampton. From
1553 to 1556 he served as Ambassador at the Emperor's Court at
Brussels, and was an eyewitness of the famous scene of Charles V's
abdication, of which he has left an interesting account.

Under Elizabeth he still retained his posts, and was restored to the
deanery of Winchester. From 1559 to 1564 he was again Chancellor
of Oxford. During the opening years of Elizabeth's reign he had the
direction of foreign policy.

At his death in 1566 he was buried at St. Paul's, leaving no issue.
Lady Mason had family by a previous husband. His principal heir
was his adopted son Anthony Wyckes, alias Mason, grandson of
Mason's mother, who succeeded him in 1574 as Clerk of Parliament,
and was in turn succeeded in that office by another Abingdonian,
Sir Thomas Smith.

Such a record of work carries with it the proof of Mason's energy
and talents. It was a wonderful thing to win and keep high offices in
such stormy times under four such monarchs as King Harry and his
three children who succeeded him. He is described as a cautious
diplomatist, but as a man who was genial in society. His most striking
talent was his cool, unerring judgement of the trend of events. His
services to his native town were very great, and their effects continue
to the present day.[1]

The population of Abingdon in early times was not large, as has Population.

---

[1] It is not quite clear if Mason held his livings as a layman, or if he had
received the 'tonsura prima' in his youth. He is spoken of as 'ecclesiasticorum
beneficiorum incubator maximus', that is, a greedy pluralist. Fuller quotes
more complimentary Latin than this concerning him. 'Vir fuit gravis, atque
eruditus.' Again,

> 'Tempore quinque suo regnantes ordine vidit,
>   Horum a consiliis quatuor ille fuit.'

> 'He saw five princes, which the sceptre bore ;
>   Of them was privy-councillor to four.'

There is a portrait of Mason in the Hospital Hall.

TOWNSEND   Q

been supposed. It is well to remember that the population of England in 1555 was about 5,000,000, and that of London less than 150,000.[1]

In 1555, just before the incorporation, there were 1,400 inhabitants in the parish of St. Helen, according to an account taken by Cardinal Pole.[2] If we subtract the inhabitants of St. Helen's without and allow for St. Nicholas' parish, the figures would not be much larger than this for the Borough.

In 1801 under the Population Act the return for St. Helen's parish was 3,836, and for the town of Abingdon 4,356. For comparison we give other figures for that year: the townships of Barton, Norcot and Shippon had 13, 69 and 128 inhabitants respectively. The four parishes of Reading had nearly 10,000; Wallingford 1,200; Wantage with Charlton, Grove and West Lockinge about 3,000; Newbury was almost equal to Abingdon.

In the census of 1901 for the enlarged borough the figures were 6,480.

Craft-Guilds.

Bacon somewhere describes craft-guilds as 'fraternities in evil', which caused the decay of many towns in the Tudor period. These guilds aimed at keeping the monopoly of trade with the boroughs. At Abingdon the Corporation in its early days exercised a rigid control over the trade of the place, as it did over the lives of the inhabitants. It distinguished between the freemen of the Borough and 'foreigners'; assigning to the latter heavier tolls and more limited opportunities of trading. This policy lasted long: in William III's reign a 'foreigner' had to pay a fine of £50 for the right to trade in Abingdon. The various trades were divided into companies, each with its master and wardens: such as those using the craft or mystery of shoemaker and cordwainer.[3]

In Charles II's reign the various trades were grouped into three Companies—the Grocers', the Butchers' and the Skinners'. Under the Tudors stringent regulations were passed by the Corporation about prentices. Innkeepers were not allowed to poach upon the trade of the baker or the brewer. In the same period fines were inflicted

Fines.

on night-walkers. Every inhabitant was expected to keep a good and sufficient club in readiness for the conservation of the peace—'Si vis pacem, bellum para'. Sunday trading was forbidden after the service-bell had rung. The Council was directed under a fine to attend Church upon the greater festivals. There were fines to prevent the

[1] *Encycl. Brit.*
[2] Establ. 1609, Borough Records.
[3] MS. in Bodley, quoted by Lysons.

wandering of hogs in the streets, in St. Helen's Churchyard and near
Burford. Fines also for Mayors and Chief Burgesses refusing to take
up their office. And fines for Burgesses attending the Council without
their gowns, or speaking unseemly words in the Council house.

In 1613 the Council ordered that the Judges and Mr. Fowler should   The Judges.
have allowed them at every assize this allowance and no more, one
hogshead and one barrell of strong beer and one barrell of mild beer,
' if less will not serve,' and for ' Mr. Fowler's horsemeat ' fourteen
shillings. The same Council cast upon the Sheriff of the Shire the charges
for setting up a booth for the Judges. In 1614 the Council granted
fourteen nobles a year to John Fyssher, sen., who had ' grown into such
decay of his estate ', to better maintain himself as a principal burgess.[1]

The danger of fire alike from summer drought and from the artificial   Fires.
heating of the winter-season has always been prominent. In 1584 a
watch was ordered as a precaution in winter nights. In 1602 the
Council provided two great hooks, twenty leather buckets and two
very long and strong ladders of firwood. In 1644–5 a great fire, causing
loss of life, is referred to in the Churchwardens' Accounts. Again in
1659 a nightly watch was rendered urgent by great fires. Two years
later the Council adopted the policy of getting stone chimneys substituted for wood and wattle in Corporation leaseholds.

In 1671 six ladders and six buckets were ordered, and four years
later three sufficient ladders—two and a half feet wide at the foot—
and six smaller ladders.

In 1679 every inhabitant had to provide a ' cowle ' of water next
his dwelling-house, while in 1697 provision was ordered to be inserted
in the leases of Corporation property in the Ock Street for the replacing
of thatch with slate or tile.

In 1722 to prevent dreadful fires in the spinning and weaving
houses no person was allowed to dress hemp or flax or to spin or weave
hemp by candle-light. This order was repeated in 1761. In 1735 it
was decreed that spinning-houses should not be thatched.

The first mention of providing a fire-engine occurs in the records of
1734, and the Sun Fire Office was asked to contribute towards the
cost. In the following year the School House was insured in the same
office. In 1742 three dozen buckets were purchased. A sum of £15
was voted by the Council in 1765 for the relief of the victims of a fire in
West St. Helen's.

[1] Borough Records.

In 1834 new leather pipes were purchased. In 1838 there was a dispute as to who was liable for the repair of several engines in the town.

In the latter half of the nineteenth century the Volunteer Fire Brigade worked in co-operation with the Corporation. The present steam-engine was bought in 1905 by subscription, aided by a contribution from the Corporation. The greatest fire of modern times was that which destroyed several houses on the north side of the Narrow in 1883 and threatened to destroy the whole of the High Street. The establishment of hydrants and rapidity of communication have diminished the old danger.

Anthony Forster.

A photograph of a letter is exhibited at the Council Chamber, addressed to an Abingdon tradesman by Anthony Forster, whom Scott, justly or unjustly, made notorious in *Kenilworth*.

' Mr. Pocok, I pray you delyver to thys berer foure elles of blak taffata for a shorte gowne and iij yards of blak vellet to gard the same whyche gowne my Lord dothe gyve to Mr. Smythe the quenes man and also iii yards quarter of crymsen satten for a dublet whyche my Lord gyvythe to the Mayre of Abyngton and xij yards of blak satten for ij dubletts whyche my lord gyvythe to ij of the mayre's brethern of the towne of Abyngton thys hartely fare you well thys xvj of Maij 1566.

Yrs
Antho : Forster.'

We do not here discuss the questions connected with Amy Robsart. Anthony Forster was Member of Parliament for Abingdon in 1572 and died that year. His monument is on the north of the altar at Cumnor Church.

The Chamberlain's Accounts.

The unpublished Chamberlain's Accounts at the Guildhall for the years 1558–81 add to our knowledge of Elizabethan times.

In 1558 there are entries for ' reparations ' to the Council House, the Guild Hall and the Jail; also an item of pay to a labourer to help up with the stocks. The same year, after the accession of Elizabeth, has an entry of ' reparacions ' to the pillory. In 1563 there is a charge for the perambulation dinner, and others for stone water-tables at the end of the Hall, for a bell in the Guild Hall, and for players on Ascension Day before Master Mayor in the Guild Hall. In succeeding years there are charges for the Queen's players, Master Wayneman's players, my Lord of Leicester's players, the Earl of Leicester's bearwards, my Lord of Shrewsbury's players, the Earl of Derby's players, and my Lord of Worcester's players. In 1565 the Dungeon was filled with gravel, the stream under Burford was scoured, benches were set up about the Checker or Exchequer, the Cage was repaired, the old Pillory was taken down, and a flew or fishing-net was distrained for two years' rent of a defaulter. There are a number of entries in that and other years concerning eating flesh in Lent. In 1568 money was spent on the Stert bridges and on the paving of the Stert. In 1569 payments were made for mending the new Market House. Many gifts are recorded to the Sheriff : e.g. in 1569 a pottle of sack and a pottle of claret wine ; in 1570 two calves bought in the market for eleven and eightpence ; and in the same year two sugar loaves at six and sixpence. Gloves were presented that year to the judges and their wives. In 1572 timber was being farmed out of the Abbey. In 1573 a pound of sugar, costing sixteenpence, was sent to my Lord Norrys at his being in the town. In that year a conference—and dinner—with Mr. Squiar about the School cost twenty-seven shillings. Our Town Clerk received £5 for pleading the Charter. In lesser matters John a Bentam was paid twelvepence for helving the pole-axe of the tything-man. In matters military money was spent on making the butts and a Turk for shot. In 1578 wine and sugar were given to the Lord Chamberlain of England the day Mr. Mayor took his oath. In 1579 seven shillings were expended for three loads of hedgewood to hedge in the folks visited with sickness at the town's end. There are some curious entries of rent depending on the head of this man or that, which recall the leases for three lives in the South of Europe.

The unpublished Accounts of the Churchwardens and Overseers of St. Helen's and St. Nicholas' for 1606 to 1634, also at the Council Chamber, afford a few more details. In the fourth year of James I a millwright was fetched from Ilsley to set up a mill to set the poor on work. Also forty-six soldiers' coats, belonging to divers persons, were sold at twelve shillings a coat ' to the erecting of a House of Correccion and other charitable uses '. Fines amounting to thirty shillings were taken by Mr. Mayor of certain bowlers bowling in the time of divine service and of others playing at unlawful games. In the next year money was spent to prove that Drayton was in St. Helen's parish. In 19 James I there are some fines for being absent from Church on the Sabbath Day.

Overseers' Accounts.

CHAPTER XI

THE CIVIL WAR AND THE COMMONWEALTH

1640–1660

Preparations for war.

AN entry in the Borough Records of 1640 sounds the beginning of the great Civil War : 'that two barrells of gun powder, sent to this town by Sir Robert Pye, be paid for by the Chamberlain, to be kept for the use of this Borough.'

The lull before the storm.

In 1641 was printed a book with the title *In honour of Abingdon, or the seaventh day of September's solemnization*, by John Richardson, serjeant of Abingdon. It is an account of the celebration at Abingdon of the accommodation with the Scots, which proved to be but the pause before the storm. 'The cvi[th] Psalm was sung by 2,000 quoristers at the crosse.' Mention is made of the figure of King David upon the cross, of 'the skilfull serjeant Corderoy', and of 'the well-known antelope in Abingdon'. The ruined battlements of the Abbey are spoken of as still in sight, and the cross is called the chief ornament of the place. St. Helen's bells are called 'Aaron's bells ', and St. Nicholas' bells 'honest Nick's low bells '. There is also a reference to 'Christ's Hospitall near churchyard wall. Where were also Roysse's fruitfull nurseries, out of which the earle of Pembroke's gardens were supplied.' Hearne bought this rare book for 2*d*. in 1727. He failed curiously to see that the literary serjeant meant Roysse's School and Pembroke College, for he states that there were no nurseries there in his day.[1]

Pamphlets.

There are many contemporary pamphlets that throw light on Abingdon in the Civil War, but they must be read as partisan documents. The town was held at the beginning of the war by the Parliamentarians.

In 1641 was published 'A Report from Abbington towne in Barkshire being a relation of what harme the Thunder and Lightning did on Thursday last [2] upon the body of Humphrey Richardson a rich miserable Farmer.[3] With an exhortation to England to repent. Also

---

[1] Hearne's *Remains*, ii. 294.   [2] December 23.

[3] i. e. a miser.

how the barne of the aforesaid man was burned downe. Warranted by John Andrewes Esquire, Justice of the Peace and Coram, living in the same shire.' The farmer is stated to have decided to pull down his barn and build a greater, when the Lord struck him and his barn.

Another pamphlet of 'Judges' Resolutions', dated October, 1642, mentions Captain Barker as bringing up from Abington to the Parliamentary Judges at Westminster the Mayor of Worcester and other delinquents 'with twenty-two hundred-pound-weight of plate'. This occurred the week before the occupation of Abingdon by the King's troopers.

A third pamphlet, also written from the Parliamentary side, is entitled 'Abington's and Alisburies present Miseries. Both which Towns being lately lamentably plundred by Prince Robert [1] and his Cavaliers. By G. H. 1642.'

'These mischievous Malignants,' according to this writer, plundered the house of Master Ashcombe and then 'the Towne of Abington, sixe miles from Oxford', and played at dice for the plunder. They seem to have set an example of violence that was followed two years later by 'those whom they were pleased to call Malignants and Roundheads'. Carlyle in his *Cromwell* remarks that you cannot pull the shirt off a man, the skin off a man, in a way that will please him.

The Churchwardens' Accounts of St. Helen's indicate that the bells of St. Helen's rang in the King's troopers on October 29, 1642; on the 31st they welcomed Prince Rupert; and on November 2 the King himself. The same Accounts have entries 'for nailes and mending the seates that the soldiers had toorne'; also of soldiers that died at Abingdon. St. Helen's Church was apparently used to shelter the troopers. *Town occupied by the King.*

The bells appear so often in the story of Abingdon as to recall the proverb in Fuller, 'England is a ringing island.' According to Fuller, there were in England 'greater and more tunable bells than in any country in Christendom.' They recall also the famous passage in Froude, in which he says that the bells, the peculiar creation of mediaeval genius, call up better than anything else the idea of the men who built and inhabited abbey and castle, and who are separated from us by so impassable a gulf. *St. Helen's Bells.*

In the troubled years of 1643–4 three Mayors had to be forced to take up their office by fine and imprisonment, and of these one died in office.[2] *Mayors fined and imprisoned.*

---

[1] i.e. Rupert, the Robber Prince.   [2] Borough Records.

The skirmish of Chalgrove (1643) and the battle of Newbury (1643) were fought within a morning's ride of Abingdon.

The Queen passes through. In 1644 the war came nearer still. On April 17 the King, with Prince Rupert and the Duke of York, brought the Queen from Oxford to Abingdon on her way through Lambourne to Exeter and France. Thus Abingdon witnessed what proved to be the final parting between Charles and his wife. Princess Henrietta was born two months later at Exeter.

Abingdon the centre of operations. On May 16 the King was at Reading; on the 18th he moved to Oxford, while his troops bivouacked on the Downs near Compton. On the 24th the foot were drawn into Abingdon, the King's cavalry being at Faringdon. The King had frequent meetings with his council of war at Abingdon, both before and after the arrival of the troops.[1]

This may satisfy the local traditions of the council of war held in the upper room of the Old Bell Inn, and at the Unicorn, an inn on the west side of East St. Helen's, pulled down early in the nineteenth century. Among those named by Walker as in consultation with the King at Abingdon are Lord Digby, the secretary of state, the Earl of Brentford, lord general, Lord Percy, commandant of the artillery, Sir John Culpepper, master of the rolls, Lord Hopton, the Earl of Lindsay, the chamberlain, Lord Richmond, and Lord Wilmot, lieutenant general of the horse. It was decided that Abingdon must be held, and the King, before returning that night to Oxford, left clear orders that in the event of an attack from the east the town should be defended, in the event of an advance by the west the troops should meet it from Abingdon and offer battle. Essex lay that night at Hagbourne, having 10,000 men in his command. His cavalry was commanded by ' faithfull and religious Lord Roberts '.[2]

The town occupied by Parliament. On the morning of the 25th, upon the advance of Essex, Lord Wilmot, who had not less than 6,000 men with him, was seized with panic and decided to evacuate the position, using the cavalry from Faringdon to cover his retreat. Sir Charles Blount, scout-master general, and another officer galloped to Oxford to warn the King of this disastrous folly. It was too late ; as Blount rode back with orders to hold Abingdon, he met the Royalist troops already in sight of Oxford. The capture of Abingdon was important, as it enabled the Parliamen-

---

[1] Sir E. Walker's *Historical Discourses*, and Clarendon's *History*.
[2] Josiah Ricraft's *Survey of England's Champions*, 1647.

tarians to break the line of the Thames, held so far by the cordon of garrisons, and it served as a post of annoyance to the King's head-quarters at Oxford until the end of the war. Essex occupied the town on Sunday, May 26, and Waller pushed towards Wantage to try to pass the river and cut off Charles from the west. Two days later Essex crossed the Thames at Sandford Ferry and camped at Islip, leaving Richard Browne as governor of Abingdon to fortify it and hold it 'just under the enemies' noses'.[1] Browne was a citizen of London, who had distinguished himself the previous year in Kent. On May 29 the Earl of Cleveland made a dash to recover the town with a troop of horse, but was driven out. On the 30th or 31st Waller sawed down the cross 'as a superstitious edifice'. On June 2 Waller forced the the passage of the Thames at Newbridge and threatened Oxford. The next day the King feigned an attack on Abingdon, forcing Waller to return to its defence. Essex had now started on his foolish campaign westward, leaving Waller and Browne in a most difficult position. If Essex and Waller had co-operated intelligently, the fall of Oxford must have followed the capture of Abingdon. The blame may be divided between Essex and the Parliamentary Committee.

<!-- margin note -->
Browne appointed governor.

On June 8 Richard Browne was constituted Major-General of the forces of Berks, Bucks and Oxon for the subduing of Oxford. 'He was a continual thorn in the eyes and goad in the sides of Oxford and the adjacent royal garrisons.'[2]

The Parliamentary Diurnals are full of the exploits of 'this his most active garrisson': e.g. at Headington, Buckland and Chalgrove. In one of these skirmishes 'the Oxford prisoners then taken, being found to be most of them base and bloody Irish, hee presently hanged according to an ordnance of parliament.'[3]

In the autumn he gave an Irish major to the same death. The Irish were regarded by the English at that time as savages, and Charles injured his cause by introducing them into the war in England.

<!-- margin note -->
Executions of Irish prisoners.

These executions excited great bitterness and gave rise to the phrase 'the old Abingdon Law, where Execution preceded Tryal'.[4]

<!-- margin note -->
Abingdon Law.

In the Churchwardens' Accounts for 1644–5 among the numerous entries of money paid for digging graves for officers and soldiers is an entry for five Irishmen. There are also entries 'for wood and candles when the soldiers were in the Church'. In the spring of 1644 there is

---

[1] Ricraft.
[2] Vicars.
[3] Vicars' *England's Worthies.*
[4] *Statesmen of Abingdon,* 1702.

R

an entry 'for ringing when the King came from Reading'; and again 'for ringing twice the bells when the King came'.

On June 29 Charles defeated Waller at Cropredy Bridge, and Waller arrived at Abingdon on July 20 'with a bare 2,500 horse and 1,500 foot', chiefly Londoners, who 'refused to stir one foot further, except it be for home'. Browne's troops were raw recruits, unpaid and ready to mutiny. A certain Colonel Birch, who was stationed at Abingdon, when he hoped for employment and promotion in one of the main armies, speaks of himself in his 'Military Memoir' as out of employment and out of health 'like a chimney in summer'.

After the decisive victory of Marston Moor (July 2) and the fall of York Manchester and Cromwell made Abingdon the rendezvous of the troops they were moving against Charles in the south-west, where he had gone on his victorious march, resulting in the surrender of the army of Essex.

One other pamphlet may be mentioned : ' The Taking of Gateshead, also the perticulars of the defeat given to the Oxford Forces near Abbington.' In this is an extract of a letter from Sunderland, August 1, 1644, stating that an attack on Abingdon had failed, and that the Royalists had lost Sir Richard Grimes, eight slain, twelve taken and sixty horses taken in the pursuit near Oxford.[1]

The *Verney Memoirs* relate that in August Sir Alexander Denton's son in a desperate sally was 'slain within a worke at Abtone as Sir Will. Waller's forces had made'. In September troops from Abingdon tried to intercept Colonel Gage, who achieved the impossible in taking relief to Basing House ; and in the same month Colonel Horton from Abingdon took part in the fierce siege of Donnington Castle, where the stubborn defence of Boys upon this and all occasions forms a splendid episode in the history of Berks. In October Charles was defeated in the second battle of Newbury, yet Manchester failed to push home his victory. Browne used the garrison at Abingdon to harass the Royalists in their retreat. During the autumn Lord Digby corresponded with

On August 28, 1644, an Abingdonian preached before the House of Commons. The sermon is published under the title 'Hierusalem or a vision of peace, preached at Margarets in Westminster before the Honourable House of Commons at their monethly Fast by Christopher Tesdale pastor at Husborn Tarrant in the County of Southampton and a member of the assembly of Divines.' In his vision of peace he urges that Achan must be stoned, Jonah must overboard, and that Jacob's voice and Esau's rough hands are best welcome to God. This turbulent Tesdale figures also in the history of Pembroke.

Browne to get him to play the traitor and surrender Abingdon to the Browne and
Digby. King. Browne answered craft with craft, and pretended to negotiate, until he had finished the new fortifications and received reinforcements. On December 19 he was able to write to Digby in terms of scorn that he had been playing with his proposals and to retort to the hanging of a spy by similar reprisals ' resolving never to be outdone either in civility or justice '. Browne's enemies did not fail to remind him that he had once been a wood-monger ; but he showed himself a capable soldier, holding Abingdon for many months against heavy odds. To him and to Waller belongs much of the credit of starting the New Model Army. At the end of December Beckman, a Swedish engineer, who had escaped from Abingdon, seized Bessilsleigh House (the seat of Speaker Lenthall from 1630) as a post of attack upon Abingdon. Browne at once recaptured it and ' used Beckman according to his desert '.[1]

On January 11, 1645, in time of flood Sir Henry Gage, the governor Sir Henry
Gage killed
at Culham. of Oxford, with 800 horse and 1,000 foot from Faringdon, Wallingford, Witney and Oxford, accompanied by Prince Rupert and Prince Maurice, attacked Culham Bridge, intending either to rush Abingdon, or to break down the bridge and fortify Culham Church and Lady Carey's house. At that time ' Paradise Lane ', which ascends the slope of Mill Hill on the London Road, was so narrow that only one cart could pass between the hedges. The attack failed after desperate fighting, which finds its echo in the records at St. Helen's Church. Gage was mortally wounded. He was an accomplished scholar as well as a brilliant soldier. There is an inscription to him in the Cathedral at Christ Church, Oxford. A simultaneous attack on the town from the west was also repulsed, and the Royalists were pursued to the entrance of Faringdon.

In April, 1645, Cromwell sent down his new guns and ammunition to Cromwell in
the district. Abingdon, and then ' shot westward ' to win another victory at Radcot Bridge. His threat to put the garrison of Faringdon to the sword, if it did not surrender, was in vain. After waiting for several hours for the arrival of infantry from Abingdon he attacked at 3 o'clock in the morning, and had to accept a repulse with loss at the hands of a burgess.[2]

Cromwell appears to have stopped at Abingdon on his return, for one of his letters to Major-General Skippon is dated ' May 3, 1645, Abington.'

[1] *The Lord Digbies Designe to betray Abingdon.*
[2] Carlyle, *Letters and Speeches of Cromwell.*

The Reads of Barton Court.

The Reads of Barton Court served the King with distinction in the war, and it is convenient to give here a sketch of their connexion with Abingdon.

At the dissolution of the monasteries Barton Manor with the house, which took the name of Barton Court, passed by purchase into the hands of Thomas Read. The Manor stretched from Pomney in Radley to Shippon, and to Sunningwell, Sugworth and Bayworth. Thomas Read appears to have been connected with Reading. John Audelett had been the lessee of Barton under Thomas Rowland, the last Abbot. His wife Katherine was Thomas Read's cousin and benefactress. John Audelett left bequests to Sarum, to St. Nicholas' and to St. Helen's, and ordered that he should be buried, with the leave of the convent, in the Abbey Church. Thomas Read's son Thomas (d. 1604), who married a Stonhouse of Radley—the estates marched together—was three times High Sheriff of Berkshire. His arms were Gules, a saltire between four garbs or. His son, Sir Thomas (1575–1650), was High Sheriff of Berks, of Oxfordshire and of Herts. Barton Court had borne the name of the King's House, and its ownership carried with it the duty and honour of entertaining the King when he visited Abingdon. Sir Thomas entertained Charles I and Henrietta Maria several times. On August 19, 1629, they passed ' Berton ' without stopping. But in returning from Woodstock on the 27th they stayed at ' Berton '. Again in 1638 there is an entry in St. Helen's Accounts : ' To the ringers when the King came to Bartonn, 16s. ; to the ringers upon the Kinge's returne, 16s.' In April, 1645, Sir Thomas was captured by the Parliamentarians near Oxford, and made his peace soon after. It was the influence of Speaker Lenthall that saved the Reads and the Stonhouses from severer treatment. It is not clear if Barton was battered down in 1644, or if it survived until two years later. It served in March, 1646, as an ambush for Royalist troops, who crept up ' between Thrupp and Norcot ' in a last attempt upon Abingdon. They were ' smoked out ' by Browne. Compton Read, a youthful grandson of Sir Thomas, distinguished himself in the defence of Barton at this or the earlier date, followed the Royalist cause until the final blow at Worcester, and was rewarded at the Restoration with a baronetcy. There are distinguished branches of the Read family in England and America. The Barton estate passed a century ago into the Stonehouse-Bowyer family.

In the summer of 1646 the fall of Oxford marked the end of the

first act in this struggle. Even Faringdon and Donnington Castle Fall of
had been forced to surrender at last. Oxford.

A few details of Major-General Browne's career after he left Abing- Browne's
don may be of interest. In 1647 he was appointed a commissioner to later career.
receive Charles from the Scots. He was said by his enemies to have
been converted by the King's discourses at Holmby. He was then
elected Sheriff of London. In 1648, like most of the Presbyterians, he
changed sides. In the Worcester campaign he was blamed for allowing
Cromwell to outflank him. Cromwell deposed him from his post as
sheriff, and he had to spend several years in prison at Windsor, Wallingford, Ludlow, &c. He says, ' I was worse used than a cavalier.' He
was concerned in plots against the Protector's dynasty. At the
Restoration he was one of the deputation of the City to bring back
Charles II, who knighted him. In 1660 he became Lord Mayor, and he
received other marks of honour and emolument before his death in 1669.

He was taxed with treachery in his dealings with Lord Digby at
Abingdon in 1644 ; but, if a commander is ever justified in meeting
guile with guile in the face of heavy odds, we must condone Browne's
diplomacy. As to his changing sides before the execution of Charles I
we cannot blame him without blaming men like Fairfax, who fought for
liberty, not for the establishment of a military tyranny, and who
brought back Charles II for the same reasons that they had taken arms
against Charles I. The most serious blot on Browne's high reputation
is his evidence at the trial of the regicides. But the period was one of
extraordinary difficulty to choose between conflicting duties. There
are contemporary portraits of Browne in Vicars and in Ricraft (both
1647).

An entry in the Borough Records of 1647 speaks of ' the money here
collected for the use of the garrison '. In May of the same year a muti-
nous regiment marched from Hampshire upon Oxford, which had then
fallen ; but Colonel Rainsborough, their leader, hurried down from
Parliament, met them at Abingdon and suppressed the mutiny.[1]

In 1648 the bells of St. Helen's rang ' upon the Victory in the North ', Church
i. e. the suppression of the Royalist rising. The inventory of the church Records.
plate that year begins ' In primis ', and then there is an ominous blank
page. However, in the Accounts of 1653 the plate reappears. Much
money was spent on the repairs of the church during the Commonwealth. There were Presbyterian preachers, but the bells, which tell

[1] Gardiner.

so much, continued to ring, particularly on March 2. Strangers passing through the town had to be provided apparently with a pass. In 1655 there is again an entry 'for a houre Glasse for the Church'. Also, 'paid to Thomas Tomkines towards the ringing of the Eight and foure of the Clock Bell—£1 0 0.'

Puritan Fines.

In that year there is a list of fines collected by the Constables and paid over to the Churchwardens (and similar fines the year following) :

	s.	d.
James Glasier of Witney for Sweareing one oath	3	4
Richard Duffine for Sweareing one oath	3	4
Elioner Duffine for Sweareing one oath	3	4
A gent. for Travelling on the Sabboth	10	0
Richard Langfield for drawing Beere on the Sabboth day	10	0

It is noteworthy that the Churchwarden's Accounts run on almost continuously during the ascendancy of the Parliament ; but many of the pages are signed by Henry Langley, Mayor. There was evidently, and inevitably, some religious persecution : note, for instance, the order, preserved at the Council Chamber, sent in 1658 on behalf of His Highness the Lord Protector to the constables and churchwardens of St. Nicholas', to give up the names and abodes of Papists to the justices at the house of Richard Eley.

There is a curious passage in Wood's *Fasti* for 1649.

Thomas Trapham.

'May 19. Thomas Trapham chirurgeon to the general of the parliament army was then actually created batch. of physic, while the said general, Cromwell and the aforesaid officers were seated in their gowns in the doctor's seats.—

This person, who was son of John Trapham of Maidstone in Kent, and had been licensed by the university to practise chirurgery, an. 1633, did practise it in these parts for some years before the grand rebellion broke forth, and became a bitter enemy to his majesty king Charles the first ; to whose body after his decollation in the latter end of Jan. 1648 (*sic*) he put his hand to open and embalm, and when that was done, he sewed his head to his body ; and that being done also, he said to the company then present, that " he had sewed on the head of a goose ". Afterwards he was chirurgeon to Oliver Cromwell at the fight at Worcester against king Charles ii. was a great man among his party and got what he pleased. After his majesty's return, he retired to the fanatical town of Abingdon in Berks practised there among the brethren, and dying an absolute bigot for the cause, in the latter end of Dec. 1683 was buried on the 29th of the same month in the presence of a great number of dissenters in the churchyard of St. Helen's there, close under one of the windows of that Church.'

Wood identifies as son of this man one Thomas Trapham, of Magdalen Hall, lately of Magdalen College, a traveller and doctor of physic, who wrote a book on Jamaica, and was living in Jamaica in 1692. ' Quaere, whether swallowed up with the earthquake in June 1692.'[1]

In 1653 Dr. Peter Heylyn (1600–62), the famous historian and theologian, settled at Lacies Court and lived there until the Restoration, taking an important part in some local matters. He was of Welsh descent, born and educated at Burford, Oxon ; and distinguished himself at Oxford by his ability, also by marrying while still a fellow of Magdalen. Of his eleven children four were living in 1683. In affairs of Church he was an ardent supporter of Laud and afterwards his biographer. He published book after book in answer to the Low Church and Puritan divines, who sometimes speak of him as ' lying Peter '.[2] To him the dust of controversy was as the breath of life. Twenty years after his death his rival biographers, George Vernon, rector of Bourton-on-the-Water, and John Barnard, D.D., rector of Waddington near Lincoln, Heylyn's son-in-law, engaged in an amusing dispute, not so much as to the facts or standpoint of religion and politics, as to the personal equation in borrowing each other's material.   Heylyn was chaplain of Charles I and Charles II, and prebendary and sub-dean of Westminster. He was engaged in 1644 by Charles to write the annals of the war in *Mercurius Aulicus*. He was captured more than once by the Parliamentarians, and was present during part of the siege of Oxford.   He narrowly escaped with his life from the resentment of his opponents. During the Commonwealth he continued to publish his books attacking the Church views of the conquerors. Cromwell's tolerance allowed these books to be published, but Heylyn ' was harassed before Oliver's Major-General for the Decimation of his Estate '.[3]

Dr. Heylyn.

At Lacies Court he spent much money in repairing and building, particularly in building a little oratory or chapel, with silk ornaments about the altar, the other part of the room plain, but kept very decent. Here he read daily the liturgy of the Anglican Church and frequently celebrated in defiance of the Government.

Heylyn at Abingdon.

' This house in Abingdon he purchased for the pleasantness of the situation, standing next the fields, and not distant five miles from Oxford,

[1] Wood's *Fasti*, an. 1649 ; cp. Clark's *Register Univ. Oxon.*, II. i. 125, and Clark's *Wood's Life and Times*, iii. 83.

[2] Carlyle's *Cromwell*.   [3] 1657–8, Barnard.

where he might be furnished with books at his pleasure, either from the Book-sellers' shops, or the Bodlean Library.'[1] 'Many devout and well-affected persons, after the manner of primitive Christians, when they lived under heathen persecutions, resorting to his little chapel, that there they might wrestle with the Almighty for his blessing upon themselves, and upon a divided, infatuated people.'[2]

One of many stories may be of interest :

'While he was arguing his cause before the Major General and his Captains, one Captain Allen formerly a tinker, and his Wife a poor Tripe-Wife, took upon him to reprove the Doctor for maintaining his Wife so highly, like a Lady ; to whom the Doctor roundly replyed ; That he had married a Gentlewoman and maintained her according to her quality ; and so might he his Tripe-wife. Adding withal, that this Rule he always observed, For his Wife to go above his Estate ; his Children according to his Estate, and himself below his Estate ; so that at the year's end he could make all even.'[3]

Heylyn saves St. Nicholas' Church. He deserves the serious gratitude of Abingdon for saving St. Nicholas' Church from destruction.

Vernon says that St. Nicholas' was disused for a time, but that 'a few years later Mr. Huish, Minister at Abingdon, had a numerous auditory of loyal persons at public prayers at Nicholas'. These services were interrupted for a time by 'factious persons', but resumed by the encouragement of Heylyn, who wrote to Mr. Huish a letter, advocating daily public prayer. Barnard gives more details :

'And likewise his good Neighbours at Abington, whom he always made welcom, if they were honest men, that had been of the Royal party, and was ready to assist them upon all occasions ; particularly in upholding the Church of St. Nicholas, which otherwise had been pulled down, on the pretence of uniting it to St. Ellens ; but in truth, to disable the sober party of the Town, who were loyal people, from enjoying their wonted Service and Worship of God in their own Parish Church, of which they had a Reverend and Orthodox man, one Mr. Huish, their Minister ; and, in his absence the Doctor took care to get them supplied with able men from Oxford. Great endeavours were made on both sides ; the one party to preserve the Church, and the other to pull it down, because it was thronged with Malignants, who seduced others from their godly way.'

Heylyn made several journeys to London and employed 'diverse Solicitors before Committees and before Oliver's Council'. Upon a premature report that the Church was to come down 'the Presbyterian

---

[1] Barnard.　　　　　　[2] Vernon.　　　　　　[3] Barnard.

party caused the Bells to be rung, and made Bonfires in the Town, to express their joy, triumphing in the Ruin of a poor Church.' Finally, St. Nicholas' was neither demolished nor 'united to St. Ellens'.

As early as 1638 Heylyn's sight was seriously impaired, and during the whole of his residence in Abingdon he was practically blind and had to rely upon an amanuensis and upon his marvellous memory. He could only dimly see the leader whom he followed in his walks. But blindness and defeat seem to have served to improve the quality of his writing. He continued to the last to treat accurately the minute details of history. Vernon speaks of him as 'a Living Library, a Locomotive Study'. He opposed the Roman Church as stoutly as the Puritans, even refusing bluntly to receive at his new house at Abingdon a former neighbour, who had turned Papist.[1] But he gave his alms freely to the honest poor of the adverse party as well as to his own side ; and sent meat from his table to prisoners in Abingdon Gaol, and attended those condemned to death : 'particularly one Captain Francis and his Company condemned with him, at Abingdon Assizes, the Captain being a well-known Royalist.'

He was visited at Abingdon by Fuller, a former antagonist, also by several 'Old Bishops before the War ', and 'new Bishops '. 'And he wanted not good company amongst his own Neighbours in Abington, particularly Doctor Tucker a Civilian, Mr. Jennings,[2] an ingenious Person, and ejected fellow of St. John's C. in Oxon, and Mr. Blower, a witty Lawyer, who were his constant Visitors . . .' (Barnard.)

Restored to his place at Westminster at the Restoration, he presented upon his knees at the Coronation the royal sceptre and saw 'with his old bad eyes the King settled upon his Father's Throne '.

It is said that he was warned of his death by his old King : ' Peter, I will have you buried under your Seat at Church, for you are rarely seen, but there or at your Study.' So he set his papers in order, provided a house by the Abbey for his wife, and died on Ascension Day, May 8, 1662. His tomb and epitaph are near his sub-dean's seat.

Henry Langley may balance Heylyn as a typical figure of the other side. He was the son of an Abingdon shoemaker, and became an Abingdon scholar of Pembroke College in 1629. In 1647 Cornish and he were sent down by Parliament to Oxford (which had surrendered

Dr. Langley at Pembroke.

---

[1] Barnard.
[2] Robert Jennings, who made a fortune as master of the Free School at Abingdon. Wood, *Fasti Oxon.*, ii. 103.

at last in the previous year) with four other ministers to change the religion and politics of the University.[1]

Opponents described these six ministers as two fools, two knaves and two madmen—Cornish and Langley being the two fools—and made fun of their Puritan mannerisms. Metford speaks of Langley's discourses as 'tedious even when shortest'. But Calamy says, 'A judicious solid Divine, not valu'd in the University according to his Worth.' In any case Langley was the rising hope of the New Model, and was put into the Mastership of Pembroke in spite of opposition. He showed himself a resolute and successful ruler of that Royalist college. At the Restoration he was naturally ejected from Pembroke as well as from Abingdon, retired to his house at Tubney in 'Bagley Wood', took pupils, and 'oftentimes preached in conventicles at Abendon'. It was at this time that the Dissenters quitted the Church of England and formed separate churches. Hitherto they had remained within the Church of England and striven to reform it according to their views. He was buried at St. Helen's in 1679. He was the first of the seven Masters of Pembroke who came from Abingdon School.[2]

The evidence appears to indicate the following position of affairs in the Abingdon churches during the interregnum :

The churches under the Commonwealth.

(i) The great church of St. Helen's was in the hands of the Presbyterians and Independents, who still regarded themselves, however, as reformers of the Church, and had not yet separated from it as Dissenters. These were the supporters of the Protectorate.

(ii) From them the Baptists seceded for political and doctrinal reasons.

(iii) At St. Nicholas' church the members of the Church of England held services, with interruptions from time to time.

An account of the sale of Bishops' Lands under the Commonwealth, declared November 14, 1659, but evidently referring to events of earlier date, has this item :

'William Stanbridge, to the use of John Pendarves, minister of St. Helen's in Abingdon   £127 10 0.[3]'

The Survey of Church Livings under the Commonwealth at the Record Office (*Berks*, vol. i) was examined and transcribed for me by

---

[1] Macleane, *History of Pembroke.*
[2] See Macleane's *History of Pembroke.*
[3] W. A. Shaw, *English Church during Civil War*, ii. 561.

Mr. H. G. Bell. Unhappily the manuscript is very faded. The date of the commission of this inquisition is April 23, 1655. It runs thus :

'Hormer hundred. Abingdon hath two churches within the said township Saint Hellens and Nicholas. St. Hellens is a Vicarage in the gift of the Lord Protectors containing the two chapellry . . . Sandford being on the whole worth thirty pounds yearly, Shippon is a small vicarage (?) but three pounds yearly but half a mile distant from the said town . . . adjoining to the parish of Bessilsleigh . . . of Saint Hellens and Mr. John . . . said church of Hellens . . . Nicholas hath a . . .'

Should the missing surname be Pendarves or Tickell ?

Lempriere's transcripts include some papers referring to the attempt to separate the two churches ' during Cromwell's usurpation '.

John Clackson and Richard Addams in their presentment to the interrogatories of the Commissioners at Speenhamland, June 21, 1655 referred to Mr. Blacknall's dotasion of St. Nicholas', on account of the unseasonable and imperfect performing of that cure by the vicar of St. Helen's, and stated that the committee of Berks on October 9, 1650 had decided that the vicar could not be the parson to officiate the daily prayer. They give the value of the donation as £13 per annum, the vicarage is worth £7 or £8 per annum, Mr. Blacknall's donation as to the ministerial performance £20 per annum. Also the parish alloweth £3 per annum.[1]

The Lord Protector had succeeded to the Bishop of Salisbury's patronage of the readership. The patrons of the donative or parsonage were now the commissioners of the great seal instead of the Lord Keeper. The patron of the vicarage was the Protector in place of the King. The proprietor of the parsonage was Dr. Kendall, of Mr. Blacknall's donation Mr. Huish. The profits of the parsonage went to Mr. Tickell, who nevertheless ' performs no office or cure of souls there by himself or by any of his appointment '.

Huish had been ' admitted to officiate dayly prayer in Mr. Blacknall's donation ' in 1643 by the Bishop of Salisbury, and is described as ' an able, painfull and godly minister '. St. Nicholas' is proudly described as of great necessity and use to the parish and as one of the neatest churches in Berks. Standing near the Guildhall, it was the church where the sermons at the assizes were always preached before the judges. The Committee of Berks, considering that the vicar of Helen's had to perform the parish duties of the cure, had declared in

---

[1] This was a mediaeval payment.

1650 that Nicholas was a distinct parish. St. Helen's is described as 'so inconveniently built, that hardly one half of the people can well hear the minister'. The demolition of St. Nicholas' is deprecated, for 'the town of Abingdon growing every day more populous than other, it would be very dangerous and unsafe in time of any infection or contagious disease, if there should be only one church left . . .' Finally they asked 'that the profit of the vicarage of Nicholas being at present void, as we conceive, may also be conferred upon' Mr. Huish.

On April 29, 1658 the jury reported that the church of Helen's was insufficient for the people of Abingdon with the four country villages of Shippon, Sandford, Northcourt and Barton; and that Nicholas was well seated, &c. But the commissioners reported to His Highness that the parishes were best united, as 'since the late war several of the parish of Nicholas have at their own will hired disaffected persons to preach and officiate to them in the said parish church of Nicholas slighting and rejecting their own minister, a person godly, able and well affected', and that 'there is convenience enough to the said church of Helen's for the inhabitants of both parishes to meet and hear the word'.[1]

Richard Wrigglesworth.

The will of Richard Wrigglesworth, dated February 7, 1647, left £800 for the maintenance of a Godly Lecture in the Public Meeting Place in Marcham in the summer season on the morning of the Lord's Day, and in the winter season in the evening 'in Abington in their Great Meeting Place', i.e. in St. Helen's Church.

'Item, my Will is while Mr. Pendarvis abide in Abingdon or in those parts if he please he may perform the said Service.'[2]

John Pendarves the Baptist.

John Pendarves (1622–56), a Cornishman, graduated from Exeter College, Oxford, in 1641, and then according to Wood 'sided with the rout'. 'At length after several changes he settled his mind on Anabaptism,' and became 'Lecturer at Wantage, and Pastor of the Anabaptists at Abingdon in Berkshire'. On September 11, 1652 he engaged in a public disputation in the church of Watlington with Jasper Mayne, D.D., but the disputation appears to have suffered from the excitement of the audience.[3]

[1] This summary is taken from Lempriere's transcripts in the possession of the Vicar of Abingdon, and it appears to state fairly the views of the two sides. St. Nicholas' was then, as now, the church of an important minority, but the minority was then the Anglican minority in its days of adversity.
[2] App. to Wrigglesworth Scheme, 1883.
[3] *Sermon against Schisme*, Mayne.

He was the joint author with some Devonshire ministers of *Sighs for Sion*, 1656. In the same year he published *Arrowes against Babylon or Certaine Quaeries. Also Endeavours for Reformation in Saints Apparrell with some Quaeries for the people called Quakers.* His funeral is vigorously described by Wood, who agrees with the details of the following account, which throws some light upon Abingdon under the rule of Cromwell. It is a pamphlet signed William Hughes, Hinton, December 26, 1656. It is worth quoting at some length.

The title-page runs:

Munster
and Abing-
don.

MUNSTER AND ABINGDON

or the

Open Rebel-⎱   ⎰Unhappy Tu-
lion there, ⎰ and ⎱mult here.

(Bred in the same wombe)

That   ⎱   ⎰ This
From Sleidans⎰   ⎱From eye and
Comm. L. 10 ⎰   ⎱eare witnesses.

With Marginall Notes of Muncer and Mahomet. Faithfully communicated to English Readers, in a Booke and Postscript, For a seasonable Caution to the Brittish Nation. And a serious check to rash and Giddy spirits. By W. H.

It was printed at Oxford by Henry Hall, University printer, for Robert Blagrave, 1657.

The Book's Request is

Heare me, but out, My Judge, before
Thou sentence pass ; I'le ask no more.

It is evidently an apology for the Protector's government, and written by one of the Presbyterian or Independent ministers, who had no liking for ' Anabaptists '.

The first half of the book is a translation from Sleidan, giving ' The History of John-a-Leyden The Anabaptist King in Muncer '. It describes the part taken by Munster in 1625 in the religious wars of Westphalia, known as the Thirty Years' War. There the war between Protestants and Roman Catholics was followed by strife and war between the Anabaptists and other sects of the Protestants. The melancholy results are held up as a warning to the parties in England.

In the second part Hughes turns to the strife among the victors at Abingdon, and in lengthy verbiage and with many texts he holds up to scorn the Anabaptists' dicta ' The Saints must rule,' ' The ungodly must come down.' He speaks ' the feares of the honest Presbyterian and Independant ', and proceeds to ridicule the various accounts circulated of the late tumult at Abingdon. His own version runs thus :

Mr. Pendarves his Death

The Riot at Pendarves' funeral.

' Mr. Pendarves late pastour to the Adversaries of Infant Baptisme in that Towne yeelded up the Ghost some weekes before in London, and changed his many quarrels here for everlasting peace (I am so perswaded from that intimacy some years agoe betwixt us) in our fathers kingdome ; after some hot debates twixt his surviving freinds about his bodies resting place on earth : was brought at last, by water (in a chest like those for sugar, fild up with sand, and lodged at a Grocers) there to deposite the remaines of death, where the service of his life had beene devoted. This brought of persons (of the same complexion with him in religious matters) out of their respect unto his memory, from most parts of the Nation, and some the remotest, a number of both sexes (both far and neere) very considerable. The State took Item of the inconveniences the concourse of so great a people (where disaffection to our present peace apparently predominates) might start at such an opportunity, and prudently to prevent the worst, assigne eight troops of horse under command to Major Generall Bridges to take up quarters, at the very Juncture, in Wallingford : a Towne within the same County, and upon the same river, seven miles below the place forenamed. All things prepared for the funerall, and the company met on Tuesday the 30 of September —56 (the day unto that worke appointed) the Corps, with meete solemnity, in a new burying-place, before a Garden (for such a one of late hath beene procured at the Townes West end, and in the Oxestreete : whether because they would not have communion with us a live or dead, or for what other reason I must be silent) is espoused to the grave. That day, saving what time attendance on this evening worke borrowed of necessity, was spent upon Religious exercises : severall, as thereunto drawne forth, taking their turnes in praying and in speaking. The morrow is as yesterday with them. But tis sad to heare at what a rate they deale with God and Man.'

Then follow instances of their furious language, blowing the match to fire the train ' against our peace and powers '. They decided that ' God's people must be a Bloody People ', and attacked especially ' the publique preachers of the Gospel ' as ' dumb dogs, members of Babylon, Anti-christian priests, and the smoake of the bottomlesse pit.' How Laud must haye smiled in his headless grave. They compared the soldiers to Irish rebels.

Tidings were sent to the Major-General who waited ' whether wisely in order to give them rope ', or upon misinformation of a certain person. On Thursday morning a Lieutenant with fifty horse was sent in to dissolve the meeting, announcing ' That they must depart unto their several habitations ; those that are strangers that is.' They refuse : the people crowd to the Market Place.

' There in the Cryers Pulpit they begin to pray and speake or rather to rant and raile in wild confusion. Abusing the Protector and the Souldiers to their very teethes.'

' We are not for Cromwels Kingdome, for Priests and Universities.' ' Whole armfuls more of Billingsgate flowers.' One man called for ' a signe from heaven '. Finally the soldiers had to pull down the speakers. ' But of all the mischief done in such a tumult, at such resistance, by Canes, and Swords (for the Guns it seemes were silent), apparently somebody was slightly scratched (as others tell us) by a Souldier in the drawing forth his sword : and another individuum vagum cut upon the hand.' ' This being over, the Major-Generall enters with his whole Brigade of horse, and having called before himselfe, and chiefest officers the principall fomenters of that Seditious Businesse, assayes, not merely by extreame civility, but friendly and affectionate tendernesse to reduce them to sobriety.'

According to Hughes only five were committed unto custody. According to the offended preachers there was serious bloodshed. We give the story, as it stands, as a vivid picture of the parties of the time.

Another sermon of William Hughes has a local interest. It is ' Magistracy God's Ministry or A Rule for the Rulers and People's due Correspondence. With something in reference to the Present Powers For restoring Dutie and Removing Discontent. Opened in a Sermon at the Midsummer Assizes in Abington, Anno 1651. By W. Hughes.' It was printed by T. M. for Geo. Calvert, at the sign of the Half Moon in Paul's Church-yard, 1652. It is introduced by a ' Letter to his Excellencie, the Lord Cromwell, General of all the Forces raised by the Parliament of the Commonwealth of England.' Then comes a preface to the reader ' in this scribbling age ' : ' Reader, three of the famous Monarchies of the world are down, the miscellany fourth, sure, is setting : make way, the fifth, the last, the everlasting one, may rise upon us.' The sermon itself is a fairly sober and scholarly argument. It contains one topical reference : ' Assizes are the Lawyers' harvest.'

A sermon of Hughes.

According to Wood, Hughes retired to Abingdon for a time at the Restoration, when he was ejected from the rich living of Hinton.

John
Tickell the
Presby-
terian.

John Tickell is spoken of by Wood as the Presbyterian preacher at Abingdon at least as early as 1651. He was born at Tavistock, and became a 'servitor of New inn'[1] after the surrender of the garrison of Oxford. He was made a student of Christ Church, took ' one degree ' in 1649 and his M.A. in 1651. In 1654 he was an assistant to the commissioners for the ejection of ' the scandalous, ignorant and insufficient ministers and schoolmasters '. At the Restoration he retired to Devonshire, and finally conforming became minister of Barnstaple and Widecombe. He died in 1694.

Some of his books have a local interest : *The Bottomles Pit, Smoaking in Familisme*, &c., by John Tickell, Minister to the Church in Abingdon, Berks. Oxford, 1652. This is dated from Abingdon, October 3, 1651. It contains some brief notes on Abiezer Coppes Recantation Sermon, preached at Burford, September 23, 1651. After the dedication to George Hughes, pastor of Plymouth, his spiritual father, he explains that he was riding by accident past Burford Church, and, seeing the church full and the pulpit still vacant, he was ' prest in the spirit ', mounted the pulpit and preached his sermon ' immediately before Mr. Coppe came in to preach'. Afterwards he waited for Mr. Coppe's counter-sermon and then proceeded to publish this critique. A parallel is furnished in Scott's *Woodstock*.

In 1656 John Tickell, M.A., published *Church-Rules, Proposed to the Church in Abingdon and approved by them.* Also, *An Essay toward the removing of some stumbling blocks laid by Anabap. Spirits.* Also, *A few Antiquaeries to Mr. Pendarves his quaeries against our Churches and Ministries in his Pamphlet called Arrowes against Babylon.* Tickell states that three months before he had decided to remove from Abingdon, but was induced to stay upon terms. The Church Rules are his ultimatum. Among his Antiquaeries to Mr. Pendarves are these :

' Did you excommunicate Mr. D., a Godly man, for any other reason, then because he Married a Wife not of your way, and came with her to heare the publick Minister ? '

' Have you not delivered in Abingdon Pulpit, that Babylon must have blood to drink ? '

Tickell is a supporter of the ' deliverer, the Lord Protector, whom your tribe abhorre.'

[1] Wood.

In the years 1654 and 1656 under the Commonwealth according to the 'Borough Records' no writs for a parliamentary election for the Borough of Abingdon were issued.   This statement is in harmony with Browne Willis' *Notitia Parliamentaria* (1715) and the later standard books.   But these lists are often defective and are of course largely compiled from contemporary broadsides, where the writs happen to be missing.   There is at Bodley ' A Perfect List of the Members Returned and Approved on by the Councill to sit in Parliament in 1654 ',[1] which gives Thomas Holt as Member for Abbington, Berks.   There is in the same library another ' Perfect List ' for 1656,[2] which gives Thomas Holt, Esq., for Abington.

Probably Holt was nominated by the Protectorate Government, as the Recorder, without the usual forms of free election.   In a third list in the same library of the Members of the previous Parliament to that of 1654, i. e. the Rump, Abingdon is missing, and for the whole of Berks there are only three Members instead of seven, of whom the last is marked with a 'starre', as 'being for the Godly, Learned Ministries and Universities '.[3]

[1] Printed for R. Ibbitson, 1654.
[2] Printed by Tho. Newcomb, Thames Street over against Bainard's Castle.
[3] London, printed by A. M., 1654.

Members of Parliament.

CHAPTER XII

UNDER THE LATER STUARTS

1660–1714

The Resto-
ration.
A double
return.

AT the close of the Commonwealth Sir John Lenthall only son of Speaker Lenthall, and one of Cromwell's baronets, afterwards High Sheriff of Oxford, was returned to Parliament for Abingdon. In 1660 he was expelled from the Convention Parliament. He is described by Wood as ' the grand braggadocio and liar of the age ', but a better memorial of him is the silver tankard among the Corporation Plate.

In 1660 it seems that there was a double return, the dispute being as to whether ' burgesses ' in the Charter meant the inhabitants. The Committee of the House decided ' Aye ', and ordered on May 23 that Mr. J. Mayott, Mayor of Abingdon (as Returning Officer) stand committed to the Serjeant-at-Arms for neglecting to give his attendance. Three days later he was discharged. At that time Mr. Edward Turnor, formerly of Abingdon School, was Clerk of Parliament.

The Restoration was marked by expenses for the ' souldiers at the Gatehowse ', and by the dismissal of Dr. Langley and Mr. Cornish, ' the nowe pretended Lecturers,' from preaching the Lecture.[1] The Solemn League and Covenant, enforced by Major-General Browne, was solemnly repudiated. The King's Arms were set up in St. Helen's Church. The bells, which Abingdonians rang and wore out so often, were rung at the first proclamation of Charles II as king, at his solemn proclamation, on his birthday and at two thanksgivings. The Churchwardens were guilty of the extravagance of 1s. 6d. ' for a Horse hyre to Oxford to gett a Minister to preach and for expenses there '. In 1663 new gowns were ordered for the Serjeants, and the Principal and Secondary Burgesses were directed under a fine to provide gowns for themselves.[2] In the same year sixteen burgesses were removed from the roll apparently for refusing to take the Oath of Supremacy.

---

[1] Borough Records.   [2] Ibid.

Boxes were erected at that time at the Council House for the preservation of the 'Town evidences ', i. e. the Charters and records.

In 1665 a watch was set at ' the Hartbridge, St. Helen's Bridge, the Ock Bridge, the Boare Street, the Wineyard, and the Abbey ', to keep out people and goods infected with the Great Plague—'which God forbidde '. Houses were ordered to be erected near the Royal Fort in Boxwell for the victims. In that year on account of the plague the Court moved from London to Oxford. ' Upon His Majesty passing through this Corporation ' of Abingdon, £60 was paid to the King and £36 12s. 8d. to his servants, including the King's Jester, as fees of homage.[1]

The Great Plague.

Royal visit.

In 1666 money was granted to seven soldiers and two drummers for services in impressing men and proclaiming the war against France. In that year Fitzharris Farm, occupied by Joane Badcock, and Steedes Farm, occupied by William Foster, were mortgaged to raise £200 for the use of the King. A further loan of £300 to the King was made the next year.[2]

In the same year the inhabitants of the parish of St. Helen's had to pay 26s. for not repairing the highway between Ock Mill and Knightsham.

In 1668 a lease was granted to John Lindsay, citizen and goldsmith of London, for £20 a year with a covenant to new-build, of premises in Birchin Lane, London, which 'were lately demolished' by the Great Fire.[3]

Samuel Pepys in his famous diary describes a visit at this time to Oxford and Abingdon :

Pepys visits the Hospital.

' (June 9, 1668.) Thence with coach and people to Physic-garden, 1s. So to Friar Bacon's study: I up and saw it, and give the man 1s. Bottle of sack for landlord, 2s. Oxford mighty fine place ; and well-seated, and cheap entertainment. At night came to Abingdon, where had been a fair of custard ; and met many people and scholars going home ; and there did get some pretty good musick, and sang and danced till supper : 5s.

10th (Wednesday). Up, and walked to the Hospitall : very large and fine, and pictures of founders, and the History of the hospitall ; and is said to be worth £700 ; and that Mr. Foly [T. Foley, of Witley Court, who was founding a hospital for 60 boys at Stourbridge] was here lately to see how their lands were settled. And here, in old English, the story of the occasion of it, and a rebus at the bottom. So did give to the poor, which they would not take but in their box, 2s. 6d. So to the inn and paid the reckoning and what not, 13s. So forth towards Hungerford, led this good way by our landlord, one Heart, an old but very civil and well-spoken man, more than I ever heard of his quality. He gone, we forward.'

---

[1] Borough Records.   [2] Ibid.   [3] Ibid.

Pepys' signature appears on an interesting local deed,[1] dated 1666, in witness of the signature of James II, at that time ' Duke of Yorke and Albany, Earl of Ulster, Lord High Admirall of England and Ireland, Constable of Dover Castle, Lord Warden of the Cinque Ports and Governor of Portsmouth '. It is a transfer of the ' White Hart Inne ',[2] which was part of the estate of John Phelps, ' a person attainted of high treason.'

In the seventeenth century, owing to the reluctance of royalty to condescend to a copper coinage, mayors, churchwardens, trading companies and private traders found themselves compelled to issue trade tokens, which have been described as the illegal money of necessity. These issues are confined between the years 1648 and 1679. Of Abingdon tokens there are eleven issues in existence. The spelling of the name of the town varies—Abington, Abingdon, Abbington and Abindon. The commonest are those of William Stevenson and of Richard Ely (the builder of the Castle Well and his father).

To quote one instance :

Obverse. Sarah. Pleydell = The Mercers' Arms.
Reverse. Of. Abington. 1667 = Her Halfe Penny. S. P.

To revert to the Borough Records—in 1670 the Recorder was desired to treat with Dr. Hall, the Master of Pembroke, concerning the not performing of the terms of the will of Thomas Tesdale in respect of the Scholars on the foundation. In 1672 there is a note of empire and emigration : a lease granted by the Council to Robert Payne, gent., ' of the Colonie of Virginia,' of a messuage in Broad Street late in the occupation of his father. In 1675 Thomas Holt was removed from the Recordship for residing at Reading, ' a place twenty miles distant.' The next year was paid 36s. 6d. for meat, drink and tobacco provided for the Corporation ; while steps were taken to exclude immigrant paupers.[3]

In 1677 the Mayor, Bailiffs, and Common Council decided to pull down the old Market House and replace it by a convenient House where His Majesty's justices might sit.[4]

[1] In the possession of Mr. E. M. Challenor.
[2] On the site of the County Gaol.
[3] Borough Records.
[4] Ibid. An older Market House is described by Leland in Henry VIII's reign: 'There is also a fair House with open Pillars covered with a Rofe of Lead for Market folkes.' The Chamberlain's Accounts in Elizabeth's reign speak of the *New* Market House.

It has been stated that the architect of the new Market House was a pupil of Wren. There is also a tradition that the designs were by Inigo Jones, who has left monuments of his genius at Oxford. If this be so—the building is worthy of him—his designs were not executed for a generation after his death.

In 1678 the Corporation ordered timber trees standing in Bagley Close to be cut and carried to the new building. As to its later history, in 1707 the Council passed a curious order, that no person be suffered to dry any clothes in the Market House.[1] In 1852–3 more than £1,000, raised by collection, was spent on the restoration of the Market Hall. Mr. Clacy, the County Surveyor, recommended that the Cupola should be removed from the roof of the Hall to the roof of the Tower, stating that it was no part of Inigo Jones' design but a late addition. The Corporation showed an excellent taste in rejecting this advice, for the Town Hall with its Cupola makes a majestic crown to Abingdon, whether viewed from rail or road or river. An unsightly gallery was removed from the centre of the fine Hall, and the ceiling was decorated with deeply recessed panels. Windows were substituted for the ugly doors in the two centre window-openings of the north front. A glance at the old prints will indicate how great an improvement this was.

Since 1886 the plain but convenient Corn Exchange of brick has replaced the Town Hall, for the most part, as the temple of political oratory and other forms of public amusement. But the Town Hall will continue to be valued as the most splendid in Berks, whether it be compared with the humbler market-houses of Wallingford and Faringdon, or Witney beyond the border, or with the modern buildings of Reading and Newbury. It escaped narrowly a terrible doom in 1849, when a number of serious people nearly succeeded in getting glazed in as a Corn Exchange the lower part of this unique building.

There is a printed letter preserved at Bodley from a Friend in Abingdon to a Gentleman in London concerning the election of a Burgess in 1679 for the ensuing Parliament. It must be interpreted as written by a partisan of the Country party. The writer states that Sir J. Stonehouse, the candidate of the Court Party, polled 171 against 297 polled by Mr. Dunch, the candidate of the popular party. This poll lasted three hours and was ordered by the Mayor, because he was not willing to decide by ' view '. The Mayor had not yet exhausted his resources : he adjourned the Court, consulted the Council, put pressure

The Market House, Town Hall or County Hall.

The Election of 1679.

[1] Borough Records.

on the tenants of the Corporation, &c., and finally decided that 171 was greater than 297, and declared Sir J. Stonehouse elected. Sir John had the support of the neighbouring Papist families.

In the riot that ensued the Mayor had to escape 'in Panic Fear' over a high wall and kept incognito a whole day in a bed of nettles. The writer is anxious to explain that the troop of 200 mounted men, who escorted Mr. Dunch, behaved in perfect order.[1]

In the previous year a night-watch was ordered by the Council 'in this time of danger iminent', and in 1683 the bells of St. Helen's were ringing 'on the King's Deliverance from the plott'. In that year the churchwardens of St. Helen's paid 2s. 0d. 'to Mary Fleetwood being a poore Minister's wife with her Childe and Mother going for Holland— By Mr. Mayor's Order.' Also 1s. 6d. 'to Goodwife Porter, Black Jack's wife, being sick.' Another detail belongs to this year : the old Guildhall was leased to a London Cheesemonger with the use of scales and weights on Mondays and Fridays for twenty-one years at 52s.[2]

Election of 1682. Another election tale may serve to illustrate these latter days of Charles II. The Letters of Humphrey Prideaux relate that in 1682 Brome Whorwood stood as a candidate 'against Lord Norris at Abington'.[3]

'We had great expectation of a tryall between ye Ld Norris and Brome Whorwood about their quarrel in the Town Hall at the election of ye Town Clerk. Brome brought an action of battery against my Lord for beateing him, and my Ld an action of "scandalum magnatum"[4] against Brome for calleing him yong fool. But the Bishop of Oxford interposeing spoiled the sport ; for in truth ye Ld Norris called Brome old fool before he called him yong fool ; and beside it was reather hypothetically then categorically etc. etc.'

This James Bertie, Lord Norreys of Rycote, was that year made Earl of Abingdon for his services to Charles II.

Charles had at that time commenced his successful manœuvre to get the control of the House of Commons by suppressing the charters of London and the provincial boroughs. Lord Norreys, a prominent

---

[1] The Dunches were connected by marriage with the family of Oliver Cromwell, held property at Little Wittenham, and for a time occupied Pusey. One of their monuments in Little Wittenham Church rehearses the virtues of a couple of the house 'now surely paradised in eternitie'. 　　　　[2] Borough Records.

[3] Lord Norreys was supporting Sir John Stonehouse.

[4] i. e. for insulting a peer.

member of the Court party, used his influence to persuade Oxford to surrender her charter and earned the hatred of the popular party. In the next reign he declined to support James II in his papist policy, and finally joined the Prince of Orange.

The first Lord Norreys of Rycote lived in the spacious days of Elizabeth. His second son is said by Camden to have served in all her wars on the Continent, and to have died in 1597 of disappointment on not succeeding William Russell as lord deputy of Ireland.

With the accession of James II Abingdon continued to be a place of excitement. In Anthony Wood's *Life* it is related that in 1685 at the time of Monmouth's rising when ' the drums beat up Abendon, a most factious town, they could get thence but four voluntiers '. St. Helen's ringers received 3s. 6d. ' when Monmouth's Army were routed ', and the like sum when he was taken. Wood says that the footmen of Merton ' went to Islip to secure the London road, and to stop all suspicious persons from going to London. At the same time the Universitie horse rode all night and dispersed themselves on the roads by Dorchester, Abendon, Farringdon,' &c. *(margin: Monmouth's Rising.)*

The troubled times are reflected in ' A Return of the Borough Constables at the Sessions, June 18, 1685 '.[1] The Constables reported that the stocks, whipping-post and pillory were in good repair, that watch and ward had been duly kept, and vagabonds punished as the law required. It concluded, ' Wee present that the Cage is out of repaire, and this is all we knowe of our owne knowledge.' This cage, which probably exposed evildoers to the contumely of the upright and the young, was ordered to be pulled down in 1710 by the Council, and a new one to be erected in the Market Place, where the pillory was.[2]

In 1686 the Council paid 50s. for wine drunk when James II was proclaimed.[3] The *London Gazette*, February, 1687, gives an address from the rulers of Abingdon to the ' Dread Sovereign ', thanking him for the Declaration of Indulgence. In that year and the next James removed and replaced many of the burgesses and officers in accordance with his policy.[4]

The march of William of Orange from Torbay has a local interest. For after lingering at Salisbury and Hungerford, he reached Abingdon *(margin: William of Orange marches through.)*

[1] Preserved at the Council Chamber.
[2] Borough Records.   [3] Ibid.
[4] Cp. letters exhibited at the Council Chamber.

in December, 1688, and rested there before turning down the river for Henley and London.

Harcourt.   In 1689 Simon Harcourt (1661–1727) was appointed Recorder, and the next year he was elected Member of Parliament. He continued to represent the Borough in Parliament for twenty years with two brief intervals.[1] He was born at Stanton Harcourt, where he succeeded to the embarrassed estates of his ancient family. He was a Tory politician, and defended Sacheverell, the 'non-resistance' divine, in the House of Lords. He purchased Nuneham Courtney in 1708, in which year he became Lord Keeper. In 1713 he became Lord Chancellor. He was greater perhaps as a forensic orator and party politician than as a statesman. He became the first Viscount Harcourt. His second son represented Abingdon in Parliament 1713–15, and his grandson was the first Earl Harcourt.

The elections of Simon Harcourt seem to have provoked the usual war of pamphlets and appeals. For instance, there is at Bodley's Library one of these leaflets :

Nov. 20, Thursday, 1701.

A Letter from Abingdon to a Friend in London.

Honest Tom,

This morning Simon Harcourt was unanimously chosen Burgess of this Corporation.

The Corporation desired him to persever in the faith, to enquire after the promoters of the late dissolution, to follow the impeachments, to procure that the Treasurers of the Navy and Land forces make up their accounts, to examine the nature, quantity and quality of the prizes, to bring the offenders to punishment.

Which the said Mr. Harcourt having promised to do : They all Cry'd, Long Live Simon Harcourt Esq. Burgess of Abingdon.

I hope other electors will follow so Good a Precedent. And am

Yours

A. B.'

The war in question was part of the Wars of the Spanish Succession, of which Blenheim Palace remains a local monument. Harcourt had a share in the Peace of Utrecht, which concluded that war.

Another pamphlet is preserved at the British Museum, dated 1702. It is entitled ' The Statesmen of Abingdon, a full answer to the True

[1] There is a portrait of Simon Harcourt at the Council Chamber.

Letter written by the body politic of that Corporation on the occasion of the election of Mr. Harcourt.'

It ridicules the idea that the little folk of Abingdon should either govern England or control a Harcourt. It is full of somewhat cheap abuse, but recalls an interesting phrase of the Civil War—'the old Abingdon Law, where Execution preceded Tryal.'

The history of Abingdon elections is a history of petitions, and particularly so in that period of the Great Revolution. For instance, in 1688 there was a petition of Sir John Stonehouse, the question of 'scot and lot' men issued in serious fighting. Sir John carried off the Borough Charter to Radley; hence the cry of 'No Radley Charter'. A new writ was ordered and Medlicott unseated. In 1689 there was another petition of Stonehouse—it was finally successful and John Southby was unseated. In 1698 a petition of William Hucks against Simon Harcourt was less successful. By the committee of the House of Commons it was 'ordered that the proceedings of Wm. Hucks is a scandalous reflection on the government and that he be committed to the custody of the serjeant-at-arms'. In 1708 Hucks had his revenge, unseating and replacing Harcourt on a petition. In that year the House of Commons passed a resolution that the voters in the borough elections should be those who paid 'scot and lot', and did not receive alms or relief. Elsewhere they are called 'potwallers', 'potwobblers', &c. In early times the member seems to have been elected sometimes by the Council, sometimes by the inhabitants.

The Borough Records afford a few details of a more domestic tone. In 1692 the Council placed a veto upon wine, ales, cakes, pipes or tobacco 'spent or eat or drunke' at the charges of the Corporation.

A hint of water-works occurs in 1696 in a lease of a plot of waste land in the Stert Street to a goldsmith to erect a great cistern. In 1714 the Corporation granted relief to a town serjeant suffering from cancer in the lip.

To this period belongs the growth of Protestant Dissent in Abingdon. Growth of Before the Restoration the Independents or Presbyterians and the Protestant Dissent. Baptists aimed at the control of the Church of England. After the Restoration they definitely left the Church and founded distinct bodies. Several well-known names occur in the pages of Anthony Wood, who writes always of them as an opponent without disguise and without restraint. Tobias Garbrand, alias Herks, a bachelor of physics and Garbrand.

Principal of Gloucester Hall, was created doctor of physic in 1648. In 1660, returning to Abingdon, he practised his faculty there. He was buried in St. Helen's in April, 1689.[1]

Danson. His son-in-law, Thomas Danson, a noted Nonconformist, after a varied career through the Civil War and the Restoration, settled and preached at Abingdon on the death of Henry Langley. There were disturbances in 1683, when he preached in the Town Hall. About 1692 he was dismissed by the brethren. The Quakers were sometimes the object of his attacks.[2]

John Garbrand, the son of the doctor, took a degree at Oxford and went to the Middle Temple. Among his writings are *The Grand Inquest, The Royal Favourite cleared* and *Clarior e Tenebris*. His support of the Duke of York spoilt his practice.[3]

The year 1700 marks a new era in the history of Dissent in Abingdon, for in that year the Baptists, the Quakers or Friends and the Independents or Presbyterians [4] each built a meeting-house or church. The **Tomkins family.** Tomkins family comprised many wealthy maltsters in the seventeenth and eighteenth centuries, who left many benefactions, chiefly to the Baptists. John Tomkins left by will in 1706 £4 a year for distribution among the poor. Benjamin Tomkins the elder in 1731 left property to build the eight almshouses in the Ock Street and £1,600 to endow them. He also left £1,000 for the poor Protestant Dissenters and for the Baptist ministers. Benjamin Tomkins the younger left in 1734-6 £200 for the Minister of the Protestant Dissenters called Baptists or Anabaptists in Abingdon ; also 20s. a year for a sermon in commemoration of the deliverance from Popery, effected by the accession of George I. Benjamin Tomkins, the grandson, left in 1751 property to the Ock Street Almshouses and to the Baptists. The separate burial-ground of the Tomkins in the old cemetery of the Baptist Church is of interest. The Clock House and Stratton House, built by this family and inhabited by them until the middle of the nineteenth century, are good examples of early Georgian brickwork.[5]

Wesley's view of Abingdonians. John Wesley, the founder of Methodism, visited Abingdon in July, 1741, and thought little of the people : ' Both the yard and house were

---

[1] Wood, *Fasti*, ii. 66.   His brass is near Roysse's tomb.

[2] Wood, *Athenae*, ii. 1016.   [3] Wood, *Oxford Writers*, ii. 1127.

[4] Now the Congregationalists.

[5] The Tomkins who held various offices in Abingdon in the second half of the nineteenth century were a different family.

full ; but so stupid, senseless a people, both in a spiritual and natural sense, I scarce ever saw before.'

As to the present chapels of the Dissenters, the chapel of the Primitive Methodists in the Ock Street was built about 1845 ; it served originally as the Welseyan Chapel. The Congregational Church in the Square was rebuilt in 1862. The Wesleyan Church in the Park was built in 1875, chiefly by the munificence of Mr. J. C. Clarke. The Baptist Church in the Ock Street was restored in 1882. The citadel of the Salvation Army dates from the early nineties. The Strict Baptists of the Abbey descend, I believe, from Mr. Tiptaft, who held the living of Sutton Courtney until his secession from the Church in the early forties. The pillars of the Congregational schoolroom are supposed to be formed from the mast of a ship wrecked in the North Sea towards the end of the seventeenth century, which had on board a minister of that church.

The cemetery of the Quakers occupied part of the present garden of Oriel House.

Buildings of the Noncon-formists.

CHAPTER XIII

IN MODERN TIMES

1714–1910

The Fifteen.
THE Jacobite rising of 1715 caused the new government of George I to take precautionary measures in the district of Oxford. Abingdon was occupied by the troopers of Major-General Pepper.[1] The movement seems to have left little mark, and we revert to local interests.

Abingdon Common.
In 1720 the rights of the inhabitants in Abingdon Common were in dispute, as on many later occasions. In the same year proceedings were ordered by the Corporation to recover an ancient common way ' from St. Hellen's Street, in Abingdon, to a place called Cole's Steps, used by the Inhabitants of this Borough for fetching water from the river of Thames alias Isis '.[2] The newer name of Isis had already become fashionable. In 1722 there was another election petition, which failed.

In 1731 the licence to sell ale or beer was limited to fifty persons except at fairs.[3]

Abingdon Races.
In 1733 a subscription of ten guineas was given by the Corporation ' for a Galloway Plate to be run for at the next race '. Similar subscriptions, sometimes larger, occur from time to time in the Borough Records down to 1800. The Abingdon race-meeting, at one time held on Culham Heath, in later time on Abingdon Common, continued until 1875. A steeplechase meeting was held in the meadows of the Thames towards Sutton during the last quarter of the nineteenth century.

In 1729 began a long attempt to recover the Bridewell from the possession of William Geagle.[4]

Polling-lists of 1734 and 1768.
In the polling-lists of 1734 and of 1768 the Dissenters are marked with an asterisk.[5] In the former list the first four voting on the losing

---

[1] J. R. Green, *Oxford Studies.*
[2] Borough Records.   [3] Ibid.   [4] Ibid.
[5] At the Council Chamber there is a certificate, October 1, 1749, by the minister and churchwardens of St. Helen's that 'Thomas Prince did take the sacrament '.

side were ' Joseph Newcome, vicar ; Wm. Fuller, anabaptist preacher ; Thos. Woods, schoolmaster ; Rich. Rose, teacher to the Quakers.' On the winning side were the Mayor and Town Clerk. In the same lists appear some quaint trade-names, such as—ale-draper, woosted-man, bacon-man, malt-plate-maker, tranter, certificate man. Of course fullers, sack-weavers, maltsters and bargemasters are frequent ; and the barber is also the practitioner in physic. In a rival list of 1734 Wm. Prince is described as ' a P—tect—d Apothecary ' ; while ' Walter Hart, Clerk, N.B. Promised to vote for Mr. Hucks, if obliged with the living of Bowthrop, then vacant.'

In and after the year 1736 there are several instances of Free-women being elected and sworn, while in 1772–80 there was a Bell-woman, who kept her night-watches by deputy, but presumably cried all the cries of the town to the utmost limits herself.[1]

Public lighting of the town first appears in the records in 1738, the lamps being ordered to be lighted October 20. In 1767 an oil lamp is mentioned in the centre of the Square of the Sheep-market. Six years later a new lamp was ordered for the Maypole in the Market-place. *(marginal note: Public Lamps.)*

In 1834 the public lamps were lighted with gas. The old gas-works stood on the island by Abingdon Bridge until 1886, when they were removed to the Vineyard. Of course the change of site is explained by the supersession of water-borne coal by railroad traffic. Ten years later the incandescent burners arrived.

In 1738–9 a watchman, as well as the bellman, was appointed to patrol the town every night.[2]

In 1742 several Mayors-Elect were either excused or fined for refusing to take office ; finally Richard Rose was elected and sworn.

In 1744 the Corporation expressed their horror of a French invasion, a Popish Pretender, &c.[3] In the next year they congratulated George II on his safe arrival in his British dominions. In the following spring they again congratulated the King on the success of the Duke of Cumberland over Prince Charlie.[4] In 1748 the bellman was paid 30s. to clear the streets of beggars and vagrants.

In 1750 a deputation waited on the Prince of Wales at his seat at Cliefden and invited him to breakfast.

In 1752 table linen was ordered for the Visitation Dinner, a sign of the approach of modern habits.[5]

---

[1] Borough Records. [2] Ibid. [3] Ibid.
[4] *London Gazette*, September, 1745 : March, 1746. [5] Borough Records.

The Rose family. The Seven Years' War, in spite of its enormous importance, has left little record in Abingdon. Richard Rose of Abingdon made three voyages to Bombay and China before he was nineteen, and served as a naval officer through the Seven Years' War in the Indian Ocean. He served afterwards ashore in India, until he was killed in action in 1768. His monument is in the south aisle of St. Helen's.

Burke states that the family of Rose, which came from Great Yarmouth, was continuously resident at Abingdon for 362 years from 1428 to 1790. They intermarried with the Hydes of Denchworth, the Bostocks, the Mayotts and the Allens of Grove. Richard Rose removed from High Wycombe to Abingdon in 1428. Hugo Rose de Abendon took the oath of allegiance with the gentry of Berks in 12 Henry VI (1433), before William, Bishop of Salisbury. John Rose was High Sheriff of Berks in 1445. Richard Rose was buried at St. Helen's in 1550, as was another Richard Rose in 1603. Another Richard Rose was a Royalist, when Charles came to Abingdon. Yet another Richard Rose was dismissed from the Council in 1687 as a strenuous Protestant. Thomas Rose settled in Charlestown, South Carolina, about 1700 ; and his son Richard returned to succeed to his uncle Richard at Abingdon in 1714. He was nine times Mayor of Abingdon, and died in 1784.[1]

We cannot help identifying with him the ' Richard Rose, teacher to the Quakers ', who voted in the Parliamentary election of 1734. He is described in the rival list as a grocer. It was a strongly Protestant family ; but Burke mentions one of the house who was a notorious gambler in the eighteenth century.

Council Chamber rebuilt. In 1758 it was ordered by the Corporation that the old Council Chamber should be pulled down and a new one built.[2] Fortunately the Abbey Gatehouse was preserved ; also the Guildhall in the lower storey, and the high-pitched roof over the great Council Chamber. But an eighteenth century façade and interior replaced the older work. A balcony was removed from the front of the Council Chamber in 1851.

In 1767 the Corporation launched out into furniture for the Town Clerk's office : Six chairs, a pair of bellows, two candlesticks, a pair of snuffers, an extinguisher, a tinder-box and candle-box, a square table about three feet seven or eight inches long and some cloak pins.[3]

Elections. In the Parliamentary election of 1768 it was alleged that the voters'

---

[1] Burke's *History of the Commoners.*
[2] Borough Records.   Ibid.

lists were tampered with,[1] and a similar dispute had occurred the year
before the election of 1754.[2] The election of 1774 was declared void,
and gave occasion for election songs, such as 'The elect were not elected',
which appear to contain more venom than merit. The Case of the
Borough of Abingdon came before a Parliamentary Committee the
following spring.

In 1774 George III granted a fresh charter to the Borough.
George III and Queen Charlotte are still 'a rare and splendid ornament' in the Council Chamber. These portraits by Gainsborough,
presented in 1808 by Sir Charles Saxton, are among the chief treasures
of the town. The portrait of the Queen is much the finer.[3] '

Gainsborough Pictures.

J. R. Green speaks of the Borough Representation as being practically in the hands of the Corporation, and of their power by bribery,
drink and influence owing to the small body of freemen. He mentions
the charter of 1774 as increasing the power of the Corporation at
Abingdon.[4]

Again, in 1789 an 'Open Letter to E. L. Loveden, Esq., M.P. for
Abingdon', contains a lengthy indictment. 'Was you not obtruded
on the Borough of Abingdon by two of the Corporation servants in the
night time?' It states that Loveden caused foxes and other vermin
to be exhibited on a gallows,[5] yet he deserted Pitt. Further, that he
acquiesced in a most destructive canal scheme. Finally, that he
expended thousands of pounds at Cirencester, Oxford and other places
equally distant from Buscot 'in articles that could have been supplied
on as good terms by your constituents'.

Mr. Loveden, M.P.

'A Lofty Answer' to the above described the writer as 'a skulking
anonymous assassin'.

The approach of the American War of Independence was marked
by a meeting in 1775 at Abingdon of the Whig freeholders of Berks,
who drew up a petition to the King protesting against the taxation of
the colonists without the grant of representation.[6] In 1781 the bells
of St. Helen's rang on the taking of Charlestown, which capture was
a slight relief in a time of gloom. J. R. Green refers to the distress felt
in this district during this war, which was increased by rigorous winters.

American War.

---

[1] Contemporary pamphlet. [2] Borough Records.
[3] The portraits of Charles II and James II were presented in 1840 by
Mr. George Bowyer. [4] *Oxford Studies.*
[5] As types of the coalition of North, Fox and Burke.
[6] *Victoria Hist. of Berks.*

The Corporation voted £50 in January, 1776, towards the relief of the necessitous poor.[1]

The Fortunate Cooper. Watson's *Geographical Dictionary* has some gossip under the heading of Abingdon which explains the print at the Council Chamber of ' The Fortunate Cooper ' :

' One Mr. Allder a Cooper and Publican of this Place had the good Fortune to obtain a Prize in the State Lottery of twenty thousand pounds. His circumstances before this lucky Event were said to be in so precarious a situation that it was imagined a Blank would have effected his Ruin ; it is certain however that his Brewer, who was his principal Creditor, remonstrated with him on the Folly and Injustice of Gaming with other People's Money. To the Coachman whom he employed to purchase the fortune Ticket he made a Present of a new Coach, and has since performed several generous Acts ; and, what is rarely the case with those, who suddenly grow rich, he has shewn that he can be liberal, without being lavish.' [2]

The Great War. The great war with the French Revolutionists and with Napoleon has left its traces in the local records. In 1794 a force of Abingdon Independent Cavalry was in existence. After Lord Howe's victory of the First of June, 1794, Admiral Bowyer, a hero of the day, who lost a leg in the action, was escorted by the townsmen of Abingdon in blue ribbons and cockades on his return to his seat at Radley, and afterwards entertained by the gentry of the neighbourhood. In 1798, the year of the Battle of the Nile, the Chamberlain was ordered to pay £300 into the Bank of England as a voluntary contribution to the expenses of the war. In 1803 the Corporation contributed one hundred guineas to the Volunteer Corps. Also in 1811 the Corporation voted ten guineas to the Committee at Lloyd's Coffee House for the British prisoners in France.[3]

In July, 1799, when the King reviewed the Berks Volunteer Corps at Bulmarsh Heath, Abingdon sent 96 men to the review out of a company of 150.[4] A bill, dated October 2, 1800, of the Abingdon Armed Association,[5] announced that William Leonard, sackcloth-maker, had been expelled the association at the Red Lion for not coming forward on September 24, ' when the Drum beat to arms.' In the Council Chamber is a list of regulations and fines of the Abingdon Volunteer Infantry,

---

[1] *Oxford Studies* and Borough Records.
[2] This William Alder or Allder was the uncle of Dr. Strange.
[3] Borough Records.   [4] List at the Council Chamber.
[5] Exhibited at the Council Chamber.

January 12, 1804. It has been well said that the defence of a country depends upon the people rather than upon the Cabinet. This Volunteer movement was so urgently needed to support the first line of defence of the fleet, that William Pitt found time to act as colonel of a mounted corps amid all his crushing burdens.[1]

In 1801 the Rev. Mr. Lempriere, Vicar of Abingdon, was thanked by the Corporation for his excellent sermon on the late peace.[2] Again in 1814 there was a local thanksgiving for the general peace.[3] In the first case the Peace of Amiens was only a truce preluding ten years of tremendous war, and in the second case the Waterloo campaign had yet to be fought.

The sermon preached on the second of these occasions at St. Helen's, June 5, 1814, is still extant. In it Henry Wintle, late Fellow of Pembroke, Lecturer at St. Helen's, dwells on the horrors of war :

' You will acknowledge the uncertain, the improper basis of joy arising from triumphs in a state of war, when I bring to your recollection that at the period when your streets were illuminated for the downfall of your tyrannic enemy, hundreds of your countrymen were breathing out their last moments in torture and wounds under the walls of Bayonne.'

In a striking passage he points out that owing to the insular position of England, ' We have, as it were, but heard of war.'

Abingdon was recognized for a long time as the chief town of Berks, Capital of and from the seventeenth to the nineteenth centuries disputed the Berks. honours with Reading.

That the Spring Assizes were held at Abingdon in 1569 is shown by the following entry in St. Helen's Register :

' 1569—buried the 3 day of Marche, Margery Towseye, widdow, who was, at the assize then holden, quite of wichecrafte layde to her charge, and dyed this day in the streete, sodenlie as she was going on her business.'

In 1669 money was spent, perhaps in bribes, to procure that the next Berks Assizes should be holden at Abingdon.[4]

[1] Half a century later there was a revival of the Volunteer movement in Abingdon, in consequence of the scare of a French invasion in 1859, when our forces had been unwisely reduced and most of the remnant were occupied in maintaining our shaken hold on India. That was the occasion of Tennyson's ' Riflemen Form '. Again in recent years there has been an important development locally owing to the Boer War, and still more recently owing to the growth of the German fleet.

[2] Borough Records.   [3] Ibid.   [4] Ibid.

TOWNSEND   X

The County Gaol. In 1803 the Corporation sold the ancient White Hart Inn to the County magistrates for a site to build the great County Gaol, which is still a prominent feature in the view of the town from the Bridge. In **The Assizes.** 1806 the Lent Assizes and Epiphany Sessions were held at Reading, the Summer Assizes and Hilary Sessions at Abingdon, the Michaelmas Sessions at Reading or Abingdon at the pleasure of the magistrates, the Easter Sessions at Newbury.[1]

In 1817 the town had to struggle to keep an alternate share with Reading in the Michaelmas or Flying Sessions for the County. Also Reading was endeavouring to get the County elections held at Reading, Newbury and Abingdon in turn. These elections had been held at Abingdon.[2]

In 1845 the County Gaol at Abingdon was threatened by the County magistrates, and after a prolonged struggle it was closed in 1868–9, and sold in 1874. It is now used for tenements and for a corn-store. The *London Gazette*, June 18, 1869, announced that Abingdon was to cease to be an Assize town.

The Prisons. The end of the eighteenth and early part of the nineteenth centuries were the most callous and ineffective times in modern history in the treatment of prisoners and of the poor, as well as in the spheres of school-life and church-life. John Howard, the great prison reformer, gives a brief description of the County Bridewell and Town Gaol at Abingdon in 1784 :

' County Bridewell Abingdon. Two dirty day rooms ; and three offensive night rooms : that for men 8 feet square : one of the women's, 9 by 8 ; the other 4½ feet square : the straw, worn to dust, swarmed with vermin : no court : no water accessible to the prisoners. The petty offenders were in irons at my last visit, eight were women. Allowance, if felons, three pence a day. Keeper's salary £18 : fees 4ˢ 4ᵈ, no table. At all my visits the prisoners had no employment.'

' Abingdon Town Gaol. Several rooms over a gateway. The first floor for debtors : above are rooms for felons etc. No court : no sewer : no water accessible to prisoners. Allowance to felons, three pence a day. Keeper, one of the serjeants at mace : no salary : fees, debtors 3ˢ 4ᵈ, felons 6ˢ 8ᵈ. No table, license for beer.'[3]

In 1798 two medical officers were appointed to inspect the Borough Gaol.[4]

[1] Lysons' *Berks*.
[3] Howard's *State of Prisons*, pp. 339–40.
[2] e.g. in 1727 and 1768.
[4] Borough Records.

In 1825 the Rules for the Government of the House of Correction or Bridewell at Abingdon were ordered to be the same as those of Reading Gaol.[1]

At that time debtors were still imprisoned. The regulations for persons under sentence of execution were very harsh.

The sentences themselves were startling in their severity. The following sentences,[2] for example, were passed at the Midsummer Berks Assizes held at Abingdon in 1820 : *(Sentences on prisoners.)*

James Bayliss, 25, house-breaking and stealing 2 gowns, 2 shawls etc. Death.

Samuel Blackhall, 17, and Robert Leech, 57, stealing 4 sheep ; also 3 beehives and 3 stocks of bees at Yattendon. Death.

Wm Bond, 21, uttering a forged one-pound Bank of England note. Transported 14 years.

Henry Bren, 22, John Holton, 24, and John Smart, 26, house-breaking and stealing several articles. Death.

Esther Bridges, 25, wilful murder of her child. One year's imprisonment.

Robert Brown, 16, Richard Cox, 18, Joseph Reeves, 19, house-breaking and stealing 10 silver spoons, 1 silver pepper-box etc. Cox evidence, Brown and Reeves death.

Geo. Foster, 29, house-breaking and stealing a copper-pot and frying-pan. One year's imprisonment.

Rich. Hall, 31, E. Macartey, 16, house-breaking and stealing a gown-piece, waist-coat, smock-frock and piece of muslin. Death.

Sarah Price, 28, receiving the above. Admitted evidence.

Francis Hagard, 18, stealing silk handkerchief. Acquitted.

Gabriel Parker, 27, sheep-stealing. Death.

Thos. Smith, 20, assault on King's highway and stealing 6*d*. Death.

Robert Stocker, 30, ' purjury.' Traversed.

Robert Welladvice, 19, house-breaking and stealing box, coat, waistcoat, breeches, &c., and 18*s*. Transported 7 years.

Robert Wenman, 50, uttering a forged one-pound Bank of England note. Transported 14 years.

Samuel Yeates, 19, privately stealing. Two years' imprisonment.

Another prisoner of note may be mentioned here : Dennis Collins, who struck William IV on the head with a stone at Ascot Heath Races, June 19, 1832, was tried at Abingdon. In the print at the Council Chamber he figures as a weather-beaten fellow with a wooden leg and beaver hat.

---

[1] Copy at British Museum.

[2] From a bill in Bodley's Library.

Trade and communications.

Agriculture.

It is worth passing in review the changes that have taken place in the trade of the town and in the means of communication. Of course agriculture has always been the chief industry of the district round Abingdon. In Norman times the town had to fight for its rights of market against Oxford and Wallingford. The Abbots' powerful patronage secured the victory. The position of Abingdon on a navigable river was especially important in the days when the roads were mere tracks and often unsafe for pack-horses. The Abbots' ships conveyed their cargoes upstream to Oxford and downstream to London.

Cloth-making.

In the fourteenth and fifteenth centuries grew up a rich cloth-making industry in Berks, of which Abingdon and Reading were the chief centres. Connected with the growth of trade was the building of the bridges at Abingdon, Culham and Dorchester, which placed Abingdon on a great trade-route from London to the West. The early writers speak of the dangerous character of the fords and ferries at Abingdon and Culham and of the navigation of the Thames generally. After the Reformation the Abbots' fulling-mill fell into decay and ruin.[1] The reversion was granted to the Corporation. The Civil War is supposed to have finally destroyed the declining cloth industry. The same war marks the rise of Leeds as the centre of that trade. Abingdon has still a considerable ready-made clothing-factory. In the eighteenth century the weaving and spinning of hemp and flax flourished in Abingdon, and the making of carpets and sacking is carried on at the present time.

Malting and brewing.

Malting and brewing have been large industries until the present day since the days when the Abbey made large quantities of malt and ale, using part and disposing of part. At the end of the Tudor period Tesdale[2] made a fortune in Abingdon by malt—'a very gainful course there.' He was also interested in cloth-making. Camden's *Britannia*, 1607, states that Abingdon 'drives a great trade in malt'.

Little, writing in or before 1627, speaks of the heavy traffic of malt passing over the bridges and causeway to the barges at Culham *en route* for London. In the seventeenth and eighteenth centuries the barges of the Tomkins family conveyed malt to London and sometimes suffered shipwreck. Lysons' *Berks*, 1806, refers to the malt sent from Abingdon to London.

The roads remained primitive right into the eighteenth century.

---

[1] Cp. Borough Charter.
[2] So also John Fyssher, Lionel Bostock and William Blacknall.

J. R. Green gives a quotation describing a prince on his travels no further back than 1734 :

' As the Prince of Orange was going from Newbury to Abingdon in order to see Oxford, and the road lying through a lane almost impassable for a coach and very dangerous, a wealthy farmer, whose estate lay contiguous, threw down the hedges and opened a way for his highness to pass through his grounds.'

The great change came in the last quarter of the eighteenth century. The stage-waggon was replaced by the mail-coach, a change rendered possible by the improvement of roads. Young in 1809 mentions the good turnpike-roads between Abingdon and other towns. In 1774 the 'Abingdon Machine' was the means of conveying a charter to London.[1] This would be a heavy waggon moving at a walking pace. In 1784 an association was formed by ' gents, farmers and others in the neighbourhood of Abingdon ' to repress highway robbery of the coaches. In 1804 the Corporation joined with that of Stroud in memorializing the Postmaster-General for a mail-coach to run directly through Abingdon to and from Stroud. There are many tales of the coaches that ran through Oxford. For instance the tale of Villebois' hound, which was being sent to the Hants Hunt, and which near Abingdon gnawed its way out of the boot of the coach and found its way back to Shrewsbury Kennels, a distance of 112 miles, the same day. Old Mr. John Bayzand was a famous coachman on the Oxford to Southampton road :

' On leaving the Angel, call at the Mitre booking-office, down St. Toll's, up Hincksey Hill. If a full load, Bayzand would very politely ask some of the passengers if they would kindly ease the horses up the hill by walking. The hill mounted, put on the skid down Sir G. Bowyer's pitch, on to Abingdon, 6 miles ; pull up at the Lamb Inn ; on to Steventon ; another walk up Milton Hill.'[2]

The ' Defiance ' coach is still remembered in Abingdon ; it ran through Dorchester from Oxford to London.[3]

In 1784 a Post Office existed in Abingdon, for its cares were accepted by the Corporation as excusing James Powell, deputy postmaster,

[1] Borough Records.
[2] *Collectanea*, IV (Oxford Historical Society).
[3] The writer mentions the ' Defiance ' with peculiar affection, because it conveyed towards Abingdon some fine engravings after Morland and some Lowestoft china, a gift from an aunt to the late Thomas Townsend.

from serving as Mayor. In 1846 the Postmaster-General was memoria-
lized for two letter-carriers to carry letters in the Borough.

Canals. The end of the eighteenth century also witnessed the development
of river and canal traffic by engineering skill. Barges had formerly
been floated down by ' flashing ', that is, drawing the weirs and taking
down the boats on the flood, a rather risky adventure for boats of
cargo. About 1775 pound-locks were introduced.[1]

Many local canal-schemes were discussed at this time, notably for
a canal from Appleton to Abingdon, to reduce the water-road to one-
third the distance. The Oxfordshire Canal, begun about 1790, gave
Abingdon a cheap road to the coal-fields of the Midlands.

The Wilts and Berks Canal was promoted in 1794, and, after serving
the trade of Abingdon for a period, about one hundred years later it
fell into complete disuse, and remains to-day as a disagreeable token
of the failure in England of waterways for heavy traffic. The rule of
the Thames Conservancy dates from 1857.

In 1829 the Corporation voted money for the widening of Abingdon
Bridge and Culham Bridge. But in 1837-8 the Corporation and
inhabitants showed less foresight in opposing the passing through
The Rail- Abingdon of the line of the Oxford and Great Western Union Railway.
way. But for this Abingdon would have been the junction of the western and
northern arms of the G.W.R., and the site of the carriage-works. A
different decision would of course have made Abingdon a wealthy
wilderness of red-brick. As it is, it has remained a small country
town, not wealthy, but picturesque and good to live in. A writer in
the *Quarterly Review* of July, 1859, describes it as ' a quiet melancholy
old place, rather going astern in these competitive days, but worth
a visit from Oxford student or sentimental traveller.' In 1842 the
Corporation repented of its decision and endeavoured to get the Oxford to
Moulsford line nearer to Abingdon, but Brunel had finally settled his plans.

Again in 1865 great efforts were made to get the G.W.R. carriage-
works here, a site between Abingdon and Radley being offered as a gift
in vain.

The branch line from Radley, opened in 1855-6, remains as the
connecting link with the railway system. This was the property of
a local company until its purchase by the G.W.R. in 1903.

---

[1] At one time the barge-traffic left the main stream of the Thames above
Abingdon Weir and passed by the smaller arm of the river at the foot of Mill Hill
to Culham Bridge.

Telegraphic communication was established in 1864, and the telephone arrived in 1896.

Many of the fairs and markets are older than the Borough, going back far into the reign of the abbots.   The fairs granted in the Charter of 1555 were on the feasts of the Translation of St. Edmund the Bishop, of St. Margaret the Virgin, of the Nativity of the Blessed Mary the Virgin, and of St. Andrew the Apostle ; also upon the first Monday in Lent.   James II granted two other fairs on the feasts of St. Mark and St. James.   A map of Berks in 1741 gives the dates of the fairs as April 25, June 9, July 25, September 2, November 30, the first Monday in Lent, and the Monday before Michaelmas.   The adoption of the New Style in Abingdon in 1752–3 put these dates eleven days later except the Lent Fair.   The change was advertised in the *London Evening Post*, *Gloucester Journal* and the *Reading* and *Northampton Mercurys*.[1]

Fairs and markets.

Of these fairs the Michaelmas Hiring Fair, now chiefly a carnival, is the most picturesque and noisy survival.   Cottages are described as in Horsspepynge, le Horsfeyr and le Horsmarket as early as 1404 in the Account-rolls.   In 1556 the horse market was held in the ‘ Bore Street ’ and ‘ Brode Street ’.   In 1692 the Council ordered that the Horse Fair called Conduit Faire be removed into the Broad and Bore Streets.[2]   Lysons’ *Berks* (1806) speaks of the Abingdon horse market as well as the corn market.

The cattle market was held formerly on the Bury, or Market Place. Sheep-pens were set up in Ock Street in 1583, and the square of the sheep market existed in 1767.   The pig market was held at the meeting of Bath Street and Bury Lane ; in 1782 the Council ordered ‘ no pigs to be killed or swelled in the Square’.   Since 1885 the cattle, sheep and pigs have changed owners in the cattle market, behind the Corn Exchange, which was built at the same time.   Until then farmers displayed their samples chiefly in the High Street and the gateway of the Lion.

The parliamentary election of Abingdon in July, 1830, was typical of the period.   A ‘ Full Report of the Speeches and Proceedings ’ was printed by C. Evans, bookseller, Abingdon, and in this the skill of a shorthand writer is manifest.

Election of 1830.

At nine o’clock in the forenoon the Mayor, Corporation and Electors proceeded with the Candidates to the Guildhall.   John Maberly, Esquire, of Shirley House, Surrey, the former Member, was nominated by Dr. Chas. Tompkins, M.D., of Stratton House, Boar

---

[1] Borough Records.   [2] Ibid.

Street, and the Rev. Mr. Nicholson ; Ebenezer Fuller Maitland, of Park Place, Berks, by William Doe Belcher, Gentleman, the Stert, and John Vinden Collingwood, butcher, the Square. The speeches refer with animation amid constant interruptions to the contemporary questions of rotten boroughs and the Miller system, to the defence of the Canadian frontier, to Catholic Emancipation and Protestant Dissent, and to the vexed questions of free trade and protection. The decline of the hemp trade in Abingdon through competition from Scotland and the Baltic made the last a burning question. The question of taxing the poor man's beer had already come to the front.

One speaker criticized freely the building of Buckingham Palace, 'that sink of public money.' The hot weather would seem to have inflamed the oratory. The Vicar, the Rev. Nathaniel Dodson, of Boar Street, was taxed with interfering in the canvassing, and replied with great vigour : he had not done so, and, if he had, he had done so rightly. There was much bandying of charges of bribery : there was talk of a local banker receiving twenty one thousand pound notes from one honourable candidate. Mr. Secretary Peel was quoted with regard to the frequency and volume of Maberly's oratory at St. Stephen's : twenty such Members and the business of the nation could not be transacted. Finally the open voting continued until 8 in the evening, and Maberly was elected by 159 to 94. On July 31 he 'was chaired in most splendid style', and afterwards sat down with his friends to a 'most sumptuous' dinner at the Crown and Thistle, and later on, in spite of the interminable vista of toasts, departed to look in at all the other dinners that were being held about the town. Maberly claimed to have most of the substantial votes cast for him, as the defeated candidate had purchased 'forty or fifty of his votes' for as little as £200 to £300. Among the voters may be noticed some coach-proprietors and post-horse keepers ; also Wm. Honey, brewer, the Stert, who is immortalized on the 'Beehive' sign; and Sir Charles Saxton, Bart., Boar Street.

Thesiger and Caulfield. A few years later came the great struggle between Sir Frederick Thesiger[1] and General Caulfield, at which an out-voter was brought up to record his open vote at the eleventh hour. In his hurry he said 'Thesiger; no, I mean Caulfield'. But the Mayor had marked him down for Thesiger. The voting resulted in a dead heat and Thesiger was elected by the casting vote.[2]

[1] Solicitor General and afterwards Attorney General.
[2] *History of Old Berks Hunt*, p. 210.

Archdeacon Pott has left a note in his Vicar's Book, November 17, 1868, on the Borough Election, which he calls 'a hideous scene of drunkenness'. The hustings now disappear, but, even with the secret ballot, there were two stormy elections in 1874 and 1880, at both of which John Cremer Clarke was returned, being the last Member of the Borough, which was merged into the County in 1885. There is much more election history and fiction in existence ; we have taken a few examples from time to time as illustrative of the manners of the day. *The last Member.*

Many of the institutions and events of the nineteenth century have already been dealt with in connexion with the earlier times, in order to present things in their sequence and growth rather than annals of disconnected scraps. It remains to deal briefly with the rest. *Details in the nineteenth century.*

At the Coronation of George IV one thousand penny cakes were ordered for the populace. This custom was continued at the Coronations of William IV and Victoria and at the two Jubilees of Victoria. The custom was to throw the buns from the roof of the Market House.[1]

In George IV's reign we find Friendly Societies and a Savings Bank established in Abingdon, events of little dramatic interest but of considerable importance.

A bill at the Council Chamber, dated August 27, 1828, gives the weights and prices fixed at the Assize of Bread. The quartern loaf was to be 4 lb. 5 ozs. 8 drs., and to be sold for 10½d. ; average price of a bushel of wheat 14s. 10d.

In 1829 the Corporation subscribed £100 to the erection of a new poor-house for the parish of St. Helen's. On June 15, 1841, Queen Victoria dates one of her charming letters to the King of the Belgians from Nuneham, then the seat of Edward Vernon Harcourt, Archbishop of York : *Queen Victoria at Nuneham.*

'This is a most lovely place ; pleasure grounds in the style of Claremont, only much larger, and with the Thames winding along beneath them, and Oxford in the distance ; a beautiful flower and kitchen garden, and all kept up in perfect order. I followed Albert here, faithful to my word, and he is gone to Oxford [2] for the whole day, to my great grief. And here I am all alone in a strange house . . .'

King Edward VII has twice been a guest at Nuneham, and on each occasion visited Abingdon. *King Edward VII*

[1] Borough Records.   [2] To receive a degree.

Dear food.   In the forties dear food and harsh interpretations of the laws caused distress and agrarian outbreaks in this district. There is at the British Museum a pamphlet entitled ' Incendiarism, an address to the Labouring Population of the Town and Neighbourhood of Abingdon. By A Man in the Ock Street, September 7, 1843. Price one penny or fifteen for a shilling. A Sermon to the poor re the burning three wheat-ricks by design very near to home.' Its only interest lies in its testimony to the state of feeling at the time.

The election addresses of 1854 contain references to the Crimean War.[1] Two years later a dinner was given to the poor to celebrate the end of that war. The gun from Sevastopol was first placed in front of the old entrance to the police station in the Abbey gateway. A generation later it was moved to the south-west corner of the Park ; and it has again migrated to the north-east of the Park.

Modern changes.   In the sixties much was done to change the appearance of the town. In 1864-5 the Albert Park was laid out by Christ's Hospital, and, now that the trees have had nearly half a century to grow, it is clear that the work was done with taste and foresight. In the *Illustrated London News* for July 1, 1865, there is an illustration of the inauguration of the monument to the Prince Consort in the Park. In a few years a crescent of houses sprang up on the Park estate, including the new vicarage and the new Grammar School.

In 1865 some less admirable work was perpetrated by a committee of the Council. This committee spent seven hours in examining the old deeds and documents of the Borough and destroyed or sold a vast quantity as valueless. Any Abingdon historian would like to be able to reconstitute that valueless collection.

In 1875-6 important schemes for modern waterworks at Old Pound and for a modern system of drainage were carried out. In 1880 a public bathing-place was fitted up on the island below the weir. In 1886 concrete paving began to replace the blue bricks, paving-stones and pebbles.

In 1887 the Cottage Hospital was founded. The building was the gift of Mr. J. C. Clarke. It is supported by subscriptions, with the aid of Christ's Hospital, Wrigglesworth's Charity and the Municipal Charities.

In 1888 the influence of the steam-roller was first felt in Abingdon, and at the same time roads and education began to pass into the hands of the new County Council.

[1] Polling Book, &c., British Museum.

In 1889 the Borough Superintendent of Police was sent out to Tasmania to fetch a fraudulent trader—not a native ; but he lost him on the homeward ship in the harbour of Rio Janeiro.[1]

In 1890 the Borough boundary was extended to the Canal, to Larkhill stream and to Northcourt.

In 1894 the Free Library was opened. In that autumn came the great flood, when boats swam along our streets, and the almsfolk had to be carried from their beds. The great flood was followed by the great frost of 1895, when carts drove on the Thames and a sheep was roasted in mid-river. This recalled many previous record frosts to long memories, but we will instance only the card printed on the Thames, February 5, 1814 :

> Behold the liquid Thames now Frozen o'er,
> That lately ships of mighty burthen bore.

In 1895 the Fishery in the Thames formerly attached to Abbey Mills was presented to the Corporation for the enjoyment of the public by Mr. C. A. Pryce. These fishing rights were a fruitful source of litigation, as may be seen in the Borough papers of the sixteenth and seventeenth centuries.

In the same year were commenced two useful works : the care of the Abbey remains by the Corporation, and the formation of a collection of Abingdon prints, portraits of past Mayors, &c.

At the Guildhall and Council Chamber there is a large collection of Corporation insignia and plate, pewter, wooden platters, badges, standard measures, staves of office, &c., which together with the portraits, prints and photographs have a great historical value. Taken as a whole, the collection ranks high among municipal collections. *Corporation plate.*

The Borough arms—vert, a cross patonce between four crosses pattées or—appear on a silver seal, which in 1605 replaced an older brass seal then ordered to be defaced.[2]

Three tiny silver maces date from the reigns of Elizabeth, Charles I and James II ; the great silver-gilt mace, replacing an older one, dates from the Restoration of Charles II.

To the seventeenth century belong two fine silver goblets, the gift of Lionel Bostock, and five tankards, given by Richard Wrigglesworth, of London, fishmonger, Sir John Lenthall, Sir George Stonehouse and Martha Stonehouse ; the fifth and smallest of 1681–2 being simply adorned with the Borough arms.

[1] Borough Records.   [2] Ibid.

To the eighteenth century belongs a large part of the plate, including four plain bowls and ladles, a two-handled cup, candlesticks, salvers, castors, salts and spoons. Among the chief donors of the eighteenth century are the Earls of Abingdon. To the end of that century belongs the great silver-gilt cup, presented by Lloyd's Coffee House to Admiral Sir George Bowyer, who commanded the *Barfleur* on the First of June, and given in 1870 to the Corporation by Sir George Bowyer, the grandson. That century saw much old plate and pewter replaced by new.[1]

The nineteenth century added tea-spoons, salt-spoons, fish-slices, a wine-strainer, a tobacco-box of the Bear Club, a Burmese bowl; and two candelabra to commemorate the Diamond Jubilee. The mayoral badge was presented in 1879 by Mr. J. C. Clarke, and the gold chain is lengthened year by year with further links.

In the present century have been added a 'Pom-pom' candelabrum —a souvenir of South Africa—and a pair of candelabra of electioneering interest.

Portraits at the Council Chamber. At the Council Chamber there are also some good portraits of historical interest : viz. a supposed portrait of Richard Mayott, the first Mayor, which is surmounted curiously by the Bostock arms ; John Roysse ; Baron Harcourt ; Admiral Bowyer ; Lord Colchester ; two portraits supposed to be of Earls of Abingdon ; the Rev. N. Dodson ; Lord Chelmsford ; Mr. J. T. Norris ; and two prints of Captain Sir Charles Saxton. Also a Martyrdom of St. Sebastian, two good portraits of Charles II and James II, and Gainsborough's George III and Queen Charlotte.

Portraits at the Hospital Hall. At the Hall of Christ's Hospital, Abingdon, are two inferior portraits of Henry VI and Edward VI ; also a picture of Geoffrey Barbour and John Hutchion building the Bridge and Causeway, and portraits of Sir Peter Bessiles, Sir John Mason, Lionel Bostock, John Perkins, Robert Orpwood, Thomas and Maud Tesdale, and Richard Curtyn. These are the work of the first half of the seventeenth century. Also a pair of smaller eighteenth-century portraits of the Rev. Walter Harte and Mistress Elizabeth Hawkins. The latter is commemorated in the great monument in the north aisle of St. Helen's, which refers to their love-story. Mr. Harte was a minor poet, the historian of Gustavus Adolphus and a fashionable tutor. His father was the Rev. Walter Harte the non-juror.

[1] *Vide* Borough Records, annis 1720, 1779 and 1800.

CHAPTER XIV

STREETS AND HOUSES

So much of the older Abingdon has disappeared from sight and from Disappear- tradition, that it may be useful to put on record some of the lingering ance of old houses. names and places, before they are changed and forgotten. Until the nineteenth century most of the streets were mere lanes and alleys. At the time of the Restoration the approaches to the town were still closed with bars or gates in the custody of gatekeepers. The Corporation records indicate the sequence in methods of road-building and paving : the pebble-pitching of the sixteenth and seventeenth centuries, the blue cubes of the eighteenth century, the triumph of macadam and of concrete pavement in the nineteenth century.[1]

To take some of the streets in detail : the Vineyard is mentioned The Vine- as the site of tenements as far back as 1184 under the spellings of yard. ' Wineerde ' and ' Wingerde de Bertona ', together with ' Schurenie Strete '.[2] The Vineyard figures also in the Obedientiars' Account-rolls of 1322, 1369, and 1440, as the Wingherd, Wynherd, Wineyarde, &c.

The Stert is an ancient name both as a stream and as a street. The The Stert. arch over the Stoerte stream is mentioned in 1184.[3] It occurs under various spellings : Sterte, Sturte, Stuyrte, &c.—in the Account-rolls from 1369 to 1450. The Stert in the eighteenth century was still an open stream, with floodgates near the Broad Street in 1770. The part by the Knowl between the Vineyard and the Broad Street was covered in by the Corporation in 1791, and the part between the Little Church and the Knowl was cleaned in the following year.[4] The miscellaneous appearance of the arches under the street suggests that the Stert was largely bridged over by the individual householders, each man bridging before his own door.

Bridge Street had formerly an island of houses below the Thistle. Bridge It figures as Butcherrow or Burford Street in the Charter of 1555. The Street.

---

[1] Cp. Borough Records in the years 1836 and 1886.
[2] Stevenson, ii. 330–1.   [3] Ibid. 330.   [4] Borough Records.

houses between Bridge Street and Schoolyard were known as Butcher Row down to the eighteenth century. Abingdon Bridge was sometimes called New Bridge, Burford Bridge and Hart Bridge. The White Hart Inn stood for centuries before 1803 upon part of the site of the County Gaol; it was already in the time of Little, 1627, 'an auntiente Inne.'

Little Bridge Street. The Little Bridge Street, whatever may have been its precise position, appears as 'Litelebriggestret' in a thirteenth-century deed of the Corporation; and as 'Lytelbrygstrete' in the Account-rolls of 1436.

Thames Street. Thames Street had a row of cottages on the river-brink until 1864. In the same street are many interesting pieces of stonework, notably a river-gate of the Abbey, which has been built into a private house.

The Abbey. Inside the Abbey gateway are many interesting houses besides the Abbey ruins. St. John's Hospital without the gate was removed, or rather its almsmen were removed, to the Vineyard in 1800 at the expense partly of Bernard Bedwell, partly of the Corporation.[1] The Gatehouse served as the prison of the Borough from 1556 until it was converted into the Masonic Room in George IV's reign.[2]

The Market-place. The Market-place has undergone many changes. 'Borewstrete,' a form of Bury or Borough, appears in a deed of 1248,[3] while 'Borewestrete' and 'la Bury' occur in the Account-rolls of 1404. The gilt stone cross was sawn down in 1644. There was a 'Cryers Pulpit' there in 1656.[4]

The old Market House of Leland's day, with its pillars and lead roof, gave place in 1677 to the present structure. Near it stood the stocks, whipping-post and pillory, as well as the cage.[5]

With them may be set perhaps the ducking-stool for which the Chamberlain paid 15s. to John Clarke in 1676.[6] The maypole was still standing there in 1773, for in that year the Chamberlain provided it with a new lamp. There were shambles in the Market-place in 1798. Until modern times St. Nicholas' Church was flanked by the Two Brewers' Inn, and the Star Inn obscured its west front from the Bury. The Queen's Arms—perhaps on the site of the New Inn or Novum Hospitium of the Abbey—did not give place to the Queen's Hotel until 1864. The Corn Exchange and the present London and County Bank

[1] Borough Records.   [2] Ibid.
[3] *Charity Comm. Rep.*, 1908, p. 121.   [4] *Munster and Abingdon.*
[5] Constables' Return, 1685, and Borough Records, 1710.
[6] Borough Records.

were not built until twenty years later. An attempt was made unsuccessfully in 1885 to preserve the entrance to the crypt under the Bank ; it ran out towards the present statue of Victoria. The ugly obelisk, which was erected in the Market-place in 1834, retired to the Square in 1887 to make room for Victoria's statue ; it has since withdrawn into privacy.

Hearne speaks of the well-known Antelope Inn in Abingdon before the Civil War.[1]

East St. Helen's Street was quite narrow at its upper end until 1812, when it was widened together with Bucklersbury. The Old Bell Inn has been restored rather severely and has reverted to its older name of the King's Head and Bell. Its *vis-à-vis*, the Unicorn, disappeared a century ago. West St. Helen's Street had formerly an island of houses near its juncture with High Street. East and West St. Helen's Streets with their exaggerated gables retain something of their mediaeval aspect. ' Westseynteleynstret ' appears in 1375, ' Seynteeleynstret ' in 1404, and ' Estseyntelynstrete ' in 1405 in the Account-rolls. Fore Street and Back Street are names still in use for East and West St. Helen's respectively. East and West St. Helen's Streets.

Banbery Court, in West St. Helen's, has a long record. In Henry V's reign it was the mansion of John Banberie the Bridge-builder. In the fifteenth century the feasts of the Fraternity of the Holy Cross were held there, until they were held at the feast-house in East St. Helen's, given them by Mr. William Dier, Vicar of Bray.[2] This latter house was in 1627 in the occupation of William Eyston, gentleman. Banbery Court was in Elizabeth's reign in the occupation of William Blacknall ; in 1627 it was the property of Richard Hide of Wick, Esquire.[3]

At the old house of the late Mr. S. I. Baker the Assize Judges were formerly entertained. Twickenham House is a good instance of early Georgian brickwork.

Also in East St. Helen's may be noted the house of Richard Ely, dated R^{R}E 1732, and the malthouse of John Tomkins, dated J 1748 T, which now forms part of ' Helnestow ' on the bank of the river.

The building which preceded the present clothing-factory was a picturesque frontage running down to the gateway of St. Helen's Churchyard. East and West St. Helen's Streets carried the triangle of houses between them almost to the north porch of St. Helen's Church, but slices have been taken off in 1795, 1864, and later.

[1] *Remains*, ii. 294.   [2] Little.   [3] Ibid.

Thames Embankment.

Until the forming of the Thames Embankment in 1883 the Anchor Inn stood out over the river, and, with the dilapidated ' almshouses over the water ' and the stone bridge over the mouth of the Ock,[1] made a more picturesque riverside than the present brick buildings and iron bridge, as may be seen in divers prints and paintings. To the west of the churchyard of St. Helen's runs the ' Long Alley ' of the fifteenth century, with its later lantern and porch—to the porch has been added a Jacobean front. To the north of the churchyard lie Twitty's Almshouses of the early eighteenth century, and to the south the galleried almshouses of the late eighteenth century.

Lombard Street.

Lombard Street figures as ' Tops Lane ' in the Borough Records of 1787, but in the Charter of 1555 it is Lumbard Street. The name suggests that it was the Jewish quarter—there was an important colony, for in 1428 the Jews of Abingdon performed an interlude before Henry VI.[2]

The High Street.

The High Street has a broad and modern appearance, but it has on the north side the pleasant ' Lion ' and Mayott's house. The west end of the High Street led to the Square through the Narrow, until the great fire of 1884 facilitated the widening of the Narrow. Traffic demanded the change ; but the beautiful coloured print of 1768 causes a regret for the old view down the street with the ' Silent Woman ' on the left hand.

The Square.

In the Square cottages have been swept away from the front of the Congregational Church. The pleasant old Rising Sun has made way for Gillett's new buildings and some very red shops. Between these and the Congregational Church was the Katherine Wheel until 1700. One of the stone fireplaces of the Rising Sun has found a home in the Hospital Hall.

The Ock Street.

Even the Ock Street, that centre of politics, has a history of changes. It appears as ' Ockestret,' ' Okkestrete ' and ' Okstret ' in the Account-rolls of 1405, 1436, &c.

Formerly, before the villas and schools sprang up, the Conduit Field lay open to the north, and its springs supplied the Carswell stream to the thirsty street. The Carswell or Castlewell was built over with an alcove of brickwork by Richard Ely in 1719.[3]

[1] There had been ' the bridge of stone ' there in Leland's time.
[2] *Jews in England*, by Hyamson, p. 120.
[3] The Corporation made him grants of £6 and £12 for this work. Borough Records.

Ock Street had formerly an unsavoury open ditch on the north as well as on the south. We fear that before the halcyon days of an urban sanitary authority the dwellers in the courts drank from the Ock, washed in the Ock and drained into the Ock. It would be tedious to recount the occasions on which the Thames and Ock Mills are mentioned : they go back into Saxon times. Reference is made in the first charter of 1609 to ' the Crosse called Riddle Crosse ' in Ock Street, and in 1673 mention is made in the Borough Records of ' Rudle Crosse '.

The Lonesome Tree is mentioned as a landmark in 1841 in connexion with a public path from the top of Boar's Street to the Spring Road.[1] It is the last of a great row of elms that ran west from Stratton House through a couple of centuries. The fancy of a recent writer has led her to make St. Edmund see visions under this Lonesome Tree. The elms of the district were apparently famous long ago, for in the thirteenth century bends of elms for ploughs were brought from Abingdon to Southampton.[2] *The Lonesome Tree.*

The present Park with its surrounding avenues and leaseholds was corn land before 1864. On the great maps in St. Helen's vestry, c. 1835, will be found some interesting names in this quarter—Larkhill, the Town Furlong, &c. There is a strip along the south side of the Faringdon Road from the Wootton Road westward marked as the Bowling Green. The triangular garden at the meeting of the Spring Road and Faringdon Road, well known as Trinity Close, is there marked as Trinity Chapel, and is presumably the site of the Chapel that figures in the Account-rolls of the Trinity Warden of the Abbey. There is a pound marked in the Wootton Road. The old farm-house of Lacies Court was leased to Thomas Meadowes in 1554 on easy terms for his services to Sir John Mason in the matter of the Christ's Hospital Charter. It has been reconstructed as a modern-antique house. The newer house, built by Mr. Bowles and occupied by Mr. Dodson, which also used the name of Lacy Court, has been removed. *The Park.*

Fitzharris Farm has passed through many hands—Bostocks, Tesdales and a host of others. The modern house still contains the kernel of the old house. It has some fine panelling with the quartered arms of the Bostocks—Sable, a fess coupé argent.

Boar Street and Broad Street appear frequently in the Account-rolls with neighbouring lanes: e. g. ' Borestret ' in 1422, ' Golafreslane ' *Boar Street and Broad Street.*

[1] Borough Records.
[2] Mrs. J. R. Green, *Town Life in the Fifteenth Century*, ii. 289.

in 1440, 'Brodestrete' in 1404, 'Barghestrete' in 1466. Bath Street appears to be a more modern name. The 'Paul's Head' was cleared from Bath Street to make the approach to the Park in the sixties.

Rhubarb Alley, in Boar Street, was distinguished in 1849 by a visit of cholera, which resulted in its partial demolition the next year.

An alley by the present Cottage Hospital and Culham Cottages was once dignified by the name of China Alley.

The Irish Lane in 'Brode Street' with 'the Brode Gate' finds a place in the first charter of 1609, which also speaks of 'the dovecotes and pidgeon houses near the Sterte'. Many old buildings have been swept out of the narrow alleys of Otwell Lane, now Queen's Street, and Bury Lane or Little Bury Street, to make room for the National School and the cattle market. At one time the National School occupied the present granary of St. Helen's Mill.

The Beehive Inn, at the corner opposite to the station gates, preserves still its much-quoted verses, playing on the name of William Honey, a former landlord :

> Within this Hive we're all alive,
> Good liquor makes us funny :
> If you are dry, step in and try
> The flavour of our Honey.

Old Prints.   Many prints perpetuate with varying charm pieces of the older Abingdon at many stages. They complement the old books and ancient documents in pourtraying with the vigour of original authorities the extraordinary continuity of the recorded life of the place through more than twelve centuries.

APPENDIX

I. ABBOTS OF ABINGDON

DATE
675. Hean.
     Cumma.
     Rethun.
     Alard.
815. Cynath.
830. Godescale.
955. Ethelwold.
963. Osgar.
985. Edwin.
989. Wulfgar.
1017. Ethelwine.
1030. Siward.
1044. Ethelstan.
1048. Sparhavoc.
1050. Ralph.
1052. Ordric.
1065. Ealdred.
1071. Ethelhelm.
1085. Reginald.
[1097. Interregnum of Motbert the
      Prior.]
1100. Faricius.
[1116. Interregnum of Warenger the
      Prior.]
1120. Vincent.
1130. Ingulf.
1158. Walkeline.
1164. Geoffrey.
1176. Roger.

DATE.
[1184. Thomas of Husselborn tem-
      porarily in charge.]
1184. Alfred.
1189. Hugh.
1221. Robert de Henreth.
1234. Luke.
1241. John de Blomeville.
1256. William de Newbury.
1260. Henry de Fryleford.
1262. Richard de Henred.
1289. Nicholas de Culham.
1306. Richard de Clyve.
1315. John de Sutton.
132½. John de Cannynges.
1328. Robert de Garford.
1332. William de Cumnor.
1334. Roger de Thame.
1361. Peter de Hanney.
1401. Richard de Salford.
1415. John Dorset.
1421. Richard Boxor.
1427. Thomas Salford.
142⅔. Ralph Hamme.
1435. William Ashenden.
1468. John Sante.
1495. Thomas Rowland.
1504. Alexander Shotisbrook.
1508. John Coventry.
c. 1512–1538. Thomas Pentecost alias
      Rowland.

II.

The following list of rectors and vicars of St. Nicholas' and of vicars of St. Helen's is taken from the Bishop's register, 1297–1836, at Salisbury. In the spellings of surnames the Bishop's register has been followed. Where further names have been added from other sources, the authority is given in brackets. To fill the gap between 1548 and 1625 in the list of rectors, it is possible that other vicars of St. Helen's besides Kisbey acted as rectors of St. Nicholas'. The lists should be read together, as several names figure in both churches. Richard Sant, 1471, was probably a kinsman of John Sante, Abbot of Abingdon.

VICARS OF ST. NICHOLAS'

Institution

1315. Henry de Heygarston, priest.
1316. John de Ely, clerk.
1321. Peter de Querendon, priest.
1321. Robert de Shelton.
Roger Chaulo.
1349. John de Mersshton.
1350. Roger Cristemasse de Garsyngdon.
1361. Henry Cogyn.

Institution.

c. 1370. John Dagat. (Stevenson papers in Bodley.)
c. 1372. John Ydesdale. (Composition in Verney Collection.)
John Venerich.
1377. John Grey.
1400. John Russell. (*V. C. H. Berks*, ii. 15.)
John Pynnok.
1407. Henry Crumpe.

At this point the vicars of St. Nicholas' cease. In 1783 William Kennedy was licensed as Reader of Prayers at St. Nicholas', the post being vacant by the death of John Stevenson.

RECTORS OF ST. NICHOLAS'

Institution.

c. 1230. Benjamin (Charters 14 and 25 in Bodley).
1310. William de Coleshull, clerk.
1316. John de Garesden.
1320. Thomas le Bottley or Botiley.
1346. Henry le clerk de Chilton.
1349. Roger de Chaulo.
1349. Richard Marye.
1361. Thomas Trace.
1365. Richard Chamle.

Institution.

c. 1372. Richard Clayvill. (Composition in Verney Collection.)
William Robers.
1393. John Lye.
c. 1400. Richard Clavill. (*Cal. Pap. Letters*, v. 275.)
1410. Henry Crompe.
Robert Burley.
1440. William Clement, A.M.
1443. John Gregory, A.M.

Institution.

1454. John Willey, also Wylley, doctor of decrees.
1461. William Hareward, S.T.B., afterwards S.T.P.
1469. Thomas Forster, A.M.
1471. Richard Sanct, also Sant, chaplain.
1474. Thomas Stephyns, S.T.P.
1489. Richard Topp, also Toppe, bachelor of decrees.
1491. William Brewe, clerk.
1492. David Jeffrey, chaplain.
    William Atwater, S.T.P.
1498. Thomas Randolf, also Randalf, licenciate in decrees.
1521. Edward Fynche, also Finch, doctor in medicine.
1526. John Mabley, also Mable.

Institution.

1532. John Wygan.
1533. John Lucas.
    Richard Otes.
1548. Richard Corbett.
c. 1622. Robert Kisbey (Marriage Register).
1625. William Webber, A.B.
c. 1636. John Stone (register of christenings).
1643. George Kendall, S.T.B.
1663. Robert Payne.
1676. Edmund Hall.
1686. Edward Redrobe.
1721. Richard Eaton.
1741. John Fludger.
1764. John Stevenson.
1775. Richard Bowles, B.D.
1804. William Smith, M.A.

VICARS OF ST. HELEN'S

Institution.

1248. Ethelmar [1] (*Half brother of Henry III*).
1284. John de Cliford.[2]
1305. William de Middletone, clerk.
1319. Hugh de Cicestr.
1333. Geoffrey de Nortone.
1349. William de Medebourn, priest.
1349. Roger de Chaulo.
1349. John Stokes.
1354. Thomas de Crendon.
1361. John Auger.
    Richard Donynton.
1376. William Hanley.
1377. Hugh de Kenynton.
    Henry Bryt.
1404. Richard Beel.
1430. William Prentys, S.T.P.

Institution.

1437. Richard May.
1468. Thomas Forster.
1471. John Mulcaster, S.T.P.
1471. William Harrewarde,[3] S.T.P.
    Robert Lathys.
1504. Henry Leshman.
1512. John Cokke.[4]
1521. Thomas Riche, A.M.
1540. John Fisher, S.T.B.
    Ralph Harteley.
1554. Robert Frauncys.
1556. John Vaun.
1561. Edmund Wolf, A.M.
1575. Robert Hollande.
1593. Stephen Cottesford.[5]
1598. Robert Kisbey.[6]
1624. Edward Reede.

[1] Matthew Paris—Ethelmar was probably rector and not vicar.
[2] Old deed.
[3] William Harrewarde is the same as Heyward on the St. Helen's brass dated 1501.   [4] 'Doctor of Laws, holding the first order of the tonsure.'
[5] Churchwardens' Accounts.   [6] Ibid.

Institution.

1629. Christopher Newstedd, A.M.
1640. Edward Reed.
1643. William Tikill.
    John Tickell.
    John Pendarves. } [1]
    John Biscough.
    Matthew Griffith.
1661. James Egglefeild, S.T.P.
1674. Miles Sutton.
1683. Richard Knight.
1686. Ezriel Burdon, A.M.
1698. Anthony Addison, S.T.B.
1719. Joseph Newcome.
1757. Andrew Portal.
1775. John Cleobury, A.M.

Institution

1800. John Lempriere, M.A.
1811. Lawrence Canniford, B.A.
1821. Charles Richard Sumner, M.A.
1822. Hugh N. Pearson, D.D.
1823. John Matthias Turner, M.A.
1824–1867. Nathaniel Dodson, M.A.
1868–1874. Alfred Pott, B.D.
1874–1878. Henry Bligh, D.D.
1878–1884. William Cobham Gibbs, M.A.
1884–1896. Robert Charles Francis Griffith, M.A.
1896–1900. Wentworth Watson, M.A.
1900. Herbert T. Maitland, M.A.

III. HEAD MASTERS OF ABINGDON SCHOOL FROM 1563 [2]

DATE

1563–c. 1570. Master Argall.
c. 1570– . Master Orpwood.
  –1597. Richard Humfrey.
1597–1600. Anthony Appletree.
1600–160⅔. John Byrd.
160⅔–1606. Degorie Wheare.
1606–c. 1624. Thomas Godwyn.
c. 1624–165⅖. Anthony Huish.
165⅖–1656. John Kerridge.
1656–1657. Interregnum of Robert Payne, usher.
1657–1684. Robert Jennings.
1684– . Richard Pleydell.
[It is not certain if Pleydell continued to 1716, or if a name is lost.]

DATE

1716–1753. Thomas Woods.
1753. Humphrey Humphreys.
1753. John Abbott.
1758. Henry Bright.
1774. Andrew Portal.
1775. William Kennedy.
1792. John Lempriere.
1810. Edward Nicholson.
1829. J. T. H. Hewlett.
1840. William Alder Strange.
1868. E. H. T. Harper, usher, master in charge.
1870. Edgar Summers.
1883. William Herbert Cam.
1893. Thomas Layng.

[1] Puritan Preachers. Cp. Chapter on Commonwealth.
[2] In this list I have followed Mr. G. W. Wallace, *Char. Comm. Report* for 1908, except in the date when Huish succeeded Godwyn. All appear to have been in holy orders except Robert Jennings.

IV

THE transcript of Plates I and II is in Stevenson, i. 33 and ii. 44. The transcript of Plates III and IV, with the abbreviations expanded, is given here by request.

PORTER DOCUMENT

PLATE III, *facing* PAGE 25

Sciant presentes et futuri quod Ego Alicia relicta Thome le porter in pura et legitima viduitate mea dedi concessi et hac presenti carta mea confirmaui Cecilie filie mee pro seruitio suo duas acras terre arabilis cum pertinentiis suis in Campis Abendōn. quarum vna iacet in burghforlong inter terram Willelmi le fwyte ex parte Occidentali et terram Walteri de Abendōn. ex parte orientali et vna dimidia acra iacet super Lauerkehulle uersus la Lyttone inter terram Johannis de forde ex parte boriali et terram Alicie de pistrino ex parte meridionali et vna dimidia acra iacet propinquius fossato contra molendinum de Ocke preter vnam inter terram monachi de opere ex utraque parte Et septem solidos et quatuor denarios annui redditus recipiendos ad duos anni terminos videlicet de tenemento quod quondam fuit Philippi le slattere in Litelebrigge stret Abendōn. inter tenementum monachi de opere ex parte meridionali et tenementum quod quondam fuit Benedicti de lardario ex parte Occidentali ad festum sancti Michaelis et ad festum beate Marie in martio quinque solidos equis portionibus Et de domo quam Radulphus dylemot tenuit in litelebrigge stret Abendōn. de feodo Benedicti de lardario que sita est inter tenementum monachi de opere ex parte Occidentali et domum quondam dicti Benedicti ex parte orientali ad festum sancti Michaelis quatuordecim denarios et ad festum beate Marie in martio quatuordecim denarios quem quidem redditum habui de dono et concessione prenominati Benedicti de lardario patris mei Habendum et tenendum totam predictam terram cum pertinentiis suis et totum predictum redditum sibi et heredibus suis de me et heredibus meis uel meis assignatis libere quiete bene integre et in pace Reddendo inde annuatim mihi et heredibus meis uel meis assignatis vnum denarium ad festum sancti Michaelis pro omni seruitio exactione et demanda Si uero dicta Cecilia sine herede de carne sua nato uel nata discesserit tota predicta terra et totus predictus redditus ad heredem meum absque contradictione reuertantur Et ego uero predicta Alicia et heredes mei uel mei assignati predicte Cecilie et heredibus suis predictam terram cum pertinentiis suis et predictum redditum contra omnes mortales tenemur warentizare defendere et acquietare imperpetuum pro predicto redditu Et ad hanc donationem concessionem et warentizationem firmiter sine dolo et fraude obseruandam hanc presentem cartam sigilli mei impressione roboraui Hiis testibus Waltero de Abendōn. Johanne le porter Ricardo de Coffesgrove tunc preposito Abendōn. Roberto bercario Matheo marescallo Johanne de forde Willelmo le porter et multis aliis

APPENDIX

CARTULARY OF HOLY CROSS

Plate IV, *facing* Page 51

Transcriptum ac de verbo in verbum verum exemplare omnium et singulorum libertatum cartarum scriptorum et munimentorum omnium maneriorum terrarum et tenementorum pratorum pascuorum pasturarum Reddituum seruitiorum et prouentuum ffraternitatis siue gilde sancte crucis Abendoniae in Comitatu Berks fundate Incipit cum dei laude Amen et primo de manerio de Seintelenes. . . .

Sciant presentes et futuri quod ego Philippus filius et heres Willelmi de Seynt Eleyne dedi concessi et hac presenti carta mea confirmaui Willelmo de Medebourn perpetuo vicario ecclesie sancte Elene de Abendon Ricardo Belle presbytero parochiali ecclesie sancti Nicholai et Johanni Buschup omnes terras et tenementa mea que habui iure hereditario in Villa de Suttone Suttone Wyk Dreyhem Wyk et in Villa de Abendon vnacum redditubus molendinis homagijs libertatibus liberorum hominum seruitijs Wardis releuijs escaetis villenagijs villanis villenagia illa tenentibus cum eorum catallis et sequelis pratis pascuis pasturis moris haijs separalibus et comunibus et omnibus vbique pertinentijs suis sine aliquo retenemento quo mihi et heredi- bus meis accidere poterint quoquomodo Dedi etiam et concessi predictis Willelmo Ricardo et Johanni vnum denarium annui redditus percipiendum de manerio de ffryleforde vnacum reuersione eiusdem manerij et cum omnibus pertinentijs suis quando acciderit quod quidem manerium Edmundus de Seynt Eleyne frater meus tenet de me ad terminum vite sue tantum et vnde reuersio ad me spectat post mortem dicti Edmundi Habendum et tenendum predictis Willelmo Ricardo et Johanni eorum heredibus et assignatis omnes terras et tenementa predicta cum omnibus pertinentijs suis predictis libere quiete iure hereditario imperpetuum ffaciendis inde capitalibus dominis feodi illius omnia seruitia que ad terras et tenementa illa pertinent pro omni seruicio seculari exactione et demanda Et ego dictus Philippus et heredes mei omnes terras et tenementa predicta vnacum redditubus homagijs liber- tatibus seruitijs reuersionibus et omnibus alijs pertinentijs. . . .

INDEX

Victoria, Queen, 161, 167.
Vincent, Abbot, 19–20.
Vine cultivation, 39.
Volunteers, 152–3.

W

Walkelin, Abbot, 20.
—— Bishop, 13.
Waller, Sir William, 56, 121–3.
Wallingford, 13, 19–21, 34, 40, 52, 114, 156.
Wantage, 114, 121.
Warenger, Prior, 19.
Waterworks, 162.
Welford, 15, 39.
Wesley, John, 146.
Westminster, 19.
Wheare, Degorie, 96.

Whipping-post, 166.
White Hart Inn, 140, 154, 166.
Wilfred of Ripon, 4.
William I, 12–15, 20.
—— II, 13–16.
—— III, 143.
—— IV, 111, 155, 161.
Winchester, 6–10, 19–21, 29.
Winter, Sir William, 69.
Wintle, Henry, 153.
Witham, 4.
Wittenham, 82, 142.
Woods, Thomas, 101, 149.
Worcester, Earl of, 69.
Workhouse, 49, 161.

Y

Young Scholarship, 106.